JERRY L. WALLS has served as a Research Fellow in the Center for Philosophy of Religion at Notre Dame. He is the author of a trilogy on the afterlife, the first two volumes of which are *Hell: The Logic of Damnation* and *Heaven: The Logic of Eternal Joy*. He is also the editor of *The Oxford Handbook of Eschatology*.

D1157078

Purgatory

Purgatory
The Logic of Total Transformation

Jerry L. Walls

OXFORD

UNIVERSITY PRESS

SMITH PRESS
11501 East 54th Street
Chicago, IL 60615

BT
843
W35
2012

OXFORD
UNIVERSITY PRESS

Oxford University Press, Inc., publishes works that further
Oxford University's objective of excellence
in research, scholarship, and education.

Oxford   New York
Auckland   Cape Town   Dar es Salaam   Hong Kong   Karachi
Kuala Lumpur   Madrid   Melbourne   Mexico City   Nairobi
New Delhi   Shanghai   Taipei   Toronto

With offices in
Argentina   Austria   Brazil   Chile   Czech Republic   France   Greece
Guatemala   Hungary   Italy   Japan   Poland   Portugal   Singapore
South Korea   Switzerland   Thailand   Turkey   Ukraine   Vietnam

Copyright © 2012 by Oxford University Press, Inc.

Published by Oxford University Press, Inc.
198 Madison Avenue, New York, New York 10016

www.oup.com

Oxford is a registered trademark of Oxford University Press

All rights reserved. No part of this publication may be reproduced,
stored in a retrieval system, or transmitted, in any form or by any means,
electronic, mechanical, photocopying, recording, or otherwise,
without the prior permission of Oxford University Press.

Library of Congress Cataloging-in-Publication Data
Walls, Jerry L.
Purgatory : the logic of total transformation / Jerry L. Walls.
p.   cm.
Includes bibliographical references and index.
ISBN 978-0-19-973229-6 (hardcover : alk. paper)
1. Purgatory.   I. Title.
BT843.W35 2012
236'.5—dc22   2011011465

1 3 5 7 9 8 6 4 2
Printed in the United States of America
on acid-free paper

JKM Library
1100 East 55th Street
Chicago, IL 60615

To Timothy and Angela Amos
And
Jonathan and Emily Walls

Angela and Jonathan, this is the third
Book I have dedicated to you.
It's not Tolkien, but it
Is a Trilogy.

Heaven is still the one you want
Even if it requires a stint
In purgatory.

He came to Simon Peter, who said to him, 'Lord, are you going to wash my feet?' Jesus answered, 'you do not know now what I am doing, but later you will understand.' Peter said to him, 'You will never wash my feet.' Jesus answered, 'Unless I wash you, you have no share with me.' Simon Peter said to him, 'Lord, not my feet only but also my hands and my head!' —John 13:6–9

CONTENTS

Preface xi
Acknowledgments xiii

Introduction 3
1. A Short History of Purgatory 9
2. Protestant Objections and Alternatives to Purgatory 35
3. Models of Purgatory 59
4. Personal Identity, Time, and Purgatory 93
5. Purgatory and Theories of a "Second Chance" 123
6. C. S. Lewis and the Prospect of Mere Purgatory 153
7. Looking Forward by Looking Back 177

Notes 183
Index 201

PREFACE

This volume is the third in a series of books on the afterlife, the first two of which are *Hell: The Logic of Damnation* (Notre Dame, 1992) and *Heaven: The Logic of Eternal Joy* (Oxford, 2002). The fact that purgatory is bringing up the rear suggests, truly, that I had no plans to do a trilogy when I wrote my book on hell. Indeed, I had no plans to write about heaven either, for that matter.

The first volume was a revised version of my PhD dissertation at Notre Dame. A few years before writing that book, the historian Martin Marty wrote an article tellingly entitled "Hell Disappeared. No One Noticed. A Civic Argument," in which he remarked that a bibliographical search for contemporary literature turned up almost nothing on the subject. In the intervening period, that has all changed, and hell is a now a matter of intense debate, particularly in evangelical Christian circles. (Indeed, several months after writing this Preface, a firestorm of controversy erupted in the evangelical world that made national news when popular pastor Rob Bell published a book on hell that challenged certain prevailing views.) Many still defend the traditional notion of eternal damnation, while others are contending for universalism, and still others are making the case that the lost will be annihilated in the end.

I did the second volume after realizing that heaven poses its own distinctive and interesting issues. Heaven has yet to generate the level of interest that hell has stirred in philosophical circles, but there are signs that it is drawing increasing attention, from critics as well as those who hope to end up there. One of the issues I discussed in that book was whether a viable doctrine of heaven needs a doctrine of purgatory. I argued that it did, and thought I was done with the matter.

Subsequent reflection proved otherwise, and again, I saw that purgatory poses a distinctive and fascinating range of issues that deserve sustained consideration in their own right. I was fortunate to return in the fall of 2009 to Notre Dame as a Research Fellow in the Center for Philosophy of Religion, where I completed this project. According to historian Jacques Le Goff, the Notre Dame school of Paris was the birthplace of the doctrine of purgatory in the twelfth century, so perhaps it is fitting in more ways than one that I finished purgatory where I started with hell.

All Souls Day, 2010
Notre Dame, Indiana

ACKNOWLEDGMENTS

Purgatory is not only a philosophical and theological concept, but an existential reality as well. Here, I limit my thanks only to those persons who have helped me gain a better grasp of the conceptual aspects of purgatory, as it would surely prove an unduly complicated exercise to recall all those who have contributed to my existential understanding of the matter, and the countless ways they have done so.

In the first place, I owe a debt of gratitude to the Center for Philosophy of Religion at Notre Dame, which awarded me a Research Fellowship to complete this book, and to Mike Rea, the exemplary director of the Center, whose encouragement and support is deeply appreciated. I am further grateful to all the Fellows I got to know during my time there, many of whom, along with other participants in the Center, offered helpful comments on various parts of the manuscript, namely: Billy Abraham, Erik Baldwin, Ron Belgau, Andrew Chignell, Paul Draper, Tom Flint, Adam Green, Mike Hickson, Mark Murphy, Jeremy Neill, Ryan Nichols, Alan Rhoda, Todd Ryan, Jeff Schloss, Amy Seymour, Patrick Todd, Chris Tucker, and Liu Zhe.

A number of other persons read individual chapters or parts of the book, and/or offered helpful comments or discussion, including Angela Amos, David Baggett, Kyle Blanchette, Ken Collins, Steve Croft, Bryan Cross, Paul Griffiths, Sam Kimbriel, Kevin Kinghorn, Brian Marshall, Kevin Sparks, Elizabeth Glass Turner, John Walls, Jonny Walls, and Jay Wood. There is no doubt the book is much better due to my time spent at Notre Dame, and is closer to perfection for having passed through the purging fire of all this criticism than it would otherwise be.

Thanks are also due to Phil Tallon not only for several conversations about purgatory, but also for suggesting, in his characteristically creative fashion, the idea for the cover art. I must also mention Trent Dougherty, who several years ago at a conference, insisted that I had to write a book on purgatory since I had already written books on heaven and hell, if for no other reason than because it might raise the probability I would be mentioned sometime in the same sentence with Dante.

I joyfully tip my hat to Notre Dame friends Claire Brown, Lesley-Anne Dyer, Brian Hall, Anna Heckmann, Eleanor Pettus, Cara Polk, Josh and Rachel Rasmussen, Tanya Salyers, Debra Thomas, Andrea Turpin, Luke Van Horn, John Wallbaum and Amanda Weppler for numerous stimulating discussions (a few of which are more accurately described as spirited arguments—some of my friends can be very contentious) about the plausibility of purgatory. During one of these disputes, Brian made a wager with me that there is no purgatory, and therefore he will spend no time there. If it turns out that he is right and purgatory is a mere fiction, I owe him a six pack of his favorite beer in the life to come. If there is a purgatory, well, I suppose the very fact that he would make such a wager surely increases his chances of spending at least a little time there.

I must also acknowledge the late Father Richard John Neuhaus, whose invitation to me to join The Dulles Colloquium several years ago was due in part to the fact that I am a Protestant who believes in purgatory. My participation in this illustrious group was not only invariably stimulating and highly entertaining, but also honed my thinking about purgatory and a number of related ecumenical issues. I hope Richard is aware that I finally finished this book, and is at least moderately pleased with the result. The fact that circumstances forced me to miss the Spring 2008 meeting of this remarkable group, not knowing it was my last chance to see both him and Cardinal Dulles is a lasting regret only heaven will fully heal.

As always, it has been a pleasure to work with Cynthia Read and the other editors at Oxford University Press who assisted with this book, namely Lisbeth Redfield, Emily Perry and Michael Philoantonie.

Purgatory

Introduction

Why all this dawdling? why this negligence?
Run to the mountains, slough away the filth
That will not let you see God's countenance.
—Dante

The comedian Jack Handy is famous for his "deep thoughts," humorous musings and scenarios that are apt to provoke reflection along with a laugh. In one such scenario, Handy tells us a story about a cowboy whose conception of heaven contained a profound absurdity.

He was a cowboy, mister, and he loved the land. He loved it so much he made a woman out of dirt and married her. But when he kissed her, she disintegrated. Later, at the funeral, when the preacher said, "Dust to dust," some people laughed, and the cowboy shot them. At his hanging, he told the others, "I'll be waiting for you in heaven—with a gun."

The absurdity here, of course, lies in the notion that anyone in heaven might be biding his time just waiting for others to arrive so he can wreak havoc—with a gun.

This is not to deny that there may be guns in heaven. We cannot be sure what forms of entertainment and enjoyment may exist to pass the time, as it were. We can, however, be sure that heaven will not include murderous desires for revenge. Heaven may not have a metal detector, but it surely has a malice detector.[1] Anyone who makes it to heaven must be free not only of sinful patterns of behavior, but also of evil dispositions and tendencies. The glorious vision of heaven in the book of Revelation emphasizes that it is a place of light and beauty, and that all forms of impurity are excluded. "But nothing unclean will enter it, nor anyone who practices abomination or falsehood, but only those who are written in the Lamb's book of life."[2]

To put this point more precisely, we can say that heaven is essentially morally perfect.[3] What this means is that it is impossible, in a very strong sense of the word, that there could be any sort of sin in heaven. We can explicate this claim in terms of the inhabitants of heaven, beginning with God himself, who is holy in his essential nature, and is therefore incapable of sin. It is not that he merely happens not to sin, or has chosen to this point not to do so. Rather, he cannot sin because he is necessarily perfectly good.[4] Likewise, if heaven is essentially morally perfect, it must be the case that the creaturely occupants of heaven are also incapable of sin. This is not to say that they are essentially good in the same sense that God is in his very nature, but it is to say that those in heaven must have at the least acquired a nature, or had their nature so transformed that it is impossible for them to sin. In traditional terminology, they must become impeccable, or immutable. They must have a settled character that is good through and through, one that is no longer vulnerable to sin.

Again to cite the language of scripture, heaven demands a kind of holiness that is like God's own. "Like obedient children, do not be conformed to the desires that you formerly had in ignorance. Instead, as he who has called you is holy, be holy yourselves in all your conduct; for it is written, 'You shall be holy, for I am holy.' "[5] And again: "Pursue peace with everyone, and the holiness without which no one will see the Lord."[6]

The requirement that we must actually become holy and thoroughly upright in spirit and character is one of the foundation stones of the doctrine of purgatory, the subject of this book. It is not enough that we be forgiven of our sins, or have righteousness imputed to us in a legal or formal fashion. Nor is the initial work of salvation in regeneration sufficient to accomplish the complete transformation we require. While regeneration begins this transformation, it does not entirely rectify our corruption or repair all our moral and spiritual deficiencies.[7] So we are left with the question of how we acquire the actual holiness that is essential for those who want to see the Lord, to know him in the deeply personal sense of enjoying a genuinely loving relationship with him.

The verse from Hebrews about the necessity of holiness for seeing the Lord was the text of a sermon in the nineteenth century by Anglican theologian John Henry Newman, later Cardinal Newman. Although he rejected the doctrine of purgatory at the time of the sermon, it is interesting to note that his reflections on this text, along with the reality that typically Christians fall so far short of holiness, led him to the gates of purgatory, even if he did not quite walk through them. His ruminations on the necessity of holiness brought into focus a common misconception of heaven, namely, the notion that just anyone would, of course, enjoy being there.

And so indeed it is widely believed that heaven is the sort of place where anyone would love to be, no matter what his tastes, inclinations, desires, and so on, as if it were some sort of cosmic version of Las Vegas that has something for everyone, whatever he likes. Newman challenged this notion sharply. "For heaven, it is plain from Scripture, is not a place where many different and discordant pursuits can be carried on at once, as is the case in this world. Here every man can do his *own* plea-sure, but there he must do *God's* pleasure."[8]

Newman goes on to illustrate his point with the phenomena of taste and percep-tion. A person whose tastes are distorted cannot enjoy the sweetest of flavors and a person whose sight is impaired will fail to appreciate the most striking beauty nature can offer. Likewise, "there is a moral malady which disorders the inward sight and taste; and no man laboring under it is in a condition to enjoy what Scripture calls 'the fullness of joy in God's presence, and pleasures at His right hand for ever-more.'"[9] So heaven indeed is overflowing with eternal pleasure, but it would not be recognized as such by the man for whom a weekend of riotous living in Las Vegas represents the pinnacle of what life has to offer. The stark implication of this insight is that heaven would not be heaven for one who has not cultivated a taste for the holy. "Heaven would be hell to an irreligious man."[10]

This does not bode well for our cowboy or anyone else who has been infected with sin. A recent book on the subject by Old Testament scholar Gary Anderson begins with the bad news that sin is a much bigger deal than merely violating a moral norm and that "the effects of sin are more extensive than a guilty conscience....A wrongful deed creates in its wake some sort of 'thing' that has to be removed."[11] Removing this thing is no simple matter, and is typically painful and difficult, as Anderson goes on to explain at length in his book.

To get a better sense of why this is so, let us spell out in more detail the effects of sin on us. According to a classic analysis of the consequences of sin, there are three destructive effects for which fallen human beings need healing. First, sin dis-orders our minds so that we turn away from God, our true source of good and happiness, and focus unduly on other things. We consequently have a distorted view of reality that keeps us from living truthfully and discerning our true good. Second, we become guilty before God because of our disregard of him and his goodness and justly deserve punishment for our actions. Third, we become weak-ened in our nature in such a way that we are more prone to sin, and disinclined to do what is good. The more we sin, the more complicated and extensive the damage we do to ourselves, and correspondingly, the more is required for repair and rehabilitation.[12]

Now let us consider our unfortunate cowboy in the light of this analysis. His excessive love of the land, not to mention women, and no doubt wine and song as well, was due to his distorted sense of values, growing out of his disordered thinking. His choice to murder his mockers left a large and ugly stain of guilt on his soul that needs to be removed. And his deeply rooted desire for vengeance reflects a weak-ened and damaged moral nature that will need extensive repair and renewal before he could truly enjoy being in the presence of a God of holy love. So let us extend his story and assume he is a Christian believer, albeit one who is obviously rough around the edges, and clearly not very faithful at this point of his life. Let us assume, moreover, that before he died he repented of his sin and sought forgiveness for his murder, and even acknowledged that his desire for vengeance was wrong.

Even if we assume all this, including that he was forgiven before he died, it is doubtful that he had cultivated a love of God and a taste for the holy such that he would be fully ready to enjoy heaven. As Newman observed, the transformation from a sinful nature to one that is truly holy takes time. Our tastes and likings are not typically changed in a moment. The gradual change of heart that leads to holiness comes in the school of learning obedience to God and following his will. "To obtain the gift of holiness is the work of a *life*."[13]

And the cowboy is far from alone in his predicament. Indeed, there are Christians of many stages of spiritual maturity and growth in holiness and many, probably most, die far short of perfection. In another sermon, Newman reflected on this reality, observing that there are many persons who may be sincere servants of God who are "dark and feeble" in their religious state. Many others repent late in life, if not on their death bed, and leave few traces of Christian fruit in their lives. And beyond all such cases as these, he pointed out that there are many others who have made a good start and persevered, yet have hardly begun the process of sanctification "when death comes upon them;—many who have been in circumstances of especial difficulty, who have had fiercer temptations, more perplexing trials than the rest, and in consequence have been impeded in their course."[14]

Faced with what seems to be this obvious empirical reality, the question remains about the fate of such persons. There are four broad possibilities. First, we might say that they go to heaven with their sins, imperfections, and the like intact, so heaven is not in fact essentially sinless. Second, we might think they will simply be lost and never make it to heaven if they die without actually becoming completely holy. Third, we might say that at the moment of death, God makes people holy by an instantaneous unilateral act, however imperfect, sinful, and immature in character they may be.[15] Fourth, we may say that the sanctification process continues after death with our willing cooperation until the process is complete, and we are actually made holy through and through.

We can rule out the first of these options rather quickly, as it is starkly incompatible with Christian teaching about heaven. The second option, although it has been defended by some theologians, is very much a minority position that is at odds with the broad consensus of Christian belief, and I will not deal with it further. The real contestants are options three and four. The first of these is the position adopted by most Protestants, and the final option, obviously, is the doctrine of purgatory, which is the position I will be exploring at length in the following pages.

We will begin our ascent of Mount Purgatory in the first chapter by way of a brief historical overview of the development of the doctrine, from ancient times to the present. It will chronicle key ideas, figures, issues, and events in the fascinating narrative of this colorful doctrine in order to set the stage for the discussion to follow. Chapter 2 will examine Protestant perspectives on purgatory, both critical and sympathetic, and will explore the various ways in which they provide alternatives to the doctrine of purgatory in their own theological systems of belief. Chapter 3 will spell out different models of purgatory, and will show that there are significantly different ways to understand the purpose of purgatory. While some of these are at odds with some of the central claims of Protestant theology, other models of the doctrine are quite amenable to at least some Protestant traditions. The fourth chapter will look at the distinctive issues about personal identity raised by the doctrine of purgatory, and will compare different accounts of personal identity and how they fare in light of the doctrine. Chapter 5 will consider the possibility of postmortem probation and repentance, a view often mistakenly identified with the traditional account of purgatory. It will analyze the relation between these two concepts and assess recent proposals that the doctrine of purgatory should be modified to include postmortem repentance. Chapter 6 will delve into the views of purgatory held by one of the most widely read Christian writers of the twentieth century, whose influence continues to grow, namely, C. S. Lewis. It will pose the question of whether his account of purgatory might have ecumenical promise as a version of the doctrine that might appeal to Protestants as well Catholics. The final brief chapter will provide a look back at key issues and summarize how our judgment on them will determine our assessment of purgatory.

Enough then for anticipating what lies ahead. Let us begin to make our way up the mountain.

1

ᴄᴠᴏ

A Short History of Purgatory

There is no better way to get at the nature of the place called Purgatory, and the belief in that place,
than to watch it being built up, piece by piece, slowly but not always surely and without leaving out
any of history's complex texture.
                                        —Jacques Le Goff

The doctrine of purgatory did not drop, fully formed, out of heaven, or hell, or
for that matter out of somewhere in between. To the contrary, the doctrine has
a long and complicated history and a significantly longer gestation period than many
other formally approved doctrines. Indeed, critics of purgatory sometimes seize on
the fact that it emerged relatively late in the history of the Church in order to emphasize that it cannot claim the same vintage as classic consensual Christian teaching.
And it is true that the doctrine was not first officially affirmed in conciliar fashion by
the Roman Catholic Church until the Second Council of Lyons in 1274. This was
several hundred years after the ecumenical councils that defined central Christian
doctrines such as the Incarnation and the Trinity. Moreover, the first great split in the
Church between Rome and Constantinople had already occurred over 200 years
earlier in 1054, and the Protestant Reformation was still a few centuries away.

In his detailed account of the origins of the doctrine, medieval historian Jacques
Le Goff locates the time and place of its birth several years before its official formulation. For him, the birth of the doctrine hinges crucially on such factors as the
emergence of the term "purgatory" as a noun. More interestingly, he thinks the
emergence of the doctrine was due significantly to factors other than theological
ones. In particular, he rejects the evolutionary view of the development of the doctrine, according to which it was present in Christian belief in embryonic form from
the very beginning, and thus it was inevitable that it would be born in due time. By
his lights, "nothing could be farther from the historical truth.... this development
was neither uniform nor inevitable. It might easily have gone awry."[1]

One's judgment on how and why the doctrine of purgatory unfolded as it did is a telling indicator of one's theological convictions. Whether or not one thinks the development of the doctrine might have gone awry, one is making a theological judgment, not merely a historical judgment, innocent of all theological commitments. Indeed, one might think the development of the doctrine, however seamless it appears, is a vivid example of pure teaching gone awry, and one might think so for distinctly theological reasons. At any rate, the point I want to emphasize is that any history of purgatory will make judgments, either explicitly or implicitly, about whether or not there is a God and how he was or was not involved in the development of the doctrine.

In the short history of the doctrine that follows in this chapter, I make no pretense of being theologically neutral. I must of necessity be selective in what I include, but I aim to give a fair account of the significant figures and factors that led to its emergence and formal acceptance in Roman Catholic theology, as well as it's rejection in other Christian traditions. The primary purpose of this chapter, however, is to provide the historical background of the issues that will be my real focus in the chapters that follow.

ANCIENT INTIMATIONS OF PURGATORY

It is hard to know where to begin in telling the story of purgatory. There are a number of parallels and intimations of the doctrine in pre-Christian sources, and some of these *may* have influenced the formation of the Christian version of the doctrine. However, unless there is clear or explicit borrowing of ideas or images or terminology, it is difficult to demonstrate such influence, especially when there are disputes about the dates of the respective documents. Moreover, to further complicate matters, judgments about which documents preceded which are sometimes based on prior judgments about which documents influenced which.

An issue of larger theological significance is that sometimes these pre-Christian sources are cited to show that Christian views of the afterlife are not unique or even distinctive, and it is further suggested that this provides reason to think that Christian views are merely human constructs that have no special status as divine or revealed truth. But of course, there are often very different ways of looking at the same data. For instance, one might think that such intimations and parallels are a divine foreshadowing of what God has revealed in definitive fashion in Christian truth. In this light, the continuities are not surprising, and indeed should be expected if Christian truth is intended for all persons in all times and places. Moreover, these foreshadows can help prepare the way for other cultures to contextualize and accept that truth for themselves.

In support of this reading, there is in fact remarkable cultural diversity in the non-Christian sources that have some parallel to purgatory, including examples that could be cited from Indian, Persian, Egyptian, Greek, Roman, Babylonian, and

Jewish texts. In Hindu thought, for instance, hell may or may not be permanent. According to the *Laws of Manu*, there are twenty-one hells, some of which involve purging of souls that may lead to future heavenly lives.[2] Furthermore, it is significant that not all the examples are from classically religious texts. Plato's *Dialogues* have passages that are reminiscent of purgatory, perhaps most clearly in *Phaedo*, where he distinguishes among the newly dead between those who are judged to be incorrigibly wicked and those whose evil may be curable. Whereas the former are cast into Tartarus with no hope of escape, the latter—such as those who may have offered violence to their parents in a fit of passion but have been penitent—may be cast into Tartarus for a limited time but eventually released.[3]

This discussion could easily be extended but there is no need to do so. The main point is already clear that the story of purgatory has some preliminary chapters in the form of interesting precedents and parallels in non-Christian sources. What to make of these is admittedly controversial theologically and in some cases historically as well, since it is in dispute whether they predate Christianity, and if so, whether they in fact played a role in the development of purgatory. But what is evident is that the broad idea of an intermediate range of persons who are neither fully good nor fully evil but may have hope of postmortem cleansing has made moral and spiritual sense to a wide range of cultures all the way back to ancient times.

BIBLICAL HINTS OF PURGATORY

For many Christians, it is irrelevant whether or not purgatory may be anticipated in other religious documents. The only document that matters when assessing the doctrine of purgatory is the Bible, and the primary question is whether it is taught in the pages of scripture. As we shall see, this is a central point of dispute among Christians of different traditions, particularly Roman Catholics and Protestants. But what is beyond dispute is that in the historical development of the doctrine, it was widely believed that scripture clearly supported it. Indeed, certain texts have regularly come up in discussion of the doctrine and have been frequently cited in its favor by its various proponents.

The first of these is a passage from the Old Testament book of Malachi that employs the imagery of a refining fire:

> For he is like a refiner's fire and like fullers' soap; he will sit as a refiner and purifier of silver, and he will purify the descendants of Levi and refine them like gold and silver, until they present offerings to the LORD in righteousness.[4]

The LORD is the one said to be employing fire to refine and purify, so it is easy to see why this text appealed to advocates of purgatory.

The next important text comes from the Apocryphal Second Book of Maccabees, a book that is accepted as canonical by Roman Catholics and Eastern Orthodox, but not Protestants. This text gives an account of a number of Jewish soldiers who have been killed, after which it is discovered that they have sinned by hiding tokens of idols under their tunics:

> So they all blessed the ways of the Lord, the righteous judge, who reveals the things that are hidden; and they turned to supplication, praying that the sin that had been committed might be wholly blotted out. The noble Judas exhorted the people to keep themselves free from sin, for they had seen with their own eyes what had happened as the result of the sin of those who had fallen. He also took up a collection, man by man, to the amount of two thousand drachmas of silver, and sent it to Jerusalem to provide for a sin offering. In doing this he acted very well and honorably, taking account of the resurrection.[5]

The meaning of this text is hardly transparent, and this is further complicated by the fact that it refers to practices that are not referred to elsewhere in scripture. What is reasonably clear, however, is that Judas Maccabeus and his fellow Jews believed that sins could be forgiven after death, and that prayers by the living could help achieve this. At any rate, this text was often cited in support of these beliefs and the attendant practice of praying for the dead, a practice that figured significantly in the later history of purgatory.

The third text is from the New Testament, and more significantly, is composed of the words of Christ himself:

> Therefore I tell you, people will be forgiven for every sin and blasphemy, but blasphemy against the Spirit will not be forgiven. Whoever speaks a word against the Son of Man will be forgiven, but whoever speaks against the Holy Spirit will not be forgiven, either in this age or in the age to come.[6]

What gives credence to purgatory here is the suggestion that at least some sins can be forgiven in the age to come. Admittedly, this is not explicitly stated, but arguably it is implicitly assumed.

The fourth text, also the words of Christ, comes from his Sermon on the Mount, where he gives instruction for dealing with anger and conflict:

> Come to terms quickly with your accuser while you are on the way to court with him, or your accuser may hand you over to the judge, and the judge to the guard, and you will be thrown into prison. Truly I tell you, you will never get out until you have paid the last penny.[7]

As we shall see in the next section, this text was taken to suggest that the prison could include the afterlife, where believers could continue to pay for their sins, before eventually being released.

The fifth crucial text is from the apostle Paul, and is particularly noteworthy because it was commented on perhaps more extensively than any other during the formative period in which the doctrine of purgatory was formulated and given its classic shape:

> For no one can lay any foundation other than the one that has been laid; that foundation is Jesus Christ. Now if anyone builds on the foundation with gold, silver, precious stones, wood, hay, straw—the work of each builder will become visible, for the Day will disclose it, because it will be revealed with fire, and the fire will test what sort of work each has done. If what has been built on the foundation survives, the builder will receive a reward. If the work is burned up, the builder will suffer loss; the builder will be saved, but only as through fire.[8]

This text was taken to describe persons who do indeed love Christ more than anything and would choose Christ if put to the test, but whose loves may not always be properly ordered in a way that is consistent with this commitment. They may love the world more than they should and may accordingly be guilty of sins that reflect this disordered love. Although such persons are saved, this text was taken to teach that they needed to pass through purgatorial fire to cleanse them and reorder their loves in such a way that fits them for heaven.

A few other texts should be noted, though their relevance to purgatory is less apparent than the five just cited. First, the story of the three Hebrew children in the fiery furnace was often given a spiritualized interpretation in order to support the notion of purgatory.[9] Next, the Old Testament story of Hezekiah's warning about his upcoming death, which was subsequently delayed, has been interpreted by some readers in support of purgatory. In particular, Hezekiah's fear of death was construed by Sir Thomas More as evidence that what he actually feared were the pains of purgatory.[10] Another text is the story of the rich man and Lazarus, which depicts those in hell as aware of those in the bosom of Abraham, and vice-versa.[11] This text inspired not only speculation about different regions between heaven and hell that may be occupied by the departed dead as they await final judgment, but also suggested the possibility that at least some of those in hell might be able to ameliorate their condition. Tertullian took the text to imply that certain of the dead might experience a certain *refrigerium interim* (interim refreshment), a special form of treatment during the period between death and resurrection, a notion that would play a fascinating role in later purgatorial speculation. Fourth, those enigmatic passages that refer to Christ's descent into hell[12] also fueled speculation about intermediate abodes preceding the final state of salvation and damnation and the possibility of deliverance from them.

My aim here is neither to defend nor to criticize the use of these texts in support of the doctrine of purgatory. This sketch is intended merely to show the biblical grounds and concepts that helped give rise to the doctrine. Let us continue this historical quest by turning now to survey key figures in the ancient Church that contributed to the formation of the doctrine.

FATHERS AND MOTHERS OF PURGATORY

The previously mentioned concept of *refrigerium* played an important role in what is perhaps the earliest document in Church history that portends the doctrine of purgatory, namely, *The Passion of Perpetua and Felicitas*. This document recounts the death of two women who were among those martyred in the persecution of Christians in Africa in 203. During her imprisonment, Perpetua had a dream in which she saw her brother Dinocratus, who had died of illness when he was only seven years old. In her dream, he was in a place of darkness, clothed in filthy rags, parched with thirst and with a sore on his face. Moreover, there was a basin of water from which he desired to drink, but it was too high for him to reach. Perpetua knew she was worthy to ask a favor on his behalf and she began to pray for him to be relieved. She awoke with a certainty that her brother was undergoing trial, but that she could assist him, so she continued to pray for him every day. A few days later she had another vision:

> I saw the place that I had seen before, and Dinocratus, his body clean, well dressed, refreshed [*refrigeranteum*], and where the sore had been I saw a scar; and the lip of the basin that I had seen had been lowered to the height of the child's navel, and water flowed out of it continuously.... Then, his thirst quenched, he began playing happily with the water, as children do. I awoke and I understood that his penalty had been lifted.[13]

This vision differs in important respects from later formulations of purgatory, particularly since there is no clear sense that Dinocratus is being judged or punished, though this may be implied by the assumption that he was under some sort of penalty. Regardless of how this is understood, he is clearly in pain and distress. The important point is that he is saved due to the prayers of someone considered worthy to intercede for him, someone who is shortly to be martyred for her faith. This text played an important role from the time of Augustine forward in the discussions that led to the formulation of the doctrine of purgatory.

A second significant figure in the early history of purgatory is Cyprian of Carthage, who died in 258. Cyprian's contribution to the doctrine arose in a pastoral context as he dealt with the very pressing issue of persecution, and particularly how to deal with believers who had denied Christ in the face of martyrdom. The issue under debate was whether such well-intentioned but weak believers could still remain in the Church and hope to be saved. Cyprian found a possible solution in the following words of Christ, cited above: " .... you will be thrown in prison. I tell you solemnly, you will not get out till you have paid the last penny."[14] To Cyprian, this suggested that weak believers could still be admitted to communion and finally saved, though they would have to pay the appropriate penance for their sins. This penance could continue in the "prison" of the afterlife if necessary, a notion that is obviously very much in accord with the doctrine of purgatory as it would later take shape. As Joseph Ratzinger, now Pope Benedict XVI, observes: "With this interpretation, that there is purification in the future life, the root concept of the Western doctrine of Purgatory is already formulated clearly enough."[15]

Let us turn now to the theologians that Le Goff singles out as "fathers of purgatory." As we do so, we immediately face a deep irony. The two fathers of the Church who have been called the "founders" of purgatory are both Greek theologians, namely, Clement of Alexandria and Origen. The irony is due to the fact that purgatory is primarily a doctrine of the Latin West rather than the Greek East, where the distinctively Roman doctrine of purgatory has been strongly rejected. These Fathers made a fundamental contribution to the doctrine of purgatory by interpreting those biblical passages in which God is described as a fire in terms of purification rather than wrath. Origen, moreover, who believed that ultimately everyone would be saved, was the first to state clearly that the soul can be purified after death. He distinguished, furthermore, between three categories of persons: first, the righteous; then, those guilty of lesser sins, whose journey through the purging fires would be brief; and finally, "mortal sinners," whose stay in the fire would be more extended.

It was partly in reaction to the notion of universal salvation that the most influential of all the fathers of purgatory was inspired to formulate his thoughts. As with so many other aspects of Western theology, it is Augustine who provided seminal thinking and significant components of what would emerge as the mature form of the doctrine. In the first place, he provided crucial terminology that would remain in the discussion through much of the Middle Ages, particularly the following adjectives as applied to divine punishment: *purgatorius*, *temporarius* or *temporalis*, and *transitorius*. He employed these adjectives in such phrases as *poenae purgatoriae* (purgatorial punishments) and *poenae temporariae* (temporary punishments).[16]

Next, Augustine offered support for one of the most crucial ideas that gave rise to the doctrine of purgatory, namely, that prayers for the dead can be effective for hastening their entrance into heaven. In a famous passage in the *Confessions*, he prays in this fashion for his recently deceased mother Monica.[17] While he was confident of her devotion and piety, he was also mindful that she had not lived in perfect obedience to God. He returned to this issue in *The City of God*, and again affirms that prayers for the dead may be effective for certain kinds of sinners, in particular, those who have already shown evidence of God's grace in their lives. As he puts it, "it is for those who, having been regenerated in Christ, did not spend their lives so wickedly that they can be judged unworthy of such compassion, nor so well that they can be considered to have no need of it."[18] It is important to emphasize that Augustine holds out no hope that prayers can lead to the salvation of the wicked who die outside of Christ.

Starting in the year 413, Augustine gave increasing attention to the fate of souls after death in response to a group of adversaries who, following Origen, held that eventually all, or at least most, would be saved. He considered this a dangerous view that encouraged moral laxity and accordingly took considerable pains to refute it. In articulating his convictions on this matter, he further developed his views not only on eternal hell, but also on purgatorial punishment. One of the principles he laid down in his (perhaps earlier) *Commentary on Psalm 37* was widely cited in subsequent discussion: "Although some will be saved by fire, this fire will be more terrible than anything that a man can suffer in this life."[19] The rigorist intent of this principle is clear. No one should put off reforming his life with the thought that it will be more painless to do so after death. To the contrary, any suffering in this life will pale in comparison to the pain of postmortem fire.

In the process of fleshing out his opinions on hell, Augustine distinguished between four classes of persons. On one end of the spectrum are the saints, martyrs, and other righteous persons who go quickly if not immediately to heaven. On the other end are the godless who are consigned to hell with no hope of any further chance of being saved. For our purposes, the more interesting types are the two intermediate groups, those who are neither altogether good nor altogether wicked. The latter, according to Augustine, go to hell but have hope that their suffering may at least be mitigated somewhat by the prayers or suffrages of the righteous, though they cannot be saved. It is the former group, composed of those who are not altogether good, who are most relevant to the doctrine of purgatory. He believed that these persons may eventually reach heaven after the appropriate time in the purgatorial fire. Augustine's fourfold distinction of postmortem fates was highly influential in subsequent accounts of purgatory, though it would require revision, as we shall see, for the doctrine to be articulated with full clarity.

How he characterized those who were not altogether good is also significant, particularly his claim that their hope for salvation was due to their general worthiness as shown in the lives they had lived before death. They demonstrate such worthiness by their efforts to improve, their good works, and their practice of penitence for sins they had committed. Augustine was the first clearly to draw the connection between penitence and purgatory, a connection that would assume great importance in the twelfth and thirteenth centuries.[20] It is also worth emphasizing that he believed that tribulations in this life could serve as a kind of purgatorial fire, along with the fire after death, which he took to be more painful than any suffering on earth.

In addition to Clement, Origen, and Augustine, there is one other person who deserves to be recognized as a founder of purgatory according to Le Goff, namely, Gregory the Great. This pontiff was characterized by both an evangelistic and an eschatological zeal. He was convinced that the end of the world was at hand and was accordingly committed to do all he could to save as many as possible, including souls who had died.[21]

Gregory was fascinated by the geography of the afterlife and his speculations on this matter are among his distinctive contributions to purgatory. In particular, he distinguished between upper hell, where the righteous rest, and lower hell, where the wicked reside. What he called the upper hell may have been what was later identified as the Limbo of the Fathers, the place where it was believed the righteous persons of the Old Testament rested until Christ descended into hell to bring them to heaven. He further fueled geographical speculation by a story he told of the

Gothic King Theodoric being carried off to hell. Although the story does not mention purgatory, it was taken as a clue to the earthly location of purgatory, since it was presumably in the neighborhood of hell.

Gregory made another novel contribution to the emerging doctrine of purgatory with his use of anecdotes to illustrate and support his claims, a practice that would later come to flourish as a means to popularize the doctrine after it was officially sanctioned in the thirteenth century. One particularly interesting feature of some of his stories is their depiction of departed persons expiating for their sins in the same place the sins were originally committed. In these stories, souls return to the scene of the crime, as it were, in order to experience the spiritual purging they need to undergo.[22] This notion was eventually rejected when the doctrine was formalized and purgatory was clearly defined as a part of the world to come, rather than this one.

In LeGoff's view, little of consequence happened during the next five hundred years in the formulation of the doctrine of purgatory. The claim has been challenged more recently by a number of historians, who contend that there were important developments in the early medieval era. One of these historians, Isabel Moreira, has made the case that the Venerable Bede was a crucial figure in giving the doctrine the stamp of orthodoxy. She cites a passage from his *Homilies,* from the 720s or early 730s, in which he presents purgatory as a simple fact, and describes it in a way that includes the essential elements of the doctrine that would be recognizable by later medieval theologians. Indeed, she contends that in his writings we first "encounter a view of purgatory that positions it theologically as an explicit expression of orthodox belief. This was Bede's contribution: to frame purgatory as an orthodox response to heresy."[23]

The specific heresy that he aimed to rebut was Origen's doctrine of universal salvation. Bede's account of purgatory framed the doctrine in such a way that it appropriated much of the spirit of Origen's view that made it so appealing. As Moreira puts it: "Purgatory was, in essence, a highly limited and circumscribed response to the appeal of universal salvation: it was an orthodox variation on universalism."[24] In particular, Bede offered the hope of salvation to a wider range of persons, including those guilty of serious sins, so long as they partook of the sacraments, confessed those sins, and were willing to do penance, even if this was delayed till their deathbed. This wider hope agreed with Augustine in denying universalism, but it held that many more persons were eligible for final salvation than he allowed.[25]

THE BIRTH OF PURGATORY

The twelfth century was the next significant period in the historical narrative of purgatory, and indeed this is where its birth can arguably be located with some precision.[26] One development in these intervening years is worth noting, however, because of its subsequent importance in the Christian calendar. This was the commemoration of the dead that grew up in the monastery at Cluny, France. Sometime in the eleventh century, probably between 1024 and 1033, Cluny began commemorating the dead in a service on November 2, the day after All Saints Day. Originally called the "Day of the Dead," it is now known as "All Souls Day." The practice quickly spread, and one effect of this was to create a solemn bond between living and dead that "cleared the ground for the inception of purgatory."[27] Throughout Christendom, this day was set aside especially to perform suffrages for the dead in the form of prayers, masses, and alms for the poor, in order to hasten their respite from the purging fires. The growing consensus emerging at this time that the living could assist the dead in this manner played a major role in the construction of purgatory as a distinct doctrine.

The stage was now set for purgatory proper to be born in the following century. According to Le Goff, this is the first time the word "purgatory" was used as a noun instead of an adjective, as in phrases such as "purgatorial fire." The figure he thinks likely coined the term, Peter Comestor, also went by the colorful name "Peter the Eater" because of his habit of devouring books! Peter was an original thinker and an important figure in the intellectual life of Paris and taught there at the school of Notre Dame. He was among the first, if not the very first, to write a commentary on Peter Lombard's *Sentences*. Le Goff is confident that Notre Dame was the specific birthplace of purgatory and that the term was first used as a noun sometime in the decade from 1170–1180.[28] The significance of this verbal change lay in the fact that it signaled a clear sense that purgatory was now recognized as a distinct place in the geography of the next world.

A critical intellectual development related to the acceptance of purgatory as a distinct place revolved around a revision of Augustine's fourfold classification of persons. His classification was reiterated by Gratian around 1140 in his work *Decretum*, which inaugurated the influential genre of literature that came to be known as canon law. Gratian's reiteration of the four categories reinforced Augustine's position, which posed a difficulty that needed to be resolved for the logic of purgatory to emerge clearly and cleanly. In short, it was necessary to simplify Augustine's classification in such a way that the four categories of persons could be reduced to three in order to correspond to three places: heaven, hell, and purgatory. This was accomplished by collapsing the two middle categories, the not altogether good and the not altogether wicked, into one intermediate group. The emergence of purgatory as a distinct place also signaled the end of the notion of the *refrigerium* and eventually the bosom of Abraham as well. The only other place that retained significance in the geography of the afterlife was the limbo of infants, for babies who had died without baptism, a place characterized by the loss of the beatific vision, but not the other pains of damnation.

Another important episode in the construction of the doctrine of purgatory occurred when the practice of auricular confession emerged as a form of penance. In 1215, the Fourth Lateran Council made auricular confession at least once a year mandatory for all adult Christians. The relevance of this practice to purgatory lies in the notion that purgatory might be the destination for persons whose venial sins were not dealt with in the confessional.

The concept of venial or minor sins is also integral to the doctrine of purgatory. The distinction between venial sins and mortal sins goes back to a passage in I John 5:16–17, which contrasts "sins unto death" with sins which are "not unto death." The New Revised Standard Version translates this passage as follows: "If you see a brother or sister committing what is not a mortal sin, you will ask, and God will give life to such a one—to those whose sin is not mortal. There is sin that is mortal; I do not say you should pray about that. All wrongdoing is sin, but there is sin that is not mortal." Although the idea of venial sins was articulated by thinkers as early as Tertullian and Augustine, it was not until the twelfth century that the term became commonplace, and not until the middle of that century that the contrast with mortal sins was worked out in a systematic fashion.

With all these concepts in place, the doctrine of purgatory readily gained a firm foothold in both the thinking and the imagination of Christendom. This is evident in two very different kinds of literature. First, purgatory was accepted in formal theological writing and literature as an integral component of Christian teaching. Le Goff identifies Peter the Chanter, an important founder of Scholasticism, and master of the school of Notre Dame of Paris who died in 1197 as the first person to integrate purgatory into theology in this fashion.[29]

The other type of literature, even more important for the popular acceptance of purgatory, was visionary stories and tales of persons who had allegedly visited purgatory and returned with lessons and morals to edify those who heard or read them. These visions were similar to apocalyptic literature of an earlier period and played a similar role. They appealed to the imagination and undercut skeptical doubts by playing the trump card of personal experience, an approach that reaches the larger populace in a way that even the best of theological arguments can never begin to do. One of the most famous of these works was *Saint Patrick's Purgatory*, written by a monk who lived in the Cistercian monastery of Saltrey of Huntingdonshire. He had first heard the tale from another monk who had been sent to Ireland to find an appropriate place to build a monastery. The tale includes an account of Saint Patrick's preaching to the Irish on the terror of hell and the delights of heaven, but without much success. In the midst of his preaching, it was alleged that Jesus showed him a round dark hole in a desolate place, where persons could spend a day and a night and observe both the misery of the wicked and the pleasures of the good. Thereby, their own sins could be purged if they had a true spirit of penitence. Patrick built a church beside the hole and also constructed a wall around it. Near the end of the twelfth century, many pilgrims began making their way to this site in hope of having their sins purged. The notion that the geography of the next world could be correlated with this one contributed powerfully to the appeal of purgatory in the popular imagination. *Saint Patrick's Purgatory* met with immediate success and was a best seller in the Middle Ages. Indeed, Le Goff goes so far as to say that the book was "in a sense the doctrine's literary birth certificate."[30]

At any rate, by the end of the twelfth century the term "purgatory" was in common use and the doctrine was well ensconced in Christian thinking and liturgical practice. The "baby" born earlier in the century showed every sign that it would grow strong and healthy and enjoy a long and productive life. Before moving on with its story, it will be worthwhile to reflect on the some of the factors that made the twelfth century ripe for giving birth to the doctrine. At least five such factors deserve mention.

FIVE FAVORABLE FACTORS

First, certain social and economic factors were arguably conducive to the birth and subsequent popularity of purgatory. As noted earlier in this chapter, Le Goff places a great deal of stress on these considerations as part of his case that the development of the doctrine was neither "uniform nor inevitable." To the contrary, it depended crucially on historical and social conditions that were contingent and might easily have taken another direction. Indeed, it is his "contention that the inception of Purgatory is the expression of a profound social change."[31] In particular, what emerged in the twelfth century were models of society based on a tripartite ideology, models with remote Indo-European roots. These models came to predominate over models based on binary pairs or opposites. As Le Goff puts it, this crucial change amounted to "the replacement of binary patterns by ternary patterns and the concomitant shift from blunt opposition, bilateral confrontation, to the more complex interplay of three elements."[32] It is readily apparent how this shift is amenable to the notion of an intermediate category of persons who are neither fully good nor evil, but who have hope of being elevated to goodness and true happiness.

A second change in the intellectual and social climate concerned new ways of thinking about time, space, and numbers. In particular, these ideas led to thinking of purgatory as a matter of moral accounting, with punishment accordingly construed in mathematical terms of proportionality and appropriate lengths of time. In the thirteenth century, these notions were further discussed and analyzed in quantitative terms, and it was only a matter of time before all this was applied to the controversial matter of indulgences as well.[33]

A third development in the twelfth century that created the matrix favorable to the birth of purgatory was the stress on justice as a value of pivotal concern, and related new ways of understanding sin and penance. Two critical distinctions were developed out of this concern for justice. First, there was an examination of the connections between sin and ignorance and a new attempt to take into account the intentions behind sinful behavior. An important historical source for this discussion was the work of Anselm of Canterbury, who had insisted that there is an essential difference between willful sin and sin that may be due to ignorance. He put the point as follows: "There is such a difference between the sin committed knowingly and the sin committed through ignorance, that a sin that one would never have been able to commit because of its enormity, had one but known, is merely venial, because it was committed through ignorance."[34] All the major theological schools of thought of the first half of the twelfth century accepted this distinction, which eventually became established as a traditional idea. This emphasis on intentionality led to a corresponding emphasis on personal responsibility, and these two combined were a major force leading to the practice of auricular confession, noted above. Auricular confession brought into focus not only one's individual responsibility before God, but also one's personal accountability for the intentions of his heart.

The second critical distinction emerging from the stress on justice was that between guilt and punishment, which is more subtle, but essential to understanding later controversies over the doctrine of purgatory, especially between Protestants and Roman Catholics. The important point for emphasis is that guilt (*culpa*) can be pardoned or remitted through contrition and confession, but the debt of punishment (*poena*) remains, and can only be satisfied by undergoing the penance levied by the Church. If the penance is not satisfactorily completed in this life, due either to negligence or untimely death, then the punishment must be undergone in purgatory.[35]

This brings us to the fourth favorable factor for the birth of purgatory, which was a fundamental shift in eschatology. Prior to the twelfth century, there was little consensus on what happened to persons who died between death and resurrection because the focus of eschatology was elsewhere. In particular, the emphasis in eschatological thought was on the resurrection and final judgment. In earlier centuries this was partly due to the belief that Christ's return was imminent. As this belief waned, and it became apparent that the time between death and resurrection might be lengthy, there was increasing interest in the intermediate period. Moreover, during the twelfth century, there was growing appreciation for this life and its goods, which made death a more poignant affair. This further intensified concern over individuals and the fate of separated souls as they awaited the resurrection. This shift in emphasis from resurrection and final judgment to the experience of separated souls in the intermediate state obviously comes to a head in vivid fashion in the doctrine of purgatory.[36]

The final notable trend of the twelfth century conducive to the formulation of the doctrine of purgatory was a new appreciation for the potential benefits of pain for personal and moral formation. Manuele Gragnolati has made the case for this point as a corrective to Le Goff's account of the history of the doctrine. He thinks Le Goff gives too much emphasis to the acceptance of purgatory as a distinct place, and the use of the term as a noun, among other matters. It is Gragnolati's contention that "the development of purgatory is tightly connected with the emergence of a new positive understanding of the productive potential of physical suffering to forge identity and meaning."[37]

All in all, it is clear that there were several factors in the social and intellectual matrix of the twelfth century that were favorable to the birth and flourishing of the doctrine of purgatory. While these factors hardly show that the emergence of the doctrine was inevitable, they do indicate that it was a natural development of certain currents of thought that had been flowing for centuries. Let us turn now to look at the formal shape of the doctrine and its systematic expression.

PURGATORY AS OFFICIAL DOCTRINE

If the twelfth century can be characterized as an era of creative foment, the thirteenth can be described by contrast as a century of organization and systematization. We can discern the trend toward order and system in the way the doctrine of purgatory took shape in this period. Indeed, it seems apparent that the triumph of purgatory met a certain reticence in Western theologians who did not seem altogether comfortable with the widespread acceptance of what was arguably a novel development in Christian teaching. This was due not only to a keen awareness that the doctrine lacked clear scriptural warrant, but also to a certain embarrassment over forms the doctrine took in popular piety and imagination. "One senses a desire to rationalize Purgatory, to tidy it up, to control it—in a word, to purge it of its offensive popular trappings."[38]

Perhaps the best example of the effort to rationalize purgatory is the work of the great Dominican theologian Albert of Lauingen, also known as Albertus Magnus. What made his work powerful and distinctive was his ability to synthesize the popular, empirical accounts of purgatory, which accounted so much for its broad appeal, with the rational academic arguments of the theologians. As Le Goff puts it, his work shows "the rationalization of a belief which, as we have seen, arose as much from imagery as from reasoning, as much from fantastic tales as from authorities, and which did not develop in any straightforward way but rather through countless meanderings, hesitations, and contradictions, culminating finally in a tightly knit fabric of beliefs."[39] That the doctrine could emerge in this fashion gave it a staying power it could not have enjoyed had it been only the bailiwick of storytellers and visionaries with colorful imaginations—or merely the product of arid arguments of intellectuals. Indeed, it is perhaps not surprising that Albert took perhaps the strongest stand among his contemporaries in declaring it a heresy to deny the doctrine of purgatory.

One of the most significant developments in terms of the desire to "control" purgatory came in the notion that priests have a certain jurisdiction over it. Alexander of Hales articulated the view that the "power of the keys," that is, the power to pardon sins given by Christ to Peter, and through him to all priests, applies to those in purgatory. Alexander also penned one of the clearest early statements on the value of suffrages for those in purgatory:

Just as the specific pain entails satisfaction for the sin, so the common pain of the universal Church, crying for the sins of dead believers, praying and lamenting for them, is an aid to satisfaction; it does not create satisfaction in itself, but with the pain of the penitent aids in satisfaction, which is the very definition of suffrage. Suffrage is in fact the merit of the Church, capable of diminishing the pain of one of its members.[40]

Alexander's argument, of course, hinges on a strong sense of the "communion of the saints," and the conviction that the intercession of the living could generate merit for the dead and expedite their purging. This notion readily lent itself to one of the most infamous aspects of the doctrine of purgatory, namely, the whole system of indulgences and the abuses that it later generated.

In a related vein, Hugh of Saint-Cher in the thirteenth century first based indulgences on the notion that a "treasury of merits" from Christ, the Virgin Mary, and the saints is available to the Church to dispense to the faithful under certain prescribed conditions. Again, the concept of the solidarity and the mystical unity that holds in the Body of Christ is the underlying theological rationale for this.

With purgatory so well entrenched in both the thinking and ecclesial practices of the Western Church, it was inevitable that it would soon receive official endorsement and affirmation at the highest levels of authority. In 1254, Pope Innocent IV sent a letter to Cardinal Eudes of Chateauroux of the Greek Church in which he defined purgatory in a way that he hoped the Greek Church could accept. Le Goff describes this letter, which follows, as "the birth certificate of Purgatory as a doctrinally defined place."[41]

> Since the Truth asserts in the Gospel that, if anyone blasphemes against the Holy Spirit, this sin will not be forgiven either in this world or in the next: by which we are given to understand that certain faults are pardoned in the present time, and others in the other life; since the Apostle also declares that the work of each man, whatever it may be, shall be tried by fire and that if it burns the worker will suffer the loss, but he himself will be saved yet as by fire; since the Greeks themselves, it is said, believe and profess truly and without hesitation that the souls of those who die after receiving penance but without having had the time to complete it, or who die without mortal sin but guilty of venial (sins) or minor faults, are purged after death and may be helped by suffrages of the Church; we, considering that the Greeks assert that they cannot find in the works of their doctors any certain and proper name to designate the place of this purgation, and that, moreover, according to the traditions and authority of the Holy Fathers, this name is Purgatory, we wish that in the future this expression be also accepted by them. For, in the temporary fire, sins, not of course crimes and capital errors, which could not previously have been forgiven through penance, but slight and minor sins, are purged; if they have not been forgiven during existence, they weigh down the soul after death.[42]

This statement is notable for its modesty and its minimalism. Notice that the Pontiff cites a couple of the classic biblical texts that had been used to support purgatory for centuries, along with what he takes to be a broad consensus among Latin and Greek Christians on the matter of postmortem purging of sins. Perhaps the most controversial aspect of the statement is his mild attempt to get the Greeks to assent to the name "Purgatory" as a place.

Another landmark in the official promulgation of purgatory is the Second Council of Lyons in 1274. This is a very significant date because it was here for the first time that purgatory received the institutional stamp of approval at the hands of a Church Council. The following statement was incorporated into the appendix of the constitution affirmed by the Council:

> However, owing to various errors that have been introduced by the ignorance of some and the malice of others, (the Roman Church) states and proclaims that those who fall into sin after baptism must not be rebaptized, but that through a genuine penitence they obtain pardon for their sins. That if, truly penitent, they die in charity before having, by worthy fruits of penance, rendered satisfaction for what they have done by commission or omission, their souls, as brother John has explained to us, are purged after their death, by purgatorial or purificatory penalties, and that, for the alleviation of these penalties, they are served by the suffrages of the living faithful, to wit, the sacrifice of the mass, prayers, alms, and other works of piety that the faithful customarily offer on behalf of others of the faithful according to the institutions of the Church. The souls of those who, after receiving baptism, have contracted absolutely no taint of sin, as well as those who, after contracting the taint of sin, have been purified either while they remained in their bodies or after being stripped of their bodies are, as was stated above, immediately received into heaven.[43]

This statement, like the one just cited from Pope Innocent IV, was formulated with ecumenical relations with the Greeks in mind. The word "purgatory" as a noun or a place does not appear, nor is there mention of fire, both of which may reflect an attempt to alleviate Greek concerns and objections.

Before concluding this section, I want to highlight the fascinating fact that purgatory was conceived in two fundamentally different ways, one of which finally prevailed in the thirteenth century. The simplest way to put the matter is to ask whether purgatory should be thought of as closer to hell or to heaven. Some theologians saw it as closer to hell, and accordingly emphasized the pain and terrors of purgatory as administered by demons, with the apparent motive of frightening sinners into reforming their lives while still alive in this world. By contrast, others represented purgatory as closer to heaven, and the element of hope comes to the forefront, with good angels serving as guides. That is, purgatory represents the hope of salvation for a broader range of sinners and emphasizes the glory that ultimately may be achieved by those consigned to it.

As a middle place, purgatory naturally teetered between the more securely established regions of heaven and hell, but the view that eventually come to predominate in the thirteenth century was the infernalized version that played more on fear than on hope. This is reflected in many of the artistic renditions of purgatory, which depict it as a frightful place hardly distinguishable from hell. As Stephen

Greenblatt points out, this presented artists with a representational challenge, a challenge that was typically met by reproducing the imagery of hell, but adding an image of rescue.[44] The frightful picture of purgatory, any of whose pains are worse than any pain in this life, readily lent itself to the sale of indulgences for persons willing to pay any (at least financial) price to avoid or shorten such horrific suffering. While even Aquinas contributed to this "infernalization" of purgatory by rejecting the view that it was somewhere above us, it is important to note that there were others whose thought tended more in the direction of paradise rather than hell, such as Saint Bonaventure and Albertus Magnus.[45]

It is perhaps only fitting that the thirteenth century ended, or rather the fourteenth began, with an event rife with symbolic as well as substantive significance for the doctrine of purgatory. In the year 1300, Pope Boniface VIII invited all Christians to come to Rome in celebration of the jubilee, a Jewish festival that was to be held every fifty years as prescribed in Leviticus 25. In honor of the Jewish jubilee, Boniface intended the year to be a time of rest in which Christians could practice penance and achieve forgiveness. As a special part of this celebration, he offered to all pilgrims who came to Rome a plenary indulgence, complete pardon for all sins, a favor that heretofore had been extended only to Crusaders. The relevance of this event to purgatory is that this plenary indulgence was extended to certain persons among the dead as well as the living. In particular, on Christmas Day of that year, it was granted to all those who had died while on their pilgrimage to Rome as well as to those who sincerely intended to take the pilgrimage but were unable to do so. The importance of this event lay in the fact that it marked the first occasion that a Pope employed the presumed power to liberate souls from purgatory, a power that had been articulated before but until this time had never actually been exercised.

It is more than a little ironic that Pope Boniface appears in the most famous literary work ever to celebrate purgatory, indeed, one of the singular literary achievements of all time. I refer of course to Dante's immortal *Divine Comedy*. The irony, however, is that Boniface appears not in the *Purgatorio*, but rather in the *Inferno*, where he is consigned to hell for his numerous offenses, including avarice, aggressively asserting claims of temporal power, and demeaning his holy office by pursuing other political purposes.[46] Indeed, Dante's placement of various persons in hell, purgatory, and heaven has itself often been seen as perhaps the high water mark of deploying the afterlife for political purposes.[47]

Dante wrote his great masterpiece sometime between his exile from Florence in 1302 and his death in Ravenna in 1321. The first two parts, the *Inferno* and the *Purgatorio*, were completed by 1319. It is hard to exaggerate the long-term significance of this poem for the fortunes of the doctrine of purgatory. Not only did Dante enshrine purgatory with cultural immortality by presenting it with unforgettable imagery and sheer brilliance, he also did so with compelling theological sophistication. For our purposes, it is important to note that Dante came down decidedly in favor of moving purgatory in the direction of paradise rather than hell. While his imagery of purgatory is colorfully and creatively frightful to be sure, the overriding mood is still one of hope and anticipation. As Dorothy Sayers has observed, "Dante (so often called 'bitter,' 'grim,' and 'gloomy,' by those who have never got further than the *Inferno*) is the supreme poet of joy."[48] And while this joy comes to its natural climax in the *Paradisio*, it is already present in preliminary fashion in the *Purgatorio*.

Dante famously depicts purgatory as a mountain, divided into seven cornices in each of which souls are purged of one of the seven deadly sins. With Virgil as his guide, Dante travels in purgatory for four days during the Easter season, the season above all that evokes victory and salvation. It is by ascending the mountain, and negotiating the appropriate pain and punishment, that sin is cleansed and disordered loves are rightly ordered so that souls can be reunited with God, their ultimate true love.

Le Goff judges that Dante not only "rescued Purgatory from the infernalization to which the Church subjected it in the thirteenth century," but also that he "more than anyone else made Purgatory the intermediate region of the other world."[49] In addition, he contends that Dante brought a truly original element to the doctrine, namely, his notion of "ante-Purgatory."[50] That is, Dante described a number of sinners who had to wait for a time at the base of the mountain before they were allowed to enter purgatory proper and begin the process of cleansing and renewal. Le Goff speculates that Dante included this element as a response to the increasingly common practice of promising purgatory to those who repented only at the point of death. This suggests that while Dante did not doubt God's mercy in such cases, he also thought it appropriate that such souls should endure some additional time of preparation before they would be ready to make the sort of moral and spiritual progress that purgatory represents. This reflects Dante's belief that ante-purgatory, like purgatory proper, is a reflection not only of God's great mercy, but also of his perfect justice. The fact that purgatory plausibly holds mercy and justice together in vivid fashion is no doubt a large part of the reason that the doctrine gained such a strong foothold in Christian theology.

PURGATORY REJECTED AND REAFFIRMED

Despite the stunning success of purgatory in gaining acceptance and popular support, it has not been without its critics, even before the time of the Reformation. The Arras heretics rejected it in 1025, as did the Cologne heretics in 1143–1144, both for reasons involving their opposition to prayers for the dead. In the thirteenth century the Waldensians repudiated it, and more ambiguously, so did the Cathari. While the rejection of the doctrine by these obscure groups may be of little consequence, the same cannot be said about the fact that purgatory has been a major source of controversy with the other major ʾanches of the Church, namely, the Eastern Church and Protestantism. While the broad rejection of the doctrine by Protestantism is well-known, it is important to emphasize that the Eastern Church has also resisted the doctrine, at least as taught by the Roman Church.

As noted early in this chapter, one of the great ironies in the history of the doctrine is that two prominent Greek theologians are among the earliest fathers of purgatory. Moreover, Eastern theology traditionally has affirmed prayers for the dead and the likelihood of postmortem purification before the final judgment. So at least in substance, it appears that Eastern theology is in agreement with the core claims of the doctrine of purgatory. Nevertheless, Eastern theology has not embraced the speculation and formalization represented by the theological tradition of Roman Catholicism. It is worth stressing, however, that official statements of the doctrine have typically been more modest than those of the theologians. As noted above, the formulation of the doctrine of purgatory by the Second Council of Lyons appears to be worded in such a way as to avoid offending Greek sensibilities. In particular, the statement did not mention fire as a means of punishment, nor did it specify that purgatory is a distinct place comparable to heaven and hell.

Purgatory was also involved in the controversies of the Council of Florence in 1439. This Council was composed of delegates from both the Latin and Greek Churches and attempted to reach agreement on a number of issues that divided them. While agreements were formally signed, the union did not last long, and a number of critics in the Greek Church saw it as a spurious union that was made under duress.[51] So while the year 1439 is another milestone in the conciliar affirmation of the doctrine of purgatory by the Roman Catholic Church, this date is also a marker of the fact that the doctrine has sometimes been a point of fiery contention between Roman and Eastern Christianity.

Although the differences between Roman and Eastern theology on the matter of purgatory are genuine ones, they are arguably minor compared to their agreement on the reality of postmortem cleansing in the intermediate state and the important role of prayers for the dead in this matter. The same cannot be said, however, about Rome and Protestantism, for purgatory has been a major flashpoint of controversy in the often volatile relationship between these two branches of the Church. Indeed, it is well-known that the doctrine of purgatory was a major factor in those epochal events that gave birth to the Protestant Reformation.

Perhaps it is more accurate to say that it was abuses related to the doctrine rather than the doctrine itself that played this pivotal historical role, but the abuses were at the time so closely intertwined with the doctrine itself that it was hard for many to make that distinction. I refer, of course, to the sale of indulgences and the reckless and scandalous manner in which this was commonly done as a means of fund-raising for the Church. As Roland Bainton memorably put it, "they were the bingo of the sixteenth century."[52] The most notorious instance of this was carried out, beginning in 1517, by a Dominican Monk named Tetzel, a highly efficient vendor in the indulgence business, whose hawking of his purgatory passes amounted to something of a traveling burlesque show.

Tetzel carried out this mission at the behest of Albert of Brandenburg, who had borrowed a considerable amount of money that he had paid to Pope Leo X as the installation fee for the position of Archbishop of Mainz. By securing this office, he became the primate of Germany. As a favor to help him repay this debt, Leo extended to Albert the privilege of granting indulgences for a period of eight years. But there was another financial consideration involved as well. Leo himself badly needed additional revenue to complete the building of St Peter's Cathedral, a project that had been started by his predecessor. The two reached an agreement that half of the funds from the sale of indulgences would go to Leo to build St Peter's and the other half would go to pay Albert's debt.

Albert's debt was not mentioned in promoting the indulgence, and all attention was focused on the noble goal of building a cathedral that would be a fitting monument to honor Saints Peter and Paul along with other saints and martyrs. The indulgence was a plenary one that offered benefits that made it a highly attractive purchase by any measure. All subscribers were promised full remission of all sins that would restore them to the state of innocence received at baptism, and thereby free them from the pains of purgatory. To make the deal even sweeter, indulgences could be purchased on behalf of those already dead to free them from the suffering of purgatory. Here is a sample of Tetzel's rhapsodic sales pitch sermon:

> Listen to the voices of your dear dead relatives and friends, beseeching you and saying, "Pity us, pity us. We are in dire torment from which you can redeem us for a pittance." Do you not wish to? Open your ears. Hear the father saying to his son, the mother to her daughter, "We bore you, nourished you, brought you up, left you our fortunes, and you are so cruel and hard that now you are not willing for so little to set us free. Will you let us lie here in flames? will you delay our promised glory?"
>
> > Remember that you are able to release them, for
> > As soon as the coin in the coffer rings,
> > The soul from purgatory springs.[53]

The couplet at the end of this quote is surely among the most infamous lines in Western history and perhaps symbolizes as well as anything the Protestant antipathy to the doctrine of purgatory. Later that year, on All Saints eve, Luther posted his Ninety-five Theses on the door of the Castle Church, in which he addressed the reckless claims made by Tetzel, among other issues. Theses Twenty-seven and Twenty–eight, for instance, read:

> 27. There is no divine authority for preaching that the soul flies out of purgatory immediately the money clinks in the bottom of the chest.

> 28. It is certainly possible that when the money clinks in the bottom of the chest avarice and greed increase; but when the church offers intercession, all depends on the will of God.[54]

Notice that Luther did not reject the doctrine of purgatory wholesale at this point of his career, but only the abuses surrounding it. It was only later that he would reject it altogether, as would his fellow reformer John Calvin.[55]

Indeed, so pivotal was the German Reformer's attack on the Dominican's Monk's traveling show that historian Carlos Eire has remarked with humorous hyperbole that however controversial the date of purgatory's birth may be, "no one can argue with the very exact date that can be given to the death of purgatory: October 31, 1517, when Luther began his challenge of Tetzel's indulgence preaching."[56] The hyperbole is evident in the fact that Eire goes on a few pages later to show how purgatory remained alive and well in Roman Catholic countries long after the Reformation.

It is important to emphasize, however, that the history of purgatory in Protestant countries is not simply a story of the total demise of the doctrine, even when it was officially repudiated. For it is arguable that the doctrine still cast its shadow and reappeared in various sublimated forms in the generations and even centuries after it was banished. In the next chapter we will look in more detail at Protestant alternatives to purgatory, but for now it is noteworthy that figures ranging from John Bunyan to Richard Baxter to John Locke articulated visions of spiritual discipline and growth that appear to be shaped in no small measure by the doctrine. Richard K. Fenn has advanced this thesis, pointing out that Bunyan and Baxter present pictures of life dominated by the prospect of heaven that are deeply reminiscent of Dante's souls in purgatory. Like Dante's souls making up for lost time and past failures, Bunyan and Baxter urge that every moment counts and must be used to advance one's journey to heaven. Indeed, he contends that Locke's theory of education, with its goal of shaping the human heart in virtue and perfecting character, is a variation on purgatory. As he puts it: "There seems to be no doubt that what Locke had in mind was a secular pedagogy that would be the functional equivalent of purgatory and would smooth the path of the individual to heaven."[57]

Indeed, the case can be made that the ban on purgatory was a significant factor in the rise of secularization and its eventual predominance in many Protestant countries. Whereas purgatory nurtured a vivid sense of connection with the departed, and cultivated a concern for the eternal world to come, the denial of purgatory put the dead out of mind, and redirected interest, resources, and energy onto this world. The related contempt for monasticism, with its focus on the invisible world, had the same effect of diminishing the significance of that world, and magnifying the importance of this one.[58]

In the wake of the Reformation, the so called Counter-Reformation emerged as the Roman Catholic Church reiterated its position at the Council of Trent on several controversial issues in response to its Protestant critics. Among the issues addressed was the doctrine of purgatory, which was reaffirmed at the twenty-fifth session of the Council in 1563. The decree on purgatory registers the impact of the Reformation by acknowledging abuses related to the doctrine and a commitment to correct them, as well as a concern to avoid sensational treatments of it.

But let the more difficult and subtle questions, and which tend not to edification, and from which for the most part there is no increase in piety, be excluded from popular discourses before the uneducated multitude....While those things which tend to a certain kind of curiosity or superstition, or which savour of filthy lucre, let them prohibit as scandals and stumbling-blocks of the faithful. But let the bishops take care, that the suffrages of the faithful who are living, to wit the sacrifices of masses, prayers, alms, and other works of piety, which have been wont to be performed by the faithful for the other faithful departed, be piously and devoutly performed, in accordance with the institutes of the church.[59]

As with other official statements of the doctrine, the modesty and reserve of what is claimed is noteworthy. The substance of the doctrine remains intact, despite the damage to its reputation done by "popular discourses" as well as peddlers for profit.

This is not to say that purgatory was stripped of its cultural clout in the aftermath of these events, nor of its enormous economic effect. Chastened as the doctrine may have been in its official post-Reformation formulations, it still retained considerable sway over the emotions and imaginations of believers in Roman Catholic countries—as well as their bank accounts. Perhaps the most extraordinary example of purgatory's ongoing power was on display in Spain, beginning with the reign of King Philip II who, between 1563 and 1596, built for himself and his successors a palace-monastery complex that was at the time the largest building in the world. It included an enormous collection of relics, along with tens of millions of years of indulgences, and was staffed by numerous monks whose sole responsibility was to offer constant masses and prayers for the king and other members of the royal family, living as well as dead. As striking as this is, there is considerable evidence that many of Philip's subjects wrote wills that reflected the same sort of extraordinary anxiety over the fate of their souls in the world to come. Indeed, the amount of money spent by Philip II, Philip III, and Philip IV, along with their subjects, in order to speed their way through purgatory is simply staggering. Eire suggests that when the total cost for this is tallied, "chances are that the amount of money spent by the subjects of these three Philips on their souls and those of their dead could easily dwarf the amount spent by the monarchs and add up to much more than several years' worth of treasure from the New World."[60]

INTO THE TWENTY-FIRST CENTURY

Once purgatory had gestated over several centuries, was born, theologically nurtured, officially affirmed, staunchly defended against its critics, artistically celebrated in the world of imagination, and enshrined in pious ecclesial practice, it was destined to enjoy a long period of popularity and influence. According to Le Goff, the "most fervent, most 'glorious' moments in the history of Purgatory belong to the period between the fifteenth and nineteenth centuries."[61] In addition to sermons and pamphlets propagating the doctrine, it was also imaged in numerous frescoes, engravings, altar decorations, and the like. During this period, purgatory remained a vivid part of Roman Catholic piety as well as a volatile point of controversy with Protestantism. We can see this reflected in the pointed polemics against purgatory from the distinguished Princeton theologian Charles Hodge, who wrote his influential systematic theology in the nineteenth century. Hodge noted that Catholic apologists wrote about purgatory in very palatable terms in articles directed at Protestant readers, while depicting it as frightening and grim in writings aimed at their fellow Catholics. Reiterating traditional Protestant skepticism about the abuses of the doctrine, he wrote that purgatory is "a tremendous engine of priestly power. The feet of the tiger with the claws withdrawn are soft as velvet; when those claws are extended, they are fearful instruments of laceration and death."[62]

When we move into the twentieth century and beyond, however, it is safe to say that purgatory no longer assumes anything even remotely like the significance in Roman Catholic thought and piety that it did in earlier centuries. Perhaps this is broadly due to increasing secularization, and to the extent that this is true, the same could be said of heaven and hell, as well as even more basic doctrines of the faith such as the resurrection. But it is still probably the case that purgatory has declined in significance for many Roman Catholics who are still generally traditional in their theological beliefs. Indeed, there is much less certainty over what the doctrine even entails. We can see this reflected in the treatment of purgatory by the great Catholic theologian Karl Rahner. In an essay on the doctrine written in dialogue style, he has this exchange:

> A short time ago one theologian said to another, "The pope insisted again yesterday on the traditional doctrine of purgatory." The other replied, "I've nothing against that. But if I only knew what exactly I am supposed to believe in this respect! Do you know? Can you look into the pope's mind to see what he was thinking? I can't. Anyway, if you could, it would presumably still be doubtful whether what the pope precisely understood by purgatory in this declaration would as such be absolutely binding on me as a matter of faith."[63]

A bit later in the dialogue, one of the theologians remarks that "it must be admitted that the doctrine of purgatory does not seem particularly important today even to the devout Christian."[64]

Despite such ambivalence and uncertainty, purgatory remains as official teaching. Vatican II, noted for bringing fresh theological winds into Roman Catholicism, reiterates the substance of the doctrine of purgatory in a statement on indulgences in the contemporary Church:

> The doctrine of purgatory clearly demonstrates that even when the guilt of sin has been taken away, punishment for it or the consequences of it may remain to be expiated or cleansed. They often are. In fact, in purgatory the souls of those "who died in the charity

of God and truly repentant, but who had not made satisfaction with adequate penance for their sins and omissions" are cleansed after death with punishments designed to purge away their debt.[65]

Of course, there is often a wide gap between official doctrine and the beliefs and attitudes of Church members, and the fact that purgatory is still official doctrine does little to tell us to what extent it remains a live conviction for contemporary Roman Catholics.

In drawing this survey of the history of purgatory to a close, it is perhaps fitting to note that the first pontiff of the twenty-first century, formerly Cardinal Ratzinger, now Benedict XVI, is a scholar of eschatology who has written at some length on purgatory. Indeed, in a chapter entitled "Hell, Purgatory, Heaven" he spends more pages on purgatory than he does on heaven and hell combined. I will engage his views in more detail later in this book, but for now it is worth pointing out that his treatment of the doctrine seeks to present it in a way that is both faithful to the tradition as well as ecumenically attractive. This suggests that at this stage of the history of the doctrine, the conditions may be ripe for it to be articulated in a way that gains acceptance beyond the circles of Roman Catholicism.

CONCLUSION

Writing the history of any concept that has developed over many centuries is a daunting task, especially when one is attempting to do so in a concise and summary fashion. The history of purgatory is particularly complex and likely to be contested because believers from different traditions have a theological stake in the doctrine, either in supporting it or rejecting it. Others, moreover, see the story entirely from a secular viewpoint and explain all doctrinal development in social, cultural, and economic terms, and so on. It is hardly to be expected that tough-minded Roman Catholics, Protestants, and agnostics will share a common understanding of the history of purgatory, even if they agree on a certain broad narrative of events in that history.

Even the narrative of key events and personalities in the story is open to argument and dispute. Le Goff singles out Clement, Origen, Augustine, and Gregory the Great as the true fathers of purgatory, while Pope Benedict XVI gives significant credit to Cyprian in the early development of the doctrine, a claim doubted by Le Goff, who sees this as an example of the evolutionary view of the doctrine, which he rejects. Moreover, what counts as the birth of the doctrine is disputed. Whereas Le Goff places strong emphasis on the use of purgatory as a noun, and on this basis traces the birth of the doctrine to the Notre Dame school in Paris sometime in the decade 1170–1180, others think he places too much stress on such factors and overlooks more significant matters. Moreira, representing more recent historians, thinks the main contours of purgatory as an orthodox doctrine emerged much earlier, particularly in the work of the Venerable Bede at the turn of the eighth century. And to complicate matters further, Le Goff himself assigns two different "birth certificates" to purgatory, in addition to his claim about the time and place in which it was born. Recall that he identifies *Saint Patrick's Purgatory*, probably written around 1190, as its "literary birth certificate" and Pope Innocent IV's letter in 1254 as the "birth certificate of Purgatory as a doctrinally defined place." Given the multiple dimensions of Purgatory, including theological concept, official doctrine, and subject of popular culture—not to mention what is at stake existentially and ecclesially—it should hardly be surprising that it would have such a fascinating, albeit complex and controversial, lineage.

2

⌥

Protestant Objections and
Alternatives to Purgatory

For as long as I can remember, I've had a theory that life on earth *is* purgatory, because life on earth seems to have all the purgatorial qualities that were once described to me by nuns.
　　　　　　—Chuck Klosterman

A s noted in the previous chapter, purgatory has been a fighting word for Protestants. The roots of Protestant disdain for the doctrine go back at least to the Reformation, where purgatory was closely linked to the most fundamental as well the most volatile issues that divided Western Christendom. It is not always clear whether it was purgatory proper or the abuses surrounding the doctrine that were the real problem for Protestant critics, but the abuses associated with the doctrine were so scandalous that the doctrine itself could not escape long-term damage and distortion. Recall that Luther did not reject the doctrine altogether in the early stages of the Reformation, but he did so later. After he did, purgatory was not infrequently the target of his characteristically colorful and barbed rhetoric. For instance:

> It must give rise to suspicion that in order to substantiate this doctrine no more than one passage could be discovered in the entire Bible; moreover this passage is in the least important and most despised book. Especially since so much depends on this doctrine which is so important that, indeed, the papacy and the whole hierarchy are all but built upon it, and derive all their wealth and honor from it. Surely, the majority of priests would starve to death if there were no purgatory.[1]

The scriptural text in question is the one from 2 Maccabees cited in the previous chapter, and of course, Luther exaggerates in his claim that this was the only text that was used to support the doctrine. Nevertheless, his claim that the doctrine lacks solid biblical warrant is a quintessentially Protestant one.

Protestant polemicists further buttressed this claim by giving an account of the origin of the doctrine in terms of sheer fancy and illusion. We saw in the last chapter that purgatory first gained a foothold in the larger populace through literary works that captured the popular imagination. Critics exploited this reality in arguing that purgatory was nothing more than a vivid work of human creativity, as opposed to a sober reality revealed in scripture. Lacking any objective grounds for its support, the doctrine was spun out of untrammeled fantasy and fabrication. In short, it was a massive piece of poetry transfigured into dogma. The great poet John Donne pointedly asserted as much, as follows: "Men that make God himself of a piece of bread, may easily make Purgatory of a Dream, and of Apparitions, and imaginary visions of sick or melancholic men."[2]

The argument that purgatory was a work of creative imagination was not, however, intended to suggest that it was a harmless fancy that could be tolerated or simply ignored. This is apparent in the attitude of Calvin, who, though less inclined to rhetorical exaggeration than Luther, attacked the doctrine with equal vigor. Indeed, Calvin criticized Luther's successor Melanchthon for not addressing the issue of purgatory in the Augsburg Confession, and he wrote as follows in a thinly veiled reference to him:

> And I do not agree with certain persons who think that one ought to dissemble on this point, and make no mention of purgatory, from which, as they say, fierce conflicts arise but little edification can be obtained. Certainly, I myself would advise that such trifles be neglected if they did not have their serious consequences. But since purgatory is constructed out of many blasphemies and is daily propped up with new ones, and since it incites so many grave offences, it is certainly not to be winked at.[3]

As we shall see, the magisterial reformers thought the notion of purgatory struck at the very heart of the gospel, a charge that many contemporary Protestants would still level at the doctrine.

Before examining more closely why many Protestants hold this conviction, it is important to stress that they offer their own distinctive alternatives to the doctrine of purgatory, and indeed they can hardly avoid doing so as a matter of theological consistency. Consider the following words of Anglican divine John Fletcher, whose views we shall examine later in this chapter:

> If we understand by *purgatory*, the manner in which souls, still polluted with the remains of sin, are, or may be *purged* from these remains, that they may see a holy God, and dwell with him forever; the question, *Which is the true purgatory?* is by no means frivolous: for it is the grand inquiry, *How shall I be eternally saved?* proposed in different expressions.[4]

As Fletcher's comments suggest, some version of purgatory is a theological necessity for any adequate Christian scheme of thought. For ultimate salvation requires that one be fully purged of all sin, and justification and regeneration, the initial components of salvation do not fully accomplish this. This is not to assume that Protestant accounts of salvation are identical to Eastern or Roman ones, nor that all Protestants understand salvation in exactly the same way, for that matter. However, there is still broad agreement among all Christian traditions that heaven is a place of perfect holiness and nothing sinful or impure can enter there. Fully to experience the presence of God in heaven we must be completely transformed after his moral image. The "remains of sin" must be dealt with in some fashion, and the question of when and how this occurs cannot be evaded. The real issue, as Fletcher says, is not *whether* purgatory is true, but *which account* of purgatory is the true one?

In what follows, I shall examine several Protestant accounts of how we are perfected and made fit for heaven. Thereby we shall consider not only the theological grounds upon which Protestants have rejected the doctrine of purgatory, but also how their theological systems address the problems that the concept of purgatory was developed to resolve. We shall focus primarily on classical sources but also look more briefly at some contemporary spokesmen.

LUTHERAN PERSPECTIVES ON PURGATORY

Purgatory is a major theme in one of the most famous documents in Church history, namely, Luther's Ninety-five Theses. Indeed, purgatory is mentioned explicitly in at least eleven of them, and is implicitly present in several others as well. Even more pervasive in the document are numerous references to indulgences, which recur throughout. Luther's driving passion throughout this document, of course, is faithfulness to the gospel. His main concern was not merely the fact that indulgences provided a flimsy cover for greed and oppression, but more importantly that they had come to obscure, if not obliterate, the true nature of grace and salvation.

In view of this, it is most interesting that Luther's numerous references to purgatory in the Ninety-five Theses take its existence for granted. He never objects to the doctrine itself, but only distortions of it, especially the notion that souls who are there can be freed from it by the purchase of indulgences. Indeed, in Thesis Thirteen, he levels a broad challenge to exaggerated claims to papal authority and related abuses of the doctrine of purgatory when he denies the claim that the dead remain subject to ecclesiastical control: "Death puts an end to all the claims of the church; even the dying are already dead to the canon laws, and are no longer bound by them."[5] The authority of the pope and the power of the keys do not extend beyond death, as Luther saw it, and if this is so, it undercuts the very roots of the theology of indulgences and the motivation many had for buying them. But while he denies that the pope has jurisdiction over purgatory and the fate of those who suffer there, he does nevertheless commend intercession for those souls and says that this is the basis on which the pope should pronounce remission of their sins.[6]

For our purposes, what is more interesting is that he offers in a few of his Theses a suggestive idea that could serve as an alternative to the Roman account of purgatory, namely, Theses Fourteen through Sixteen:

> 14. Defective piety or love in a dying person is necessarily accompanied by great fear, which is greatest where the piety or love is least.

> 15. This fear or horror is sufficient in itself, whatever else might be said, to constitute the pain of purgatory, since it approaches very closely to the horror of despair.

> 16. There seems to be the same difference between hell, purgatory, and heaven as between despair, uncertainty, and assurance.[7]

Given the nature of this document, Luther does not, of course, develop his thoughts in any sort of detail. It is worth noting, however, that the background for his notion that defective love and piety produce fear is the text from I John which reads: "There is no fear in love, but perfect love casts out fear; for fear has to do with punishment, and whoever fears has not reached perfection in love."[8] The larger context of this scriptural passage involves the day of judgment and how we may be perfected in love so that we will not fear the coming of that day.

Luther's emphasis here on fear and uncertainty is a highly significant one that goes to the very heart of the Reformation. One of the hallmarks of Protestant theology is an emphasis on assurance, that we can know our sins are forgiven and we are accepted by God. Luther's own struggles with fear and a guilty conscience were, of course, a major motivating factor in his own recovery of the New Testament doctrine of justification by faith and its liberating power. By contrast, Roman theology, especially in its abusive forms at the time of the Reformation, played heavily on fear and uncertainty, and the doctrine of purgatory epitomized many of these tendencies. Roland Bainton contends that Luther's well-known bouts with depression can be explained by the fact that medieval religion deliberately induced tensions in believers by playing alternately on their hopes and fears:

> Hell was stoked, not because men lived in perpetual dread, but precisely because they did not, and in order to instill enough fear to drive them to the sacraments of the Church. If they were petrified with terror, purgatory was introduced by way of mitigation as an intermediate place where those not bad enough for hell nor good enough for heaven might make further expiation. If this alleviation inspired complacency, the temperature was advanced on purgatory, and then the pressure was again relaxed through indulgences.[9]

In light of this, it is more than telling that Luther equates purgatory with uncertainty in Thesis Sixteen. Moreover, it is hardly surprising that Protestant theology should find the doctrine of purgatory discordant with its theme song of faith and assurance.

This also helps to explain why classic Reformation theology sees justification rather than sanctification as the essence of salvation, and takes pains not to make justification in any way dependent upon sanctification. Whereas justification was understood as an all or nothing matter, sanctification was a matter of degrees. Because justification is by faith, one could be certain that he is completely forgiven of his sin and delivered from any threat of condemnation. By exercising faith in the merits of Christ, one could know he was accepted by God, despite the fact that sanctification is at best only partial in this life. As the Formula of Concord puts it:

> For because this inchoate righteousness or renewal in us is imperfect and impure in this life on account of the flesh, no one can therewith and thereby stand before the tribunal of God. Only the righteousness of the obedience, passion, and death of Christ which is reckoned to faith can stand before God's tribunal.[10]

And yet, the authors of the classic expressions of Lutheran theology never tire of emphasizing that they do not mean to downplay the importance of sincere repentance that issues in a changed life and good works. Indeed, the lack of such repentance and good works is clear evidence that one does not have true saving faith.[11]

Now what is highly interesting for our concerns is that Melanchthon developed the concept of repentance in such a way that it addresses the doctrine of purgatory, and provides an alternative to it. Although purgatory is not mentioned in the Augsburg Confession itself—to Calvin's dismay, as noted above—it is critically discussed in the Apology of the Augsburg Confession, particularly in Article XII on penitence. In this article, Melanchthon criticizes at length the Roman view of penitence for its undue complexity and its failure to provide the assurance of forgiveness for troubled consciences. The Roman view, he notes, consists of three steps: contrition, confession, and satisfaction. The third of these is particularly relevant to purgatory, as we shall see in more detail in the next chapter, for in order for satisfaction to be achieved, some appropriate punishment or compensation must be paid for sins, either in the form of works of supererogation such as pilgrimages, rosaries, or the like, or in the purchase of indulgences. If such satisfaction is not achieved in this life, the appropriate punishment is meted out in the next life in purgatory.

In contrast to the complexities of the Roman account, Melanchthon points out that Lutheran theology gives penitence just two parts: contrition and faith. A person who is sincerely contrite can by faith claim absolution and know that his sins are forgiven and that he is accepted by God. Among the scripture passages cited to defend this account of penitence is Colossians 2:11–12, which speaks of putting off the sins of the flesh and being raised with Christ through faith. Melanchthon expounds this text as follows:

> Mortifying, quickening, putting off the body of sins, being raised—we are not to understand these terms in a Platonic sense as counterfeit changes; but mortification means genuine terrors, like those of the dying, which nature could not bear without the support

of faith. Thus what we usually call contrition Paul calls "putting off the body of sins" because in these troubles our natural lust is purged away. And quickening should not be understood as a Platonic figment but as consolation truly sustaining a life that flees in contrition. There are therefore two parts here, contrition and faith.[12]

Note especially that the terrors of dying have the effect of mortifying our sinful nature, of "purging" away our natural lust. This notion is reminiscent of Luther's suggestion that the terror of death is sufficient to constitute the pains of purgatory, only here the pain occurs in this life rather than the next.

Melanchthon makes the connection to purgatory more explicit later in the Article when he discusses confession and satisfaction. He rejects the Roman view that sinners need to make satisfaction for their sins on the grounds that the death of Christ provides satisfaction for both human guilt and the punishment we deserve. Nevertheless, Melanchthon grants that there is a sense in which punishment is necessary for true penitence. This punishment is "not as a merit or price, as our opponents imagine satisfactions to be. But in a formal sense revenge is part of penitence because regeneration itself takes place by constantly mortifying the old life."[13] Similar to his point cited above, he holds that terrors of conscience that are felt in the human heart have a mortifying effect on human sinfulness and thereby result in real moral and spiritual transformation. These terrors reveal the wrath of God and are punishments in a deeper sense than the satisfactions required by canonical law. "Who would not put on armor and seek out the church of St. James or the basilica of St. Peter rather than undergo the unspeakable power of the grief that comes over even the simplest people in true penitence?"[14]

The trials of life and ultimately death itself are means by which God punishes sin and brings spiritual renewal into our hearts. In view of this reality, Melanchthon sees no need for purgatory in the afterlife. In support of their view, Roman Catholic theologians cited the example of David, who had to undergo a specific temporal punishment for his particular sin of adultery and murder. Melanchthon thought too much was made of this example. "From the particular penalty imposed on David it does not follow as a universal rule that over and above our common troubles there is a special penalty in purgatory, where the particular punishment fits the particular crime."[15] Later in the Article, he contends that the Patristic decisions about satisfactions were a matter of ecclesiastical discipline, not to remit guilt or punishment. "By their references to purgatory in this connection they did not mean a payment for eternal punishment, or a satisfaction, but the cleansing of imperfect souls."[16]

Notice, Melanchthon is more than willing to embrace purgatory as the cleansing of imperfect souls. So understood, purgatory is a reality to be experienced in the course of the "common troubles" that afflict us in this life, rather than a matter of punishment in the life to come. In these troubles, the wrath of God is felt in a deeply existential sense that has the effect of mortifying our lustful desires and renewing us spiritually. Receiving "punishment" in this sense is not a matter of payment for sins or a matter of merit that achieves satisfaction. Full satisfaction for our sins was accomplished by the death and merits of Christ, and the punishments we experience in the afflictions of life are necessary to true penitence only in the sense that true penitence inevitably has the effect of mortifying our sinful tendencies.

And yet, "purgatory" so understood is at best a partial affair according to Lutheran theology. Sanctification is incomplete in this life, so the perfection that heaven requires must still occur at or after death. This is clear from the passage below from Luther's Large Catechism, which expands on the claim that holiness is only possible through the Church, where the gospel is proclaimed:

> Meanwhile, since holiness has begun and is growing daily, we await the time when our flesh will be put to death, will be buried with all its uncleanness, and will come forth gloriously and arise to complete and perfect holiness a new, eternal life. Now we are only halfway pure and holy. The Holy Spirit must continue to work in us through the Word, daily granting forgiveness until we attain to that life where there will be no more forgiveness. In that life are only perfectly pure and holy people, full of goodness and righteousness, completely freed from sin, death, and all evil, living in new, immortal, and glorified bodies.[17]

Only the death of the body and its resurrection to immortality will be sufficient to make us perfectly pure and holy. The Catechism suggests that sin and impurity reside in our flesh, and until we die, we can at best be only halfway holy. Death and resurrection are the ultimate stages in God's plan to make us perfectly holy. There is no entire sanctification short of glorification.

REFORMED PERSPECTIVES ON PURGATORY

As noted above, Calvin thought that theological issues of crucial significance hinged on the doctrine of purgatory, and he was critical of Melanchthon for not rejecting the doctrine forthrightly in the Augsburg Confession. At stake for Calvin was nothing less than the work of Christ for our salvation. As he put it, "purgatory is a deadly fiction of Satan, which nullifies the cross of Christ, inflicts unbearable contempt upon God's mercy, and overturns and destroys our faith. For what means this purgatory of theirs but that satisfaction for sins is paid by the souls of the dead after their death?" Like his Lutheran cohorts in the Reformation, Calvin judged it an issue of critical importance to insist that the death of Christ provided complete satisfaction for our sins. To be clear on this is to reject the Roman view of satisfaction, and thereby to dismantle the very foundations of the doctrine of purgatory. If one agrees that "the blood of Christ is the sole satisfaction for the sins of believers, the sole expiation, the sole purgation, what remains but to say that purgatory is simply a dreadful blasphemy against Christ?"[18]

Calvin also gives particular attention to the other central Protestant objection to purgatory, namely, that it is not taught in scripture. Indeed, he addresses one by one the texts that have been cited to support the doctrine, and argues in each case that the text, properly interpreted, does not in fact teach purgatory.[19] But it remains clear that his primary theological objection to the doctrine is soteriological, and ultimately Christological. According to Calvin, purgatory is at odds with the doctrine that we are saved entirely by faith in the work of Christ. Any suggestion that postmortem suffering is necessary for final salvation discredits the incalculable worth of the passion and death of Christ.

Indeed, it is arguable that Calvin's view of unconditional election is a further consideration that places his theology sharply at odds with the doctrine of purgatory. As Paul Griffiths has observed, predestinarian views "sit uneasily with purgatorial thought." It would be putting it too strongly, however, to say that there is an outright incompatibility between the two positions, for a predestinarian could hold that God has predestined some to go through purgatory, and has moreover determined how those persons will respond to their purgatorial sufferings. Such a claim would be no more implausible than the predestinarian claim that God determines who will "freely" respond to the call of the gospel and be saved and who will not. Still, the concept of purgatory, with its emphasis on individual responsibility for personal choice, "sits" more naturally with theological views that have a stronger view of human freedom than predestinarian views such as Calvin's.

In light of Calvin's strong opinions on purgatory, it comes as a bit of a surprise that the doctrine is not more expressly repudiated in the classic Reformed confessions of faith.[20] Indeed, given Calvin's criticism of Melanchthon for not addressing the doctrine in the Augsburg Confession, there is at least mild irony in the fact that it is not even mentioned by name in the most famous Reformed statement of faith, the *Westminster Confession*. Nevertheless, purgatory is denied in that famous document, albeit indirectly, as we shall see.

As in Lutheran theology, the issue arises in connection with the doctrine of sanctification. Like their Lutheran counterparts, the Westminster divines affirm that a real change takes place in the elect through the Word and the Spirit dwelling in them. The dominion of sin is destroyed and lustful desires are more and more weakened and mortified. They ever increase "in all saving graces, to the practice of true holiness, without which no man shall see the Lord." And yet, their sanctification remains "imperfect in this life," so that there is a "continual and irreconcilable war, the flesh lusting against the spirit, and the spirit against the flesh." This is, however, a war in which holiness shall prevail. For "through the continual supply of strength from the sanctifying Spirit of Christ, the regenerate part doth overcome: and so saints grow in grace, perfecting holiness in the fear of God."[21]

There is an ambiguity here, if not a contradiction, between the claim that the spiritual life is one of "continual and irreconcilable war" and the claim that the regenerate part overcomes and grows to such a degree that saints can be described as "perfecting holiness in the fear of God." It is hard to know what to make of a condition in which one is simultaneously "perfecting holiness" while also being in a state of "continual and irreconcilable war." This perplexity is only deepened when we consider that, according to the Westminster divines, God's sovereignty entails that he "by the most wise and holy counsel of his own will freely and unchangeably ordains whatever comes to pass."[22] This means that God determines whatever degree of holiness all persons achieve, both in this life and the next. He can make them as holy as he wishes, whenever he chooses, or as unholy. At any rate, the *Westminster Confession* teaches that perfection is only achieved for the elect when their souls "immediately return to God" at the moment of death, as the following passage makes clear:

> The souls of the righteous, being then made perfect in holiness, are received into the highest heavens, where they behold the face of God in light and glory, waiting for the full redemption of their bodies; and the souls of the wicked are cast into hell, where they remain in torments and utter darkness, reserved to the judgment of the great day. Besides these two places for souls separated from their bodies, the Scripture acknowledgeth none.[23]

Part of what is interesting about this passage is its clear affirmation of an intermediate state between death and resurrection in which the soul consciously exists without the body. Soul sleep is explicitly rejected in the previous, unquoted line of the chapter. Lutheran confessions, by contrast, are more ambiguous on this matter.[24] Recall that increased attention to an intermediate state was a crucial aspect of the change in eschatology in the Middle Ages that lent itself to the development of the doctrine of purgatory. Reformed theology has a clear account of an intermediate stage, but it is one in which departed souls are immediately either perfected in holiness and received into heaven, or cast into the torments of hell. The possibility of purgatory is obviously ruled out by these mutually exclusive alternatives.

In the nineteenth century, Charles Hodge reiterated this perspective, stating flatly that "the Protestant doctrine is that the souls of believers are at death made perfect in holiness."[25] He rejected the argument that there could not be a sudden change from imperfect moral excellence to perfect, since progress in moral excellence is gradual by its very nature. Hodge insisted, to the contrary, that such an objection supposes that salvation is a natural process, and that the objection loses all its force if in fact salvation is a supernatural work. Just as Christ can immediately cure a man of leprosy by supernatural means even though normally such a cure is an extended process, so he can instantly cleanse a man of his moral imperfections in a moment.

But let us come back to the issue of sanctification and how this relates to our ultimate salvation. Here let us consider another classic Reformed spokesman who held rather stringent views on this matter, namely, Jonathan Edwards. His account is fascinating because he articulates the necessity of holiness for entering heaven in theological terms that are strongly metaphysical. The very nature of things is such that there is no possibility of compromising on the necessity of holiness. The text for his sermon is from the prophet Isaiah: "And an highway shall be there, and a way, and it shall be called the way of holiness; the unclean shall not pass over it."[26] Early on, Edwards warns his readers that they should be under no illusion that there is an alternative route to heaven. It is not the case that some take the hard way of self-denial and mortification while others take the easy road of self-indulgence. There is only one possible way, and all who wish to go to heaven must follow it.

It is clear, moreover, that the holiness Edwards insists upon is not merely of the legal or the imputed variety. That is, it is not enough for one merely to be declared righteous while remaining sinful in reality. No, Edwards insists that all of us need to be convinced "of the necessity of real, hearty and sincere, inward and spiritual holiness, such as will stand by us forever and will not leave us at death, that sinners may not be so foolish as to entertain hopes of heaven, except they intend forthwith to set about repentance and reformation of heart and life."[27] Edwards defines holiness essentially as conformity of heart and life to God and to his laws and commands. When our hearts and lives are so conformed, we desire those things that are truly and inherently just, right, excellent, and lovely, and we abhor the truly evil, unjust, and unreasonable. The standard for achieving this is a demanding one indeed: "It must become natural thus to be, and thus to act; it must be the constant inclination and new nature of the soul, and then the man is holy, and not before."[28] Such a standard of transformation in which it becomes one's nature, where it is one's constant inclination, to be and to act holy, sounds very much at odds with the *Westminster Confession*'s picture of a "continual and irreconcilable war" in the soul.

Edwards goes on to explain in more depth why holiness is necessary for enjoying the happiness of heaven. The highest joy of heaven is to be united to God, whose nature is holy. Near the end of his sermon, Edwards describes the profound attraction of holiness, and why this truth illuminates the inherent pleasure of heaven. "Holiness is a most beautiful, lovely thing. Men are apt to drink in strange notions of holiness from childhood, as if it were a melancholy, morose, sour, and unpleasant thing; but there is nothing in it but what is sweet and ravishingly lovely."[29] By contrast, sin necessarily causes misery. It produces a disorder in the soul so pervasive that it inevitably disturbs the mind, fills it with confusion, and robs it of peace and joy. Given the very nature of God, and our own nature as created in his image, there is no other way for us to be truly and deeply happy unless we are loved by him and love him in return. Indeed, "if it were possible that God should desire to make a wicked [man] happy while he is wicked, the nature of the thing would not allow of it, but it would be simply and absolutely impossible."[30] This is a strong view of necessity indeed. Not even God can make a wicked man happy so long as he remains wicked. Happiness and holiness are necessarily connected at the very deepest levels of reality.

It is important to note that despite the lofty view of holiness that Edwards endorses, and the apparent possibility of achieving it in this life, he holds, like the other Reformed spokesmen we have noted, that sanctification is only perfected after death. His reason for asserting this is that remnants of sin remain with us so long as we are in the body. The believer longs to be free from this remaining corruption but can only be fully delivered when his soul is set free in the moment of death. "Now when the body is forsaken, 'tis all cast behind: he shall nevermore be afflicted with the loathsome and abominable thing, sin." Edwards goes on to describe the perfection of sanctification with the image of God putting the finishing touches on a lovely work of art:

> At death, the believer not only gains a perfect and eternal deliverance from sin and temp-
> tation, but is adorned with a perfect and glorious holiness. The work of sanctification is
> then completed, and the beautiful image of God has then its finishing strokes by the
> pencil of God, and begins to shine forth with a heavenly beauty like a seraphim.[31]

What is interesting and perhaps also raises problems here, as well in the other Reformed and Lutheran accounts we have examined, is the notion that the body itself is somehow inescapably sinful and our spirit can only be pure when the body is left behind. Earlier in his sermon, he described the body as "a rotten, filthy, loathsome, infected house of clay" and wrote that when the body is put off, "the soul ascends pure into the hands of its maker as it at first came pure out of them."[32] Edwards seems here to be influenced by something like a Greek version of body-soul dualism that condemns the body as inherently more evil than the soul, or worse, a sort of Gnosticism that would locate evil in the body. The resur-rected, glorified body will not of course be sinful in any way, so there is not a thorough body-soul dualism of the variety that denigrates the body altogether, but the notion that the spirit immediately can be pure once it leaves the body is still troubling if it taken to imply that sin dwells exclusively, or even primarily, in the body.

WESLEYAN PERSPECTIVES ON PURGATORY

John Wesley defended a distinctively different picture of salvation from that of his fellow Protestant leaders Luther and Calvin. While Luther and Calvin rediscovered justification by faith, and articulated this doctrine in a way that was at odds with Roman Catholic conceptions of salvation as a process, Wesley fashioned an account of soteriology that combined Catholic and Protestant emphases. Although his doc-trine of justification by faith was very similar to that of the continental Reformers, the accent in his account of salvation was more on sanctification than on justifica-tion. Whereas the Reformers tended to see justification and imputed righteousness as the very essence of salvation, for Wesley, justification was only the beginning. Indeed, regeneration is simultaneous with justification, and for Wesley this work of God in renewing the human soul is "initial sanctification," the beginning of the pro-found transformation that God ultimately intends for us. It is real, imparted righ-teousness and represents the inchoate version of what God will accomplish in our hearts and lives when his work has reached its full flower.[33]

The question of when this work is complete separates Wesley from the theological traditions of the continental Reformers, and marks one of his most notable contributions to historical theology. In their view, as we have seen, sanctification in this life is at best only partial or "halfway," as Luther put it. By contrast, Wesley argued for the possibility of "entire sanctification" in this life. This represents a fascinating alternative to both the Roman doctrine of purgatory as well as the typical Protestant view that the work of sanctification is only completed when the soul leaves the body, or is resurrected with a glorified body.

Wesley's doctrine of entire sanctification has a distinctively Protestant flavor, however. Indeed, in his *ordo salutis*, entire sanctification is received by faith in a manner analogous to the way in which justification is received by faith. Wesley highlighted this parallel in response to his critics who charged that he taught sanctification by works. "Exactly as we are justified by faith, so we are sanctified by faith. Faith is the condition, and the only condition of sanctification, exactly as it is of justification."[34] This means that sanctification can be received in an instant, as soon as a person has the faith to accept it.

But coming to this point of faith usually requires a process of gradual sanctification before one is prepared to receive it. Here is where the Catholic side of Wesley's *ordo salutis* comes into play to complement the Protestant emphases. Just as prevenient grace leads up to the moment when justification is claimed by faith, in a similar fashion progressive growth in grace normally precedes the moment when entire sanctification can be claimed by faith. This gradual sanctification involves a number of components. The first Wesley termed "evangelical repentance," which is an awareness not merely of our acts of sin, but of the deeper reality of our sinfulness itself, our sinful tendencies that erupt into acts of sin if not controlled. Growth in grace and gradual progress in holiness goes deeper than changes in our overt actions to the transformation of our natures themselves. Moreover, Wesley urged the necessity of works suitable for repentance in the form of works of piety and mercy, such as searching the scriptures, fasting, and working to relieve both the physical and spiritual needs of the poor. By these very active means, Wesley urged believers to "wait" on full salvation from all their sin.

And yet, as strongly as Wesley emphasized the importance of such works of repentance, he did not insist they were absolutely essential for sanctification. Rather, "these fruits are only necessary *conditionally*, if there be time and opportunity for them. Otherwise a man may be sanctified without them."[35] It is easy enough to think of such cases where time and opportunity may be lacking. A person converted late in life, or a person who dies shortly after being converted may not have much opportunity to undergo the gradual changes that result in deep transformation and thereby make one ready to claim by faith entire sanctification.

Now at this point, it may be suggested that the doctrine of purgatory could resolve this difficulty for Wesley, for it can offer the time and opportunity that may be lacking in this life. Purgatory extends the time available for the process of salvation to run its course, and is arguably a natural development of a view of soteriology that requires real transformation and human cooperation in achieving it. Unlike Reformed theology, with its teaching that God unconditionally chooses who will be saved, Wesley insisted that God offers saving grace to all persons, and that all have a genuine chance to receive salvation. While God elicits and enables our response, he does not determine it, and our free response is required. Whereas it is natural for Reformed theology to hold that sanctification is completed after death by a unilateral act of God, such a view does not cohere easily with Wesleyan theology. The notion that sanctification continues after death with our free cooperation, however, appears to be a natural extension of Wesley's thought.

In fact, however, Wesley had no more sympathy for purgatory than his fellow Protestant leaders. While he was more ecumenical than many clergy of his era,[36] there were still considerable tensions between Protestants and Roman Catholics at the time he lived. Moreover, the Anglican Church, in which Wesley was ordained, officially rejected purgatory, at least in its Roman form. While the Lutherans and Reformed may have winked at the doctrine in their official confessions of faith, the moderate Anglicans expressly repudiated it in their Articles of Religion: "The Romish Doctrine concerning Purgatory, Pardons, Worshipping and Adoration, as well as Images as of Relics, and also Invocations of Saints, is a fond thing, vainly admitted, and grounded in no warranty of Scripture, but rather repugnant to the Word of God."[37] Further to complicate things for Wesley, because of his strong emphasis on sanctification, he often had to defend himself from charges that he was a "papist" who taught salvation by works.[38] So it is hardly surprising that he chose to reject the doctrine of purgatory, for in his context, any version of it would likely have been viewed as a "Romish" invention "repugnant to the Word of God".

What does surprise, however, is that his reasons for doing so sometimes sound no different from those of his Reformed counterparts. For instance, in one of his works, he reproduces a Roman Catechism with his own replies to the various questions. In his reply to the question of what happens to a soul who dies in a state of grace but who is not sufficiently purged of his sins, he writes: "That those that die in a state of grace are yet in a state of torment, and are to be purged in the other world, is contrary to Scripture and antiquity." He goes on to cite several verses from the Epistle to the Romans to the effect that there is no condemnation for those who are in Christ and that those who are justified will be glorified.[39] He then comments as follows: "As justification and condemnation are here opposed by the Apostle, so are condemnation and glorification; and he that is justified, upon the same reason that he cannot be condemned, shall be glorified. Now, the elect are justified before they go out of the world; and consequently shall have nothing laid at their charge in the next."[40]

What seems out of character here for Wesley is that he appears to be thinking of the essence of salvation in terms of justification, rather than his more characteristic emphasis on sanctification. To be justified ensures that one will be glorified. Wesley does not even hint at sanctification, or of the need for believers to be transformed so that their affections may be rightly ordered and they may love God and their fellow persons as they should. Recall that the question posed has to do with those who die in a state of grace but are not sufficiently purged of their sins. Here Wesley appears to be assuming, like his Lutheran and Reformed colleagues, that in such cases sanctification is perfected instantly after death by a unilateral act of God. Whether or not this is the case, the fact that such a person is not condemned does not explain how the remains of sin are purged.

There is, however, another move in Wesley's arsenal that allows him to deny both the doctrine of purgatory and the typical Protestant view that sanctification is only perfected after death. He advanced this suggestion in a letter to someone who had questioned whether believers who died before their sins were fully cleansed were lost. Wesley's answer, consistent with his reply above, was that such a person was not in a state of damnation or under the judgment of God. Rather, so long as he believes, he retains favor with God.

But here he adds another claim to the mix: "Neither would I say, 'If you die without it [entire sanctification], you will perish'; but rather, Till you are saved from unholy tempers you are not ripe for glory. There will, therefore, more promises be fulfilled in your soul before God takes you to Himself."[41] Later in the letter, he expressed the belief that "none that has faith can die before he is ripe for glory."[42] He took a similar position in a conversation when the following question was raised: "What will become of a Heathen, a Papist, a Church of England man, if he dies without being thus sanctified?" Wesley answered as follows: "He cannot see the Lord. But none who seeks it sincerely shall or can die without it; though possibly he may not attain it, till the very article of death."[43]

It is important to underscore this last claim. Even though Wesley urged believers to expect entire sanctification and to claim it by faith, he also held that it normally happens just before death. Indeed, in a letter to his brother Charles, he expressed the opinion that the instant of entire sanctification "generally is the instant of death, the moment before the soul leaves the body."[44] Why this should be the case he does not make altogether clear. If believers have been sincere in seeking it, and it can be claimed by faith, it seems odd that most should not receive it until the moment before death.[45]

The point I want to emphasize is that Wesley's position requires him to assert a highly speculative claim about divine providence, namely, that no one who is seriously seeking entire sanctification dies until he has received it. Theoretically, he seems to say, anyone who dies without being fully sanctified "cannot see the Lord." But in reality this possibility is never actualized for any true believers. No one dies until she is "ripe for glory," until the work of sanctification is complete.

Now the fact that Wesley thinks entire sanctification typically occurs right before death raises the question of whether his position is, in reality, substantially different from the typical Protestant position. Whereas he thinks it typically occurs the instant before death (which is apparently what he means by "the very article of death"), they hold that it occurs immediately after death. The similarity may seem even more striking when we consider that Wesley held that certain kinds of imperfections are inevitable so long as we live in our bodies in this fallen world. It is important to highlight this point, or otherwise Wesley's understanding of entire sanctification will be misunderstood. While he used the term "Christian perfection" as a synonym for entire sanctification, he carefully qualified the term in a number of ways to make clear what he did not mean by the term. It does not mean, for instance, absolute perfection, nor the sort of perfection that Adam and Eve enjoyed before the fall. Nor is it a kind of perfection that is free from human infirmity, such as the sort of failures that may result from misjudgment or physical embodiment. One can have perfect love and a pure heart and still make mistakes of various kinds due to faulty thinking and other sorts of frailties. As Wesley put it, "Indeed, I do not expect to be freed from actual mistakes, till this mortal puts on immortality. I believe this to be a natural consequence of the soul's dwelling in flesh and blood."[46]

Here again, it is arguable that Wesley's position is very similar to his Lutheran and Reformed colleagues, especially when we consider that the shortcomings and mistakes he acknowledges in the entirely sanctified are sins, strictly speaking, and require the atonement of Christ. Sinless perfection does not occur in this life, but must await the time when "this mortal puts on immortality."

Despite the fact that there may be little practical difference between believing entire sanctification typically occurs the instant before death as opposed to the instant after death, there is a real theological difference in Wesley's view that full salvation can occur earlier, though for most it does not. Moreover, his conviction that it is possible to receive it by faith in a manner "exactly" analogous to justification also sets him apart from the Lutheran and Reformed traditions. Our main concern here has been to show that his doctrine of entire sanctification gives him a theological rationale to dispense with the doctrine of purgatory, though he does not develop this point in any sort of explicit fashion.

However, the point was developed in some detail by his close friend and colleague John Fletcher, who wrote a systematic defense of Wesley's theology in a series of essays known as *Checks to Antinomianism*. The last of these he entitled "A Polemical Essay on the Twin Doctrines of Christian Imperfection and a Death Purgatory." What he dubs "death purgatory" is, of course, the view held by the Lutherans and the Reformed that death perfects us in holiness. Recall the quote from Fletcher at the beginning of this chapter, in which he insists that the question of purgatory is by no means frivolous, but rather is another way of posing the question of how we may be eternally saved. Indeed, he tells us in the preface to this essay that in the pages to follow, "The Scriptural doctrine of purgatory is vindicated, and the newfangled doctrine of a death purgatory is exploded...."[47]

The scriptural account of purgatory, according to Fletcher, is the one taught by the Anglican Church. Fletcher cites his church's *Homily on Prayer* for a concise expression of the true doctrine of purgatory:

> If death cleanseth us from indwelling sin, it is not Christ's blood applied by the Spirit
> through faith. But the only purgatory wherein we [Christian men] trust to be saved, is

the death and blood of Christ, which, if we apprehend it with a true and steadfast faith, purgeth and cleanseth us from all our sins. "The blood of Christ," says St. John, "hath cleansed us from all sin."[48]

The bulk of Fletcher's argument is a biblical and theological case that the doctrine of Christian perfection is not only the true account of how we are purged from the sin that remains in our hearts and lives after conversion, but also that this doctrine is a faithful expression of Anglican theology.

In addition to offering a positive case for Christian perfection, Fletcher also puts forth some suggestive arguments for why death cannot cleanse us from sin. In one such argument, he points out that we may mistakenly think that moral and spiritual disorders are akin to bodily disorders, or at least closely correlated with them, as if, to use a couple of his examples, "obstinacy were a crick in the neck" or "raging anger a fit of the toothache." If this were so, then death could reasonably be thought to cure our moral and spiritual maladies. But, Fletcher insists, there is no such correlation between the moral and the bodily, and consequently "death has no more power to cure our pride, than old age to remove our covetousness." He continues to elaborate the point in a rather eloquent fashion:

> When old drunkards and fornicators are as unable to indulge their sensual appetites as if they actually ranked among corpses, do they not betray the same inclinations which they showed when the strong tide of their youthful blood joined with the rapid stream of their vicious habit? Is this not a demonstration that no decay of the body,—no, not that complete decay which we call *death*, has any necessary tendency to alter our moral habits?[49]

When we recall that demons do not have bodies, and the most serious sins have traditionally been thought to be sins of the spirit rather than sins of the flesh, Fletcher's point seems to have considerable force. Separating a sinful spirit from its corruptible body will not automatically make it pure.

Fletcher goes on in the next section of his essay to chide the notion that God would ever appoint death to play such a glorious role as perfecting our sanctification. Granted, he admits, since God can do things that surprise us, such as command iron to swim, perhaps he could also "command the filthy hands of death to cleanse the thoughts of our hearts." But Fletcher sees nothing in scripture to indicate that death, the final enemy to be defeated, has been promoted to such a lofty position. "And we shall think ourselves far more guilty of impertinence, if we nominate either death or hell to do the office of the final purifier of our hearts, than if we ordered a sexton to do the office of the prime minister, or an executioner to act as the king's physician."[50]

Before concluding this section, it is worth pointing out that one of Fletcher's arguments against "death purgatory" poses difficulties for Wesley's view that entire sanctification typically occurs the instant before death. The nature of this experience, he contends, requires more stamina, both mental and physical, than is characteristically present when a person is on the threshold of death. Full sanctification, he writes, "springs from a peculiar degree of saving faith" and moreover "from an operation of the 'Spirit of burning'" that is sometimes so intense that it is difficult for a healthy man to bear it. "It seems, therefore, absurd to suppose that God's infinite wisdom has tied this powerful operation to the article of death, that is, to a time when people, through delirium or excessive weakness, are frequently unable to think, or to bear the feeble operation of a little wine and water."[51]

Recall Wesley's concession that some, if not most, may not receive entire sanctification "till the very article of death." Fletcher's argument here, and elsewhere, is that the "article of death" is too late to experience what is involved in entire sanctification. Most persons, the moment before they die, are unlikely to have the mental energy to exercise the degree of faith required for entire sanctification, not to mention the physical strength to absorb the vivid personal experience that sometimes attends the powerful transforming work of the Holy Spirit. Or so, at any rate, Fletcher thought, and this was another reason that entire sanctification should be claimed well before death. By urging that sanctification should occur before the moment of death, he distinguishes his position cleanly from the advocates of "death purgatory" who contend that it occurs the moment after death.

CONTEMPORARY PROTESTANT PERSPECTIVES ON PURGATORY

Given the fact that the doctrine of purgatory has been overwhelmingly rejected in classical Protestant theology, it is hardly surprising that it is still roundly criticized by many Protestants today. What may be somewhat surprising, however, is that there are signs of openness to the doctrine in some Protestant circles and a willingness to consider reformulated versions of it.

Those who continue to reject the doctrine usually do so for the same sort of reasons that Luther, Calvin, and Wesley did, namely, that it is not clearly taught in scripture, and that it is allegedly a form of salvation by works that is incompatible with the Reformation doctrine of justification by faith. Baptist theologian Millard Erickson, for instance, admits that the doctrine has a certain appeal because it just does not seem right to us that we should have free admission into heaven without any suffering on our part. As he sees it, this is just a symptom of how hard it is for us truly to own the reality of salvation by grace. "But it is the teaching of Scripture that must prevail, not what appears to us to be logical and just; and on this basis, the concept of purgatory—and indeed any view which posits a period of probation and atonement following death—must be rejected."[52]

Erickson's fellow evangelical theologian Donald Bloesch rejects purgatory for similar reasons, adding that the doctrine unnecessarily induces anxiety about one's salvation. "Whereas evangelical Protestants have assurance that they will be with Christ at the moment of death because of faith in his atoning blood, Catholics can only hope that eventually they will see the glory of heaven."[53] Bloesch does, however, gesture in an ecumenical direction by urging that evangelicals must seek to discern the truth in the doctrine of purgatory, which in his view is that salvation does indeed entail purification by the Holy Spirit. Keeping with his evangelical convictions, he insists that "this purifying work takes place in the daily life of the Christian. We can surmise that it is consummated at death or in the very brief transition from death to paradise."[54]

Indeed, Bloesch expresses the view that the differences between Protestants and Roman Catholics on the issue of purgatory are not insurmountable. He offers another conciliatory suggestion based on the notion that hades is an intermediate state in which the great majority of people who die outside of the Christian faith reside after death. It is his view that we may hope for the eventual salvation of many of these people. And here we see one of the main theological motivations of Protestants who are open to a reexamination of the doctrine of purgatory; namely, they see it as a way to conceptualize the final salvation of persons who were not believers in this life. We shall explore this matter in detail in a later chapter, so here I merely make the point in a preliminary fashion. In short, Bloesch expresses the hope that "the restoration of hades as an intermediate state in which we wait and hope for Christ's salvation may speak to some of the concerns of those who embrace Purgatory."[55]

Another prominent Protestant critic of purgatory is the Anglican New Testament scholar N. T. Wright. Following the Reformers, he rejects the idea of purgatory as a place, a time, or a state, and insists that bodily death is the end of sin in a person. "Death itself gets rid of all that is still sinful; this isn't magic but good theology. There is nothing then left to purge." Wright goes on to contend that Paul's teaching that there is no condemnation for those who are in Christ rules out purgatory altogether. Showing a comic side akin to Luther, he writes: "And if you still want to say that Paul really meant 'though of course you'll probably have to go through purgatory first,' I think with great respect that you ought to see not a theologian but a therapist."[56] The adversities of this life, he argues, provide all the purging we need to prepare us for our glorious future, and he offers the theory that purgatory became popular because it was a projection of present suffering into the future done with great imaginative appeal. Moreover, in an ironic sort of ecumenical twist, he points out that leading contemporary Roman Catholic spokesmen have radically diminished their claims about purgatory in a way that moves them closer to Protestant theology. It is therefore unnecessary and perhaps even counterproductive for Protestants to embrace the doctrine in order to enhance their relationship with Roman Catholics.

While these sorts of objections no doubt represent the majority report, there is a substantial minority report that must be considered to get an accurate measure of contemporary Protestant attitudes toward purgatory. Indeed, we can find examples of theologians from earlier generations who thought Protestants may have been too hasty in discarding the doctrine. Writing several decades ago, the noted Scottish theologian P. T. Forsyth expressed the hope that many people who may not be fully converted in this life could have their moral eyes further opened after death and be thoroughly converted in the long run. "We threw away too much when we threw purgatory clean out of doors. We threw out the baby with the dirty water of its bath. There are more conversions on the other side than on this, if the crisis of death opens the eyes as I have said."[57] Forsyth is another instance of those who see purgatory as a helpful way to conceptualize the hope that salvation may ultimately embrace more persons than it appears to us in this life.

More recently, the German theologian Jurgen Moltmann has written sympathetically about purgatory in a similar vein. Moltmann notes that the basic idea of Purgatory is suggested in the famous beatitude that promises that "the pure in heart shall see God."[58] The doctrine of purgatory allows a person's history with God to continue until the purity of heart necessary to see God is achieved. This is a specific aspect of the more general truth that God will continue until completion of the good work he has begun in our lives. Moltmann is hopeful that this promise applies not only to the fortunate of this world, but also to those whose lives were cut short by tragedy or were otherwise stunted or maimed by adverse circumstances. He rejects the notion of purgatory as a place of punishment or a place to perform penitential acts, but affirms the idea of an intermediate state in which God can advance his purpose for our lives. "So I conceive" he writes, "of that 'intermediate state' as a wide space for living, in which the life that was spoiled and cut short here can develop freely. I imagine it as the time of a new life, in which God's history with a human being can come to its flowering and consummation."[59]

Another eminent Protestant thinker who has embraced a version of purgatory is John Polkinghorne, the Cambridge physicist turned theologian. Polkinghorne invokes purgatory in a discussion of how a theologically construed account of the end of the world must include elements of continuity as well as discontinuity. He points out that relativity theory combines space, time, and matter in one package and suggests this will be true of the world to come as well. That is, resurrected beings will be embodied in a new kind of "matter" as well as located in "space" and immersed in "time."[60] Moreover, the modern recognition of the role of "becoming" in the unfolding of the present order gives us reason to believe that this will also characterize God's new creation:

> Among other things, this recognition seems to require some recovery of a suitably demythologized concept of purgatory. The hope of purgation must be part of the transforming process that fits human beings for everlasting encounter with the reality of God. It will surely not be brought about by an instantaneous act of divine magic.[61]

It is worth emphasizing here that what Polkinghorne sees as "magic" his fellow Anglican N. T. Wright sees as "good theology." It is also noteworthy that Polkinghorne uses the word "everlasting" to describe our encounter with God. This denotes his view that the beatific vision will not be a timeless experience of bliss, but rather an unending exploration of the infinite riches of God's nature.

A third example of a contemporary Protestant proponent of purgatory is the evangelical theologian Clark Pinnock. He contributed several years ago to a multi-authored volume on hell in which each of the authors defended different perspectives on damnation, and then responded to each other. Three of the authors were evangelicals of various stripes, and the fourth was Roman Catholic theologian Zachary Hayes, whose essay was a defense of the doctrine of purgatory. While his other two fellow evangelicals were critical of purgatory for standard Protestant reasons, Pinnock, by contrast, was clearly sympathetic. As a preliminary point, he noted that most evangelicals believe that babies who die in infancy end up in heaven. Presumably, however, they do not remain infants forever, but grow to maturity. If so, Pinnock notes, there must be occasion for growth and maturity in the afterlife. This point applies more broadly to adult believers who typically die before their characters are perfected. "Therefore, it is reasonable to hope that there might be a perfecting process after death. Without discounting the decisiveness of decisions made in this earthly life, a doctrine of purgatory would allow for continued growth in the same direction."[62]

As Pinnock recognizes, a crucial issue in how one thinks about these matters is one's view of human freedom and whether or not our cooperation is necessary for our salvation. If we believe that God's work to make us holy in this life is achieved by eliciting our freely given love and obedience in response to his loving initiatives, then it is natural to think that the sanctification process will continue in the same vein until it is complete, in the next life if necessary. Indeed, Pinnock sees this as a straightforward implication for Wesleyans and Arminians. "Attaining holiness takes time and cannot be done automatically by superior power. . . . Is a doctrine of purgatory not required by our doctrine of holiness?"[63]

CONCLUDING REFLECTIONS

We have seen that Protestant objections to the doctrine of purgatory, both classic and contemporary, characteristically involve the claims that it is not taught in scripture and that it is a form of salvation by works that denies justification by faith and devalues the work of Christ to save us. These objections reflect differences between Protestants and Roman Catholics with respect to fundamental issues of theological authority and the nature and conditions of salvation.

As a preliminary observation, it is worth pointing out that contemporary Protestants who still object to the doctrine of purgatory tend to conceive of salvation primarily in terms of justification, whereas those who are more sympathetic to the doctrine tend to stress sanctification and the transformational dimensions of God's work to save us. Those who see salvation in forensic, legal terms emphasize that there is no condemnation for those in Christ and reject purgatory on the grounds that it undermines this claim. But for those who conceive salvation primarily in terms of real moral and spiritual transformation, freedom from condemnation is only the beginning of salvation, crucial as it is.

Protestants such as Wesley who emphasize sanctification can hold that justification is by faith just as certainly as their Reformed counterparts. (Recall, too, that Edwards insists on real holiness no less stringently than Wesley). Moreover, they can, and do, insist that sanctification is just as much the work of Christ to save us as justification. The grace by which we are saved is not merely God's choice to forgive us for the sake of Christ, but also to restore us to his likeness. Unless grace is limited to forgiveness and justification, the claim that the doctrine of purgatory represents a version of salvation by works is simply misguided.

In the same vein, it is simply beside to the point to appeal to the blood of Christ and the atonement as grounds for rejecting purgatory, unless one assumes the whole point of purgatory is punishment to satisfy the justice of God. As we shall see in more detail in the next chapter, there are different models for understanding purgatory, some of which emphasize sanctification. If the issue at stake is how to purge and rectify our sinful tendencies and dispositions that remain after regeneration, it is not sufficient to appeal to the doctrine of justification, and the fact that forgiven sinners are no longer under condemnation. Forgiveness alone is not an adequate measure to deal with sinful dispositions and desires. These must somehow be purged and displaced by holy dispositions.

In his aforementioned essay on purgatory, Hayes makes the observation that Protestants who insist that the doctrine is not taught in Scripture are seeing the issue strictly through the lens of a Reformed view of justification. "What is really at issue, then, is not whether in the light of Scripture purgatory is possible or impossible, but whether the Reformation theology of justification provides the only appropriate optical lens for interpreting the Scriptures."[64] Those who think not have one less reason to dismiss purgatory out of hand.

As Hayes's comment indicates, there is a close connection between how salvation is understood and the issue of whether purgatory is taught in scripture. On the latter issue, it is noteworthy that contemporary Roman Catholics seem little inclined to defend the claims of their theological forebears, who thought explicit textual support for the doctrine could be found. In an article on the doctrine in the *New Catholic Encyclopedia*, the section on purgatory in the Bible makes very modest claims on its behalf. The author concedes that the Old Testament support is scant but contends that several texts in the New Testament can at least be understood as referring to it indirectly. He concludes that "In the final analysis, the Catholic doctrine on purgatory is based on tradition, not Sacred Scripture."[65] Likewise, Hayes makes no attempt to demonstrate that the doctrine of purgatory is explicitly taught in scripture. As he assesses the matter, "Roman Catholic exegetes and theologians at the present time would be inclined to say that although there is no clear textual basis in Scripture for the later doctrine of purgatory, neither is there anything that is clearly contrary to that doctrine."[66]

Some Protestants, of course, would reject this claim, and insist that scripture decisively rules out purgatory.[67] In doing so, they must be careful not to mimic the mistake of earlier generations of Catholics, who tried to get too much mileage out of ambiguous texts in supporting the doctrine. That is, critics of purgatory must avoid a simple proof text strategy in attempting to refute the doctrine, and its proponents must do the same in defending it.

Now, if this is correct, there is no direct way to settle the issue by straightforward biblical exegesis of isolated texts. But this hardly means there is no way to argue the matter theologically or to arrive at a biblically grounded view on the issue. For the question remains whether the doctrine coheres with things that are clearly taught in scripture, or can even be inferred from them as a reasonable theological conclusion. Such inferences must, of course, involve some degree of speculation, and should be held with an appropriate degree of modesty. But theology can hardly avoid such inferences, especially when dealing with eschatological issues, where explicit biblical data is often sparse.

Here it may be instructive to compare another issue on which traditional Christians are largely agreed, both Protestant and Catholic, namely, the fall of Satan. As with purgatory, earlier generations of believers found texts that were taken to teach the fall of Satan quite explicitly, texts that contemporary exegetes do not typically read in that way.[68] Nevertheless, many contemporary Christians still hold to the belief that Satan was originally a good angel who fell. The question is, on what grounds do they do so? One obvious answer is that the fall of Satan is a theological inference from important theological truths that are clearly taught in scripture. In particular, scripture teaches that God created all things that exist, other than himself, and that all he created was good. Now if this is so, Satan must originally have been good and somehow turned evil. If one also believes that God's goodness precludes him from causing or determining Satan to turn evil, then it is reasonable, if not inevitable, to conclude that he must have done so by his own free choice. So if one takes seriously the existence of Satan, one must account for his existence in a way that is compatible with crucial truths about God's goodness and the nature of his creation. The fall of Satan is a rational theological inference along these lines.

Likewise, purgatory may be defended as a rational theological inference from other important biblical and theological commitments. Recall Pinnock's question above: "Is a doctrine of purgatory not required by our doctrine of holiness?" It is agreed on all sides that holiness is necessary for us to see God, and it is generally agreed that many, if not most, or even all believers are not perfectly holy when they die. Some account must be given of how these believers are made perfectly holy in order to see God.

As we have seen, most Protestants think that this occurs at death, immediately before or immediately after. Some of these accounts seem to assume that sin resides in the body itself, as if the very act of separating the soul from the body allows it to be pure. Others seem to assume that holiness is perfected by a unilateral, instantaneous act of God, so that sanctification is consummated simultaneously with glorification. These accounts, of course, are characteristic of the Reformed. And such an account of a unilateral act of God is quite consonant with the Reformed view that God unconditionally elects whom to save and determines all their choices that lead to salvation. Such a unilateral act of perfecting holiness does not, however, cohere so easily with the view that God requires our undetermined free cooperation in salvation. If God takes our freedom seriously in his work of transforming us in this life, it is reasonable to think he will continue to do so in the next.

In short, purgatory is a perfectly rational theological inference for those who take seriously the role of human freedom in salvation. Moreover, it is important to emphasize that those who do so typically hold that God truly desires to save all persons and does everything he can, short of overriding freedom, to do so. By contrast, the Reformed hold that God unconditionally chooses to save the elect and passes over the rest, consigning them to damnation. What this means for this debate is that one's view of the plausibility of purgatory will hinge on a number of deeply rooted theological commitments, not the least of which is one's view of the love and goodness of God.

Recall, too, that one of the main theological motivations of contemporary Protestants who are sympathetic to purgatory is the need to make theological sense of how persons may ultimately be saved who are not clearly converted in this life. Again, the deep theological issue here is a conviction about the love and goodness of God and his desire to save all persons. By contrast, those who hold to unconditional election will likely assume that those who are not converted in this life are simply not elect and will not be inclined to hold out the hope for their ultimate salvation.

To sum up then, the debate over whether purgatory is taught in the Bible is finally a debate about fundamental theological convictions involving the nature of salvation and the role of human freedom and cooperation in this matter. Even more fundamentally, this dispute hinges on differing accounts of God's goodness and his love for all persons. Since purgatory is never explicitly mentioned in Scripture, addressing it intelligently will require far more than citing isolated texts, either to prove or to disprove it. This debate will inevitably be a profoundly theological one that will involve one's reading of the whole biblical narrative and of the nature and purposes of the God who drives it.

3

⚯

Models of Purgatory

On the Seven Cornices of Purgatory Proper, the 'punishments' are purgative rather than penal. Accordingly, as we have already seen, they are not terminated or remitted from without, but come to an end as soon as the cleansing is completed from within.
    —Dorothy Sayers

A s noted in the last chapter, the doctrine of purgatory has been embraced in recent years by some leading Protestant thinkers and theologians, albeit in a qualified, and sometimes tentative, fashion. What has historically been a fighting word, loaded with intense emotional baggage, made even heavier by long-standing historic rivalry and suspicion, may be emerging as a matter of potential ecumenical agreement. At the very least, the fires of controversy ignited by the doctrine may be dying down, and the possibility of a fresh look at the issue may be on the table.

It would be much too hasty, obviously, to suggest that Roman Catholics and Protestants have come to a meeting of the minds on the doctrine of purgatory. For even when Protestants express some degree of openness to purgatory, they typically take pains to make clear that they are not endorsing the Roman Catholic version of the doctrine. Clark Pinnock, for instance, who is quite sympathetic to the notion of purgatory, wrote: "Evangelicals would not think of purgatory as a place of punishment or atonement because of our view of the work of Christ, but we can think of it as an opportunity for maturation and growth."[1] Donald Bloesch is more specific in spelling out his rejection of what he takes to be the misguided aspects of Roman Catholic teaching on the matter. His suggestion that we may conceive of the intermediate state as one in which we wait and hope for salvation is at best an ecumenical gesture in the direction of purgatory, but hardly an endorsement of the doctrine, as he makes clear. He goes on to comment pointedly as follows:

We must, however, continue to resist the allegation that the debt of punishment that one incurs through sin has not "necessarily been cancelled" by Christ's sacrifice on the cross and that it can be paid for by the "expiatory suffering" of still struggling believers. Evangelicals can never accept the view that the temporal penalty for sin is remitted "by the willing bearing" of penances and disciplines imposed by the church.[2]

A few lines before this passage, Bloesch reiterates the Reformed doctrine of the "imputed" righteous of Christ, and insists that while suffering may play a role in our purification, it does not in any way "render us acceptable to God."

More recently, philosophers of religion have entered the discussion with the aim of stating more exactly the differences between those accounts of purgatory which are acceptable to Protestants, and those which are not, particularly Roman Catholic views. Justin Bernard has contrasted and attempted to distinguish clearly between what he calls the "satisfaction" model, which he ascribes to Roman Catholicism, and the "sanctification" model, which he argues is the only model that Protestants should accept. The satisfaction model, he contends, is at odds with standard Protestant commitments about the work of Christ for our salvation, while the sanctification model is not.[3]

Bernard's attempt to clarify and distinguish the two models, however, has been sharply criticized by Neal Judisch, who contends that Protestants who have recently embraced a version of the doctrine of purgatory do not really understand where the differences between the two traditions actually lie. They have thus both arrived at a doctrine of purgatory but "in wildly different ways and for irreconcilably opposed reasons."[4] The seeming agreement on purgatory turns out to be illusory in his analysis, since the way Protestants characterize things only highlights a radical underlying rift that seems to be as deep as ever. Ironically, however, Judisch goes on to argue that the rift is not so insurmountable after all. Indeed, the central contention of his essay is that "the Satisfaction Model and the Sanctification Model amount to the same thing, so long as the Satisfaction Model is appropriately understood."[5] The contemporary Catholic understanding of purgatory, in other words, is equivalent to the sanctification model, as spelled out by Bernard.

We can put this contemporary debate in historical context by noting that it mirrors to a large extent a debate within Roman Catholic theology that has been going on for some time between two competing models of purgatory, broadly speaking. In an article published in 1922, M. F. Egan drew a contrast between what he called the two "theories" of purgatory, defending the second of the two, which he characterized as the minority position among his fellow theologians. It is most interesting, for our purposes, that the view he saw as dominant among the theologians essentially lines up with the satisfaction model, whereas the view he identifies as the popular one among ordinary believers (the "minority" view which he defends), is closer to the sanctification model, though distinct from it, as we shall see.[6]

The purpose of this chapter is to delineate the various distinct models of purgatory as clearly as we can, and to compare and assess them. We will also assess them in terms of their compatibility with Protestant theology. We will begin our comparative analysis with the satisfaction model, but first I want to lay out more carefully some of the central theological concepts at issue, especially the heavily contested battleground of penance.

PENANCE AND THE RATIONALE FOR PURGATORY

A good place to start here is with Judisch's account of how Protestants perceive and depict the differences between Protestant and Roman Catholic views of salvation, and how these differences shape the way they perceive the purpose of purgatory. As Protestants see it, he says, the Catholic view of purgatory has its roots in their view that salvation is more or less by works, as opposed to the Protestant view that salvation is by grace. Protestants believe that the merits of Christ's death are imputed to them by faith, so their debt of punishment is canceled and they are thereby put right with God. The purpose of purgatory, consequently, is only to finish the process of making actually holy a person who is already fully forgiven, right with God, and bound for heaven. By contrast, on the Catholic view, even a person who is bound for heaven may still have debts to pay for some of his sins because he has not done the requisite good works to atone for them. Such a person "may then 'enter into the joy of his Lord' (Matthew 25:21), but only after his Lord, by way of preparation for the joyous homecoming, has exacted an appropriately agonizing amount of vengeance upon him for a suitable stretch of time."[7] In essence, Protestants believe that Christ has paid the full penalty for their sins, thus freeing them of all punishment, whereas Catholics think that they must pay part of the penalty themselves. Following Bernard, Judisch notes that on this picture purgatory has a "backward looking" purpose of remitting past sins, whereas the Protestant view is a "forward looking" one, concerned only with making us fit for fellowship with God in heaven.[8]

Judisch's picture, apart from a bit of rhetorical hyperbole, seems to be a fairly accurate account of Protestant attitudes toward the Roman Catholic rationale for purgatory, as suggested by the quotes from Protestant spokesmen at the beginning of this chapter. But whether the satisfaction model is a product of Protestant caricature is another question altogether. So let us turn now to examine some classic Roman Catholic sources that explain the theological ground for the doctrine of purgatory.

One such source of large historical significance is the statement on purgatory that was incorporated in the appendix of the constitution affirmed at the Second Council of Lyons in 1274. Recall from chapter 1 that this was the first time purgatory was officially affirmed by a Church Council. Part of that statement, cited earlier, describes how those who fall into sin after baptism may receive pardon for those sins:

> That if, truly penitent, they die in charity before having, by worthy fruits of penance, rendered satisfaction for what they have done by commission or omission, their souls, as

brother John has explained to us, are purged after their death, by purgatorial or purificatory penalties, and that, for the alleviation of these penalties, they are served by the suffrages of the living faithful, to wit, the sacrifice of the mass, prayers, alms, and other
works of piety that the faithful customarily offer on behalf of others of the faithful
according to the institutions of the Church.[9]

For our concerns, notice particularly the notion that those who have not "by worthy
fruits of penance, rendered satisfaction" must face the "purificatory penalties" after
death.

Let us turn now to the prince of Catholic theologians, Aquinas himself, to see his
rationale for the doctrine of purgatory. It appears in the passage below, concisely
articulated in the larger context of his claim that immediately after death all souls
receive either punishment or reward, according to their merits. The highest reward,
man's ultimate beatitude, is the vision of God, which is given to those who are thoroughly purified. Aquinas notes that this cleansing takes place in this life by penance
and the other sacraments, which God can use to purify us of our disordered attach-
ments to things other than himself. However, he observes, this purification is not
always perfected in this life, in which case "one remains a debtor for the punishment, whether by reason of some negligence, or business, or even because a man is
overtaken by death." Various reasons, then, may explain why we may not be perfected in this life, some of which may be our fault, such as negligence, while others,
such as an untimely death, may not be. So long as unrepented mortal sin is not
involved, these failures do not deprive one of his eternal reward, for the necessary
purgation can still take place after this life, as Aquinas explains:

> This purgation, of course, is made by punishments, just as in this life their purgation
> would have been completed by punishments which satisfy the debt; otherwise, the neg-
> ligent would be better off than the solicitous, if the punishment which they do not
> complete for their sins here need not be undergone in the future. Therefore, if the souls
> of the good have something capable of purgation in this world, they are held back from
> the achievement of their reward while they undergo cleansing punishments. And this is
> the reason we hold that there is a purgatory.[10]

Notice that Aquinas's essential reason for affirming purgatory here is because it
makes sense of how punishments can be applied to persons to satisfy moral and
spiritual debts that they failed to pay in this life.

Moreover, it is important to emphasize the rigorist motivation here as well.
Aquinas invokes purgatory to undercut any sort of moral or spiritual laxity and any
sort of presumption that we can evade the punishments we must undergo to pay
our moral debts. If there were no purgatory, the negligent who fail to pay their debts
in this life would be better off than the conscientious. This point is underscored by
Augustine's dictum, also endorsed by Aquinas, that any pain of purgatory is worse
than any suffering in this life.[11] Not only are the negligent not exempt from the

punishment due them, but it will be worse than any punishment in this life would have been.

Let us examine these points more fully in their immediate theological context by looking more carefully at Aquinas's doctrine of penance, which is the sacrament particularly designed to absolve Christians of sin after their baptism. Recall from the Introduction that Aquinas identified three damaging effects of sin that need to dealt with for our relationship with God fully to be restored. First, our mind and thinking are disordered because the choice to sin is the choice to turn away from our true good. Second, we incur the guilt of punishment because God's justice requires the punishment of every fault. Third, the natural good of our nature is damaged because we become more prone to evil, and more reluctant and resistant to the good.

Penance has three parts that correspond to these three damaging effects. First, contrition is the reordering of the mind, the turning back to God, which is at the same time a turning away from sin, and a genuine sorrow for committing it and a resolve not to do so again. Sinners who turn to God in this fashion are enabled by grace to do so, and as they turn to God, they cling to Christ, whose merit is sufficient for the forgiveness of all our sins. But here Aquinas offers an important qualifier. Not all achieve the perfect remission of sins that comes from turning fully to God, but rather, "each achieves it in the measure in which he is conjoined with Christ suffering for sins."[12]

This somewhat difficult phrase is clarified when Aquinas goes on a bit later to explain how our grace-enabled repentance varies in degree from person to person, with correspondingly different results in how fully we are united with Christ. "For there can be a turning of the mind toward God, and to the merit of Christ, and to the hatred of sin which is so vehement that a man perfectly achieves the remission of sin, not only with regard to wiping out the fault, but even with regard to remission of the entire punishment."[13]

It is very important to be clear that Aquinas is talking here about temporal punishment, not eternal punishment. Mortal sin entails not only temporal punishment, but eternal punishment as well, which is the loss of our relationship with God, the true end for which we were created. When mortal sin is forgiven, the eternal punishment is remitted altogether, and the sinner is restored to grace, but temporal punishment remains. Venial sin, by contrast, does not entail eternal punishment, although it does entail temporal punishment, even after it has been remitted. Aquinas is concerned here with the temporal punishment that remains for the contrite sinner. In the passage above, he appears to be describing a sort of repentance that is so thorough that the previous faults of the sinner are altogether rectified. Notice especially that in this case the (temporal) punishment is entirely remitted, as well as the fault completely repaired.

Aquinas goes on, however, to observe that "there sometimes persists an obligation to some punishment to maintain the justice of God which requires that fault be ordered by punishment." This leads immediately into the second part of penance, which is confession. The connection here is forged by the notion that if punishment is required, someone is needed to determine what the punishment shall be—in particular, someone who can exercise judicial power as an agent of Christ. Ministers of Christ are so designated because they have been given "the keys of the kingdom of heaven,"[14] along with the authority to hear confession and pronounce absolution. It is their responsibility to make the judgment to dismiss part of the debt of punishment that remains after contrition.

However—and this point is crucial for our concerns—the remainder of the debt must still be resolved, and the minister has the right and the responsibility to hold the penitent responsible for the balance of his debt. "And this fulfillment of the obligation is called *satisfaction*, which is the third part of penance. By this a man is entirely freed from the guilt of punishment when he pays the penalty which he owed."[15] Satisfaction, then, is achieved when the penitent sinner submits to the authority of the minister of Christ, and accepts whatever punishment the minister judges appropriate to maintain the justice of God. This part of penance Protestant theologians have particularly found objectionable, and these concerns are at the heart of why most of them have rejected the doctrine of purgatory, and why, even when they affirm some version of it, they make clear that they reject the Roman account.

Recall from chapter 2 that Melanchthon criticized the Roman view of penance and contended that the Lutheran view, with its two parts of contrition and faith, provided assurance of absolution in a way that the more complicated Roman view could not match. The notion that penitent sinners must play some role in making satisfaction for their sins, in particular that they must be punished in some way for the guilt of punishment to be remitted, is the claim that seems to them to undermine the work of Christ. And the problem is only exacerbated by the notion that if sinners fail to make satisfaction in this life, then they must make it good by suffering in purgatory in the next.[16]

Now before turning to examine satisfaction models of purgatory, it is important to emphasize that we should not automatically assume that when Aquinas speaks of "satisfaction," he is using the term in the same way as it is employed in those models. This is not to deny that Aquinas can be interpreted in this fashion, or that spokesmen for satisfaction views claim his support, as we shall see. We will return to Aquinas in a later section, but the point for now is just to caution against a hasty interpretation of how he understands the role of punishment and satisfaction.[17]

SATISFACTION MODELS

With this background in place, let us turn now to identify the content and contours of a full blown satisfaction model of purgatory. Such a model has indeed been widespread, perhaps even prevalent in Roman Catholic theology during at least a significant part of its history, according to the article from 1922 that I cited early in this chapter. The author begins his essay by quoting Dom S. Louismet, who rejects the view he deems favorable to the popular mind, namely, that purgatory exists as a means whereby imperfect Christians gradually acquire purity and saintliness. By contrast, Louismet asserts that "the theological truth is that a man, not a reprobate at the hour of death, becomes a perfect saint the moment after, whatever be his debts to the divine justice, which indeed will have to be paid to the last farthing."[18] Egan, the author of the article, goes on several lines later to characterize this view as holding that "the Holy Souls are, in themselves, perfectly fitted for the vision of God," but they must be held back from enjoying that vision until they have thoroughly and completely paid their debt to divine justice. The distinction between the two views, he notes, is a sharp one.

Now, an obvious question here is how these "Holy Souls" are perfected and made fit for the vision of God according to this position. Egan's account is that among the Scholastics the view emerged that the soul is cleansed of all its defects by an act of love for God that is elicited as soon as the soul leaves the body. This act of love is apparently enabled to a significant extent by the very fact that the soul is no longer united with its body. Without the body hindering the soul, it is able to turn to God in the fullness of its spiritual powers, and to love him with an intensity it could not before.[19]

The most prominent name associated with this view, according to Egan, is Suarez, the only theologian of first rank to hold the position. It is important to underscore how extensively and thoroughly this act of love is said to purify a soul from the various effects of sin. As Egan describes his view, Suarez held that when a soul passed into eternity "bearing upon it the guilt of unrepented venial sin, the 'remains' of mortal sins forgiven but not altogether purged, and imperfect or evil inclinations due to past sins, all these are completely obliterated by the act of divine love which that soul immediately elicits."[20] Notice, not only are evil inclinations and the remains of mortal sins that have been forgiven cleansed, but so is the guilt of venial sins that were not repented. So why should a soul in such a purified condition have to spend any time in purgatory? Suarez's answer according to Egan: "Nothing remains except the *reatus poenae*, the debt of justice."[21]

This view represents a distinctively satisfaction picture of purgatory. This is not to deny that part of the purpose of purgatory is purification and cleansing on this view, but again, that is accomplished immediately when the soul leaves the body and enters purgatory. Suarez highlights the ease and speed with which purification can be accomplished in his opinion that an adult who dies immediately after baptism or martyrdom, or even after gaining a plenary indulgence, goes straight to heaven, regardless of how imperfect his dispositions. God can instantly remove the blemishes of a soul and heal its defects, just as he sometimes heals bodily illness in an instant. He can do so in a number of ways, either by infusing the appropriate virtues to counter the vices, or by removing the "influxus conservativus" (conserving influence) from the faulty habits, or even by simply admitting the soul into the light of glory, where all shadows disappear.[22]

Notice, among the options here are certain metaphysical changes God could make that would have large moral consequences, namely, withholding his "conserving influence" from faulty habits. The point is that God's conserving influence is necessary for any choices we make, and this conservation makes possible both the rants of the blasphemer as well as the praise of the saint. If God simply withdrew his conserving influence from our bad habits, they would immediately disappear, according to Suarez.

Similarly, souls can be instantly purified by an intense act of love for God the moment they enter purgatory, and the only reason they must continue for a longer period is to satisfy the demands of justice. The fate of such souls is similar to that of a convicted criminal who is sentenced to ten years in prison, without parole. Suppose he has a profound moral and spiritual conversion and becomes a thoroughly transformed person his first day in prison. He may still have to finish his sentence to satisfy the demands of justice for his crimes against society.

I reiterate that Egan rejects this view, and in his article defends the "popular" view that purgatory is a primarily a place of purification and the gradual healing of spiritual damage. However, he acknowledges that the view he attributes to Suarez was held by many theologians of his time. This perception is confirmed by the article on purgatory in the *New Catholic Encyclopedia*, whose author claims that, until quite recent times, the preponderance of Catholic thought held that the guilt of venial sin was forgiven by the intense act of love of God that is elicited when the soul enters purgatory. Reminiscent of Egan's account, he remarks: "In this state a divided, partial allegiance to God would be unthinkable."[23] The only suffering that remains is the temporal punishment due to his sins.

To understand this position more fully, let us examine a fully explicit, modern example of this view as expressed in a volume published in English around the midpoint of the twentieth century, after going through seven editions in French, by theologian Martin Jugie.[24] Jugie's first chapter is entitled "The Catholic Doctrine of Purgatory," and it is clear that his intention in his book is simply to present and defend orthodox Roman Catholic teaching on the doctrine. He cites classical sources and official Church teaching in support of his exposition, and it is apparent that he has no interest in originality or novelty.

In explaining the rationale for purgatory, he lists three possible reasons that a soul may go there: first, because of venial sins not remitted on earth; second, because of vicious inclinations that may remain in a soul due to habits of sin; third, because of the temporal punishment due to every sin, venial or mortal, committed after baptism and not sufficiently atoned for in this life. Now, what is interesting is that he eliminates the second reason, except as a theoretical possibility. For vicious inclinations do not themselves constitute sins, and more importantly, he holds that "these inclinations do not survive the first instant that follows separation of soul and body," a view he says is held by the majority of theologians, including St. Thomas.[25] The same applies to the first reason, since the act of perfect contrition that occurs at death is enough to wipe out the *guilt* of venial sin.

Here it is crucial to recall the distinction that Catholic theologians draw between the guilt and the punishment of sin, noted in chapter 1. While guilt may be wiped clean by contrition, punishment may not be, and remains to be exacted as a matter of justice. This distinction may seem artificial, and it may be thought that if guilt is pardoned, punishment should also be forgone. Many Protestants, moreover, will be inclined to think that both guilt and our debt to punishment have been resolved by the atonement of Christ, even if they accept this distinction. Jugie, however, accepts this distinction to defend the need for temporal punishment, so his rationale for purgatory reduces to the third of the reasons he distinguished to explain why a soul may go there. Here is how he summarizes the matter:

> It follows from all this, that the principal—one might even say the unique—reason for the existence of Purgatory, is the temporal punishment due to sins committed after Baptism, since neither venial sin nor vicious inclination survives the first instant that follows death. Immediately on its entering Purgatory, the soul is perfectly holy, perfectly turned towards God, filled with the purest love. It has no means of bettering itself nor of progressing in virtue. That would be an impossibility after death, and it must suffer for love the just punishment which its sins have merited.[26]

Given this account of purgatory, it is clear that Jugie understands the rationale for its existence in starkly satisfaction terms.

Let us consider three further points he makes that underscore this claim. First, he draws a "marked" difference between the concepts of *purification* and *expiation*, and insists that it leads only to confusion to use the two terms interchangeably. The term "purification," he notes, signifies the removal of some sort of stain, blotch, or imperfection. When applied to the moral realm, the term describes the removal of a stain of the spiritual order. So used, however, he notes that it is a metaphor, and not a term that is truly native to moral discourse. By contrast, the notion of "expiation" is a distinctively moral term and finds its literal application in reference to free agents. Expiation aims to repair a fault by some sort of pain or chastisement that the guilty party imposes on himself, or accepts as imposed by the person he has offended. Crucially, the point of expiation is not the moral improvement or growth of the person undergoing the punishment. Rather, its entire aim is to make amends to the person offended at the cost of the one who offended him. So after the brief instant of purification that the soul experiences the moment it leaves the body, whereby it is immediately perfected, the remainder of time spent in purgatory is "consecrated to one single object—to *expiation*. Expiation is a debt for sins committed, which is paid by suffering; it is a reparation offered to the holiness and the justice of God, offended by sin."[27]

Second, one's suffering in purgatory depends on the both the gravity and number of sins not atoned for by penance and good works. "The just judgment of God on each soul is the measure of its Purgatory, as regards the nature of its pains, its intensity, its duration."[28] In some cases, God may shorten the time in purgatory, but increase its intensity. Jugie speculates that this may be true especially of souls in purgatory on the eve of the final judgment.[29] But the general point is that the suffering of purgatory will be exactly proportioned to one's debt of punishment. Jugie underlined this point by expressing his judgment that modern priests generally do not impose satisfaction that is long and severe enough "to allow us to hope for a complete remission of the temporal punishment due for our sins."[30] If the satisfaction they require is too light, the debt of punishment must be made up in some other way. Jugie goes on to point out that the deficit may be supplied by indulgences, by voluntarily inflicting penance on oneself, and by accepting in a spirit of penance the trials of life that God may send our way.

This brings us to his third point, namely, that the expiatory nature of the suffering in purgatory is confirmed by the conviction that the Church Militant can pay the debts of the Church Suffering by offering suffrages, sacrificing the Mass, as well as through indulgences. If the aim of purgatory was the improvement of the sufferers or their progress in perfection, it would be "incomprehensible" that we could suffer in their place, mollify or shorten their pain, or even end it altogether. But if what needs to be resolved is an objective debt, it is altogether intelligible that fellow members of the same mystical body should share and relieve the burden of debt incurred by their errant siblings in the faith. "In a word," Jugie sums up, "Purgatory must be looked on as a liquidation of the past, not as a march with face lifted towards a future, towards an ideal not yet attained."[31]

One final observation must be made to round out Jugie's account of purgatory. He stresses that the essential pain of purgatory is the delay of the beatific vision. While the Church has also affirmed that purgatory involves pains of sense, he notes that no particular definition has been given of those pains. Indeed, he speculates that the pains of sense are in fact consequences that flow from the delay of the beatific vision, so that in some way, perhaps the delay is actually the only pain. He characterizes this pain as the product of an intense desire to see God, a desire that is frustrated and hindered by its debt of sin. He wishes to follow Aquinas in affirming that the pain of purgatory surpasses the greatest pain of this life, but at the same time says that purgatorial pain is of a different order and cannot be compared with the pains of this life. Given the perfection of the souls in purgatory, they suffer their pains willingly, even joyously, as a sort of love offering to the "outraged love" of God. "The great desire to offer to that love a just reparation, devours them. At the same time, their hunger and thirst for the Beloved pierces them with the agony of longing. That is their great torment—a torment of which our earthly loves can give but a pale idea."[32]

ASSESSMENT OF SATISFACTION MODELS

Now, by way of assessment, it is clear in the first place why this view of purgatory would be unacceptable to Protestants. Even if they do not hold the view that the righteousness of Christ is imputed to those who have faith in him, they will hold that the gift of salvation through Christ pardons them of sin in such a way that they are no longer required to pay any sort of debt of punishment. So as an account of purgatory for ecumenical consideration, this model offers very little, if any, promise. It is moreover, quite clear that the satisfaction model is not merely a Protestant caricature. It is a historical issue beyond the scope of this book to determine when and to what degree this view was accepted among Roman Catholic theologians, and moreover, whether it is a faithful interpretation of official Church teaching in past decades or centuries. But it appears to have been accepted by many theologians as orthodox Catholic doctrine until relatively recently.

Second, it is striking that the claim that the soul is instantly purified when it leaves the body is essentially the same as the view of most Protestants, who hold that the sanctification of believers is immediately perfected after death, or immediately before. Indeed, if purgatory were understood only as the instant of purification that occurs when the soul leaves the body, Protestants would likely find nothing to dispute in the doctrine. In chapter 2, I noted Charles Hodge's defense of the Protestant view that the souls of believers are immediately made perfect at death. Here it is worth noting that his defense of this claim is similar to the claims made by Catholic writers in this regard. He notes that the Apostle Paul was immediately changed by an encounter with the glory of Christ on the road to Damascus, and asks if it is strange in light of that to think "that the souls of believers, when separated from the world and the flesh, and redeemed from the power of the devil, and bathed in the full brightness of the glory of the blessed Redeemer, should in a moment be purified from all sin?"[33]

Third, the notion that perfected souls have an extensive debt of punishment to pay is morally dubious, and perhaps incoherent at points. It is clear that part of what motivates Jugie's account of purgatory, as well as many others, is a desire to challenge moral and spiritual indifference and sloth. The doctrine of purgatory is a pointed threat to any who ignore the call to holiness and who make sanctification and spiritual growth a low priority. Purgatory is a guarantee that those who do so will end up regretting their choices and wishing they had pursued perfection more earnestly. If purgatory did not exist, Jugie observes, God would treat the slackers and the spiritually fervent the same. "Such a doctrine would favor laxity: it would be the ruin of the life of perfection."[34]

Now the idea that lax Christians receive the very perfection at the instant of death that they neglected in this life seems odd if the primary purpose of purgatory is for the temporal punishment of sins committed after baptism, especially if part of the threat of purgatory is to motivate a life of perfection. This seems even more puzzling if that very perfection is the main reason for the suffering in purgatory. Recall that the delay of the beatific vision is the essence of the pain of purgatory, according to Jugie. This pain is keenly felt precisely because souls have been perfected and now have an intense love for God and a desire to behold him in heaven. Without this love and perfection, they would not suffer with the sort of intensity they do. Indeed, the less perfect they were, the less they would suffer from the delay of the beatific vision, for if their love were less, their desire for it would not be as strong. Indeed, the bestowal of perfection seems itself to be part of the punishment, or at least essential to it, on this account.

This account of the pain of purgatory also leads to odd results for the notion that God could shorten the duration of purgatory by intensifying the pain. Again, if the pain is due to frustrated desire for the beatific vision, then the most obvious way to intensify the pain would be to intensify the desire and accordingly cause or allow a correspondingly deeper sense of frustration. The desire could be intensified by an increase in clear thinking or an increase in cognitive capacities. As one's reflection deepened, and his understanding enlarged, his desire for God would also intensify and increase his pain. The upshot again, is that a deeper degree of holiness is the pre-condition for the intensified suffering.

One way to resolve these paradoxical, if not incoherent, implications would be to propose that the gift of perfection is not received until the end of one's time in purgatory. It would make more moral sense if the souls in purgatory experienced punishment and pain precisely as the persons who still had the moral defects and blemishes as well as the guilt of their sins to expiate. One might suggest that the pain of purgatory was solely a matter of justice for the temporal punishment of sin that remained in the soul of the sinner. At the end of purgatory, perfect sanctifica- tion would be granted in something like the manner suggested by Suarez or Jugie. This would remain a starkly "satisfaction" model of purgatory that would still be fundamentally at odds with Protestant theology, but it would seem to make more moral sense than the view that holds that purgatory metes out great suffering to souls that are spiritually perfect.

Before moving to the next model, it is worth noting that at times Jugie seems to slip into language that is more fitting for a "sanctification" model. Recall that he insists that the purification aspect of purgatory happens instantly when the soul leaves the body and first enters purgatory, after which the sole purpose of remaining there is for expiation. Purification, moreover, is merely a metaphor, whereas expiation is the sober literal truth about purgatory. This distinction that Jugie wants to draw is dubious, however, for expiation is also typically expressed using metaphors. Whereas sanctifi- cation in purgatory is expressed using metaphors of healing, cleansing, and purifica- tion, satisfaction or expiation of moral debt is conveyed using financial or legal metaphors. Indeed, the notion of debt itself in this context is a metaphor.

It is perhaps at least suggestive that Jugie has trouble making full sense of the extended stay in purgatory in strictly "satisfaction" terms that he sometimes uses cleansing metaphors. He asks whether it would not be extremely boorish to attend a royal feast or a wedding in ragged and dirty clothes. That is how a holy soul must see itself in the light of God's glory. "The divine light reveals to the soul that which she owes to the justice and sanctity of God, so that of herself, with great eagerness, she flies towards the place of expiation, where she can be cleansed, and appear without a blush of sensitive shame before God and His saints."[35] It is hard to know what to make of these mixed metaphors. Is the debt of justice that is still owed to

God some sort of impurity? If so, then how are we to understand the claim that the soul is filled with an intense love of God that immediately corrects all wrong inclinations, and purifies the soul completely? Perhaps it makes sense to say the soul might still have a sense a debt that needs to be paid, but to picture this in terms of dirty and torn clothes seems misleading if the soul is indeed fully upright and purified as a result of an intense of love for God. By trading on this ambiguity, and smuggling suggestions of sanctification into his model, he obscures his explicit claim that the need for expiation is the sole reason that souls must stay in purgatory for extended periods.

SATISFACTION/SANCTIFICATION MODELS

Recall that Egan's article about the "two theories of purgatory" argues against the view we have just discussed, in favor of what he calls the popular view, albeit a minority position among theologians. The alternative he defends, however, is not an exclusively sanctification model, by any means. As he puts it: "The other theory does not deny the debt and payment, but it asserts that the payment is the means, the normal though not absolutely necessary means, by which God cleanses their sores and gives them the perfect spiritual health which their future life with Him requires."[36] This theory deliberately employs metaphors of cleansing and healing, along with those of debt and payment, to describe the purpose of purgatory, with the accent on the former.

Now let us return to our discussion of Aquinas's account of penance to see how this model might be worked out. Recall that the three parts of penance correspond to the three damaging effects of sin, and that satisfaction is the third part of penance. Above, I quoted part of his explanation of satisfaction. Now I want to repeat part of that quote and continue with Aquinas's further comments:

> By this a man is entirely freed from the guilt of punishment when he pays the penalty which he owed; further the weakness of the natural good is cured when a man abstains from bad things and accustoms himself to good ones: by subjecting his spirit to God in prayer, or by taming his flesh by fasting to make it subject to the spirit, and in external things by uniting himself by giving alms to the neighbors from whom his fault had separated him.[37]

What I want to emphasize here is the latter part of this quote, where Aquinas addresses the issue of how penance deals with the third damaging effect of sin, namely, that it weakens our nature and makes us more inclined to sin, and less disposed to do the good. Earlier in his chapter on penance, he had described it as a "spiritual healing of a sort" and as "a kind of spiritual alteration."[38] The passage just quoted provides some helpful detail to understand how penance can work healing to the damage done to human nature by sin.

In an earlier chapter describing "how man is freed from sin," Aquinas observed that "it is not only necessary for man to abandon sin in the external act, but also to renounce it in his will, for the purpose of rising again from sin."[39] And in his account of sanctifying grace, he remarks that man cannot be brought to his final end of seeing God in his essence "unless he be united with God by the conformation of his will," which he says is "the proper effect of love."[40] Now going back to his comments about how penance can cure the weakness of the natural good, it is helpful to read his examples not as mere acts to perform in some legalistic fashion, or as only punishments to be born, but more fundamentally as means to reform the will so that it conforms to God's will. Sinful habits and dispositions need to be corrected and displaced by holy habits and dispositions, and these can be cultivated, as a means of grace, by the sort of actions and practices Aquinas suggests.

To flesh this out and provide a little more detail about the connection between these practices and their positive effects, let us consider one of Aquinas's examples, namely, that of subjecting one's spirit to God in prayer. It is arguable that the very essence of prayer is a matter of submitting our will to God, as suggested not only by the "Our Father," where we pray "thy will be done," but also by the prayer of Christ in the garden, where he embraced his suffering by praying: "Father, if you are willing, remove this cup from me; yet, not my will but yours be done."[41] As this prayer of Christ clearly shows, such submission of our wills to God can be painful and even agonizing. Moreover, submitting our will to God cannot be accomplished by mechanical repetition, or occasional, haphazard prayer. Rather, it is the habit of prayer that reminds us that the will of God is perfect, and reinforces this truth that we are often prone to forget. Prayer as a discipline is what deeply aligns our will with that of God so that we become truly "accustomed" to the good, as Aquinas put it.

It is also very much to the point to notice that in his discussion of "how man is freed from sin" that he makes the same point, in almost the same words, as he does in his later discussion of penance, namely, that in some cases repentance is so deep and so thorough that it remits not only the fault, but the punishment as well. What this shows is that Aquinas believes that God is most concerned with a true repentance that turns our hearts and minds away from whatever keeps us from our true end of loving God, and back to him. It is only in the absence of such repentance that punishment is necessary, as he explains:

> For, as may be gathered from things said earlier, the punishment that a person suffers after the remission of sin is necessary so that the mind may adhere more firmly to the good; since man is chastised by punishments, these punishments are, then, like remedies. It is also necessary so that the order of justice may be observed, in the sense that he who has sinned must stand the penalty.[42]

Notice the twofold "necessity" for punishment here. First, it is necessary that the mind may adhere more firmly to the good. Again, where the displeasure with sin and the corresponding attachment of the mind to God are sufficiently strong, there is no need for punishment. It is only when these are absent that punishment is a necessary means to that end. But second, it is also the case that persons whose repentance is only half-hearted also remain liable to punishment because it is necessary that the order of justice be observed and upheld.

Now if the point of punishment, and of penance generally, is not only to satisfy justice, but also to reform the will and conform it God, we should not be surprised if there is an organic connection between these two purposes. Aquinas draws this connection explicitly in another passage where he is discussing how sinful acts leave a stain that must be cleansed:

> As to the taking away of the stain of sin, clearly this cannot be wiped out except by the soul being rejoined to God; it was by drawing away from him that it incurred the impairment of its own splendor, which, as already established, is what the stain of sin is. Now the soul is joined to God through an act of the will. The stain cannot be taken away from a person, therefore, unless his will embraces the order of divine justice; either he spontaneously takes on himself some form of penance to atone for a past sin or he patiently bears with one imposed by God. In either case the punishment has the quality of satisfaction.[43]

While this passage casts punishment in terms of justice and satisfaction, its larger emphasis is on how penance removes the stain of sin and joins a soul to God. Notice, Aquinas says the act of will necessary is for the soul to "embrace the order of divine justice," whether this means willingly accepting some form of penance, or patiently bearing with "one imposed by God."

It is important to recognize that this passage is not explicitly about purgatory, but the principles Aquinas affirms here readily apply to postmortem punishment. The key point to recognize is that punishment by itself cannot automatically guarantee that the stain on a soul will be cleansed, any more than rote performance of penance in this life will mechanically produce this result. But if the will embraces the order of justice, the will is aligned with God's will and thereby is sanctified and united with God. So when punishment is freely embraced in this fashion, it has a transforming effect on the person receiving it.

Given the necessity that the punishment must be freely embraced for the cure to be accomplished, the cure may take longer and be more complicated, depending on how deeply rooted sinful habits have become. Aquinas does make this point explicitly about purgatory in an earlier writing in which he contends that some venial sins have more "adhesiveness" than other such sins if the affections have become more attached to them. "And since those sins that have more adhesiveness are purged more slowly, some are tormented in Purgatory for a longer time than others, to the extent that their affections have become more steeped in venial sins."[44]

Aquinas's account of purgatory, then, appears to be a satisfaction/sanctification model, with the accent falling on satisfaction. While his theory of penance, and of punishment more generally, gives prominence to the purifying and sanctifying aspects of these disciplines, when he explicitly discusses the punishment of purgatory he explains its rationale more in terms of the satisfaction of divine justice than the reform of the sinner's will. Either way, it seems clear that he sees no tension between the two elements of satisfaction and sanctification, and views them as fully compatible, indeed as complementary. And again, as noted above, even when Aquinas uses terms like "satisfaction," it should not simply be assumed that he is using those terms in the same sense as the satisfaction model we examined above. Elements of that theory, however, seem to be present, even if it is debatable to what extent that is the case.

However we may interpret Aquinas on this score, the most famous account of purgatory of all seems more clearly to place the emphasis primarily on purging and sanctification. Dorothy Sayers has argued that this in fact is the case in her introduction to her translation of Dante's *Purgatory*. Indeed, she quotes the passage above from the *Summa Theologiae*, along with its larger context, and claims that Dante closely followed Aquinas's definition here, and deployed his literary genius to construct narrative and images "to illumine this apparently arid theme."[45] She contends that Patristic and official definitions of purgatory up to and including the Decree of the Council of Florence in 1429 placed the emphasis on the purgative instead of the penal dimension of punishment, but this order of emphasis was reversed immediately after that. "If Dante's teaching appears more 'modern' and liberal than that of his successors, it is not because he was 'a Protestant before his time', but because he was following the older Catholic tradition."[46]

Sayers notes that the purgative nature of the punishment is dramatized in one of the most famous differences between how Dante depicts hell, on the one hand, and purgatory, on the other. Whereas there is no sense of time or the passage of time in hell, the passage of time is a central theme in purgatory. This difference signals something fundamentally different between the two places, namely, that the souls in purgatory are changing and being transformed, as opposed to the damned in hell, who are unalterably fixed in their wickedness. As Sayers notes, the pains in purgatory are hardly different in themselves from the pains of hell; indeed, they are strikingly similar. "The sole transforming difference is in the mental attitude of the sufferers. Dante has grasped the great essential which is so often overlooked in arguments about penal reform, namely, the prime necessity of persuading the culprit to accept judgment."[47]

Let us pursue this further by returning to a point from chapter 1 pertaining to factors that were favorable to the development of purgatory as an official doctrine in the thirteenth and fourteenth centuries. Recall Manuele Gragnolati's contention that a key factor, overlooked by Le Goff, was the emergence of the idea of productive pain, by which he means pain that could play a positive role in the formation of identity and meaning. Gragnolati argues at length that Dante's conception of purgatory is the consummate expression of such productive pain and how it plays an essential role in purging the remnants of sin and preparing redeemed persons fully to enjoy heaven.

This is not to say that Gragnolati denies that Dante also believed that the pain of purgatory paid a debt of punishment for the purpose of satisfying divine justice. Indeed, the very geography of purgatory, which is described as an enormously tall mountain with the garden of Eden at its summit, situated on an island in the middle of the ocean in the Southern Hemisphere, is suggestive of this. By placing purgatory on the earth, Dante pictures it as the natural continuity of penance that was not completed in this life.[48] One of the most explicit passages that depict purgatory as satisfying a moral debt occurs in Dante's description of the terrace of the proud. There we see characters whose punishment consists of being weighed down under the heavy burden of a large rock that they must carry through this stage of purgatory. Here is Dorothy Sayers's translation of the relevant lines, in which one of the proud explains why he is being punished:

> I am Humbert; and my arrogance beguiled
> To loss not only me, but all my kin
> It dragged down with it, ruined and reviled.
> Therefore, till God be satisfied for sin,
> It here behooves me bear among the dead
> The load I bore not among living men.[49]

The notion of suffering to pay a debt of punishment is clearly evident in the claim that he must bear his burden as long as necessary to satisfy God. And the further claim that he must bear the load because he failed to do so in this life shows how the debt of punishment carries over from this life to the next if appropriate penance is not made.

While Dante's depictions of the punishment of purgatory in explicit terms of satisfaction are relatively rare, there is one other notable example that must be mentioned. In chapter 1, I noted that Dante's account of purgatory contains one notable innovation, namely, his notion of what is called "ante-purgatory," where certain souls are detained before they are allowed to enter purgatory proper. Ante-purgatory contains those souls who put off repentance until the end of their lives, along with persons who have been excommunicated, and princes who placed too much value on earthly things. Whereas Dante wants to highlight God's mercy in saving even such careless sinners as the negligent and the excommunicates, he also makes clear that God's justice is not flouted in such cases. The emphasis on justice is highlighted by the fact that persons must stay in ante-purgatory for a specifically quantified, formulaic amount of time, corresponding to one's desert. In particular, the excommunicates must remain in ante-purgatory thirty times the number of days or years they have been excommunicated, while those who delayed repentance until the end of their lives must wait the exact amount of time as they lived on earth. The only way this time can be shortened is through the prayers of devout persons. Here are the lines that pertain to those who delayed repentance until the end, spoken by such a tardy penitent:

My lifetime long the heavens must wheel again
Round me, that to my parting hour put off
My healing sighs; and I meanwhile remain
Outside, unless prayer hasten my remove—
Prayer from a heart in grace; for who sets store
By other kinds, which are not heard above?[50]

According to Sayers, there is a distinct connection between the nature of this punishment and the efficacy of prayer to shorten it; "for this punishment, just because
it is merely penal, may be remitted by a simple act of Grace on God's part."[51]

By striking contrast, the cleansing, transforming punishment of purgatory
cannot be codified or reduced to some sort of mathematical formula. It is a matter
of personal transformation, and such transformation depends on the free responses
of the sinner, so how long it takes will be more complicated and subjective. As
Sayers puts it: "Purgatory is not a system of Divine book-keeping—so many years
for so much sin—but a process of spiritual improvement which is completed precisely when it is complete."[52]

The distinction between the satisfaction model and this one can be vividly highlighted by noting how they both believe that purgatory lasts "precisely" as long as
necessary, but for profoundly different reasons. Whereas Jugie held that the punishment of purgatory is exactly as long, and as intense, as needed for God's perfect
justice to be satisfied, Sayers held that it is precisely as long and involved as necessary
to complete the spiritual transformation that will fit us for heaven.

So let us turn now to examine an example of the "productive pain" that Dante
pictures as the necessary means to purge and heal the souls in purgatory proper, the
pain of sense (*poena sensus*) that goes beyond the pain caused by the delay of the
beatific vision (*poena damni*), the only pain in ante-purgatory. Purgatory proper, of
course, is constituted by seven ascending terraces, each of which is devoted to
cleansing one of the seven deadly sins, those fundamental dispositions or habits of
mind from which all acts of sin spring. These dispositions are not only present in us
from birth as fallen people, but they become more or less entrenched, and leave
more or less traces on our character, depending on our choices. As Paul Griffiths
has put it, "Even when a sin is no longer being committed and has been confessed
as such, it may still have lingering effects upon the will and affections, much as long-
past gastronomic indulgences may have on the figure."[53] Purgatory might be pictured, then, as a regimen to regain one's spiritual health and get back into moral
shape, to undo the self-destructive effects of previous sinful choices.

In view of this, let us consider the terrace of gluttony. This is most apt, not only in
light of Griffiths's comment, but also because this terrace of purgatory is considered
to be the one that most vividly captures the nature of purgatorial punishment as the
exact opposite of the sin to be purged.[54] Thus, the gluttons are pictured as extremely
emaciated as they undergo a prolonged experience of hunger and starvation. Among
these persons Dante recognizes an old friend, though with some difficulty because of

the physical deformity, and he asks him why these souls suffer as they do. His friend's answer is a classic expression of productive purgatorial pain:

> And he: "By subtle virtue I'm refined
> That from the eternal counsel whence it springs
> Falls on the tree and water there behind;
> And all this multitude that weeps and sings
> By dearth and drouth is here resanctified
> From an excessive greed of life's good things.
> Craving for food and drink's intensified
> By the sweet smell of fruit and of the spray
> Which from above sprinkles the foliage wide;
> And not once only, as we make our way
> Around this path, our pain is thus renewed—
> I call it pain: solace I ought to say;
> For that which draws us to the tree's green wood
> Is that desire which gladdened Christ to cry
> 'Eli' when He redeemed us with His blood."[55]

A number of points need to be made about this passage. First, it is acknowledged that the pain they experience from their frustrated longing for the fruit of the tree and the water that Dante and his companions have left behind[56] is caused by God's "eternal counsel." God, in other words, is recognized as the cause of their suffering. Second, the paradoxical combination of both weeping and singing in response to the divinely ordained dearth has the effect of "resanctifying" them. Though their pain is intense, they rejoice in the transformation that is taking place in their souls as they continue to make their way around the path: "I call it pain: solace I ought to say."

It is not clear whether their joy is the *result* of the progress they are making, or the necessary *condition* for the pain to be productive.[57] Perhaps all that is necessary as an initial condition is a willingness to accept the pain as God's means of transformation, and a desire to be healed and cleansed through it. The joy is perhaps a result that may then further enable ever deeper transformation, and accordingly, ever deeper joy. Whatever the case may be on this matter, it is clear that the essential nature of productive pain is that which is embraced as justly imposed, and thereby results in transformation. Dante had suggested this point earlier, at the end of their journey through the first terrace of purgatory proper, that of the proud, when contrasting the way pain is experienced in purgatory from the way it is in hell:

> As we turned thither, voices in our ear
> Sang out *Beati pauperes spiritu*:
> No tongue could tell how sweet they were to hear.
> What different passes these from those we knew
> In Hell! for there with hideous howls of pain,
> But here with singing we are ushered through.[58]

This brings us to a third important point from the passage above. The transformation is not merely of the moral variety, in terms of classic virtues, but rather, it is distinctively Christological in nature. Notice, the desire which draws these emaciated figures along is that "which gladdened Christ to cry 'Eli' when He redeemed us with his blood." This is an allusion, of course, to the cry of Christ from the cross, "Eli, Eli, lema sabachthani?," "My God, my God, why have you forsaken me?"[59] The paradoxical experience of the gluttons-in-transformation who simultaneously weep and sing in some sense parallels that of Christ, who suffered the profound sense of being forsaken by God in the midst of his gladly taken choice to redeem the world. Their desire for God is like Christ's own desire for his Father, frustrated as it seemed to be as he was dying on the cross. As Gragnolati puts it, the reason that the pain of purgatory is productive is "precisely because it allows the soul to conform to the crucified Christ, whose blood liberated (and still liberates) humankind from sin and who is the ultimate paradigm of redemptive suffering."[60] And of course, to become like Christ prepares one to be united with the Father, like Christ himself.

Two other points before leaving Dante for now. First, it is noteworthy that he emphasizes the progressive nature of sanctification, which he pictures several times in terms of the increasing speed and ease with which he climbs the mountain. At his entrance to the terrace of gluttony, for instance, he writes as follows:

> And lighter-footed than I'd felt before
> At any pass, following with ease complete
> Those two swift spirits, on and up I bore.[61]

This is a powerful image of the renewal of genuine freedom, one of the things lost in the Fall. The growing ability to ascend the mountain with ease and speed pictures a restoration of moral and spiritual strength and energy, and freedom from bondage and weakness that allows us to pursue and achieve our true end of loving God and seeing his face.

Second, it is significant that Dante highlights righteousness or justice at both the beginning and the end of his account of the terrace of gluttony. Here are the final lines of his account:

> "Blessed are they whom so great grace illumes"
> I heard it said, "that in their bosom's core
> The palate's lust kindles no craving fumes,
> And righteousness is all they hunger for."[62]

Compare Allen Mandelbaum's translation of these lines, which perhaps makes the point more clearly:

> And then I heard: "Blessed are those whom grace
> illumines so, that, in their breasts, the love
> of taste does not awake too much desire—
> whose hungering is always in just measure."[63]

The righteousness or justice that is commended here is a matter of having the right amount of hunger. It is a matter of having rightly ordered and proportioned love, which amounts to loving things in the appropriate degree. The gluttons were unrighteous in loving food and seeking the satisfaction of their appetites to a degree that was disordered, and therefore unjust. Their willing acceptance of the punishment they received reordered their desires and their loves and restored them to a condition of righteousness or justice.

Analysis of Dante could, of course, go on virtually forever, or at least as long as purgatory, but for our purposes we have said enough for now. Before we turn to assess satisfaction/sanctification models, however, it is worth noting that variations of this model, with the accent on sanctification, seem to have been recovered as the predominant model among Roman Catholic theologians sometime in the twentieth century, in preference to satisfaction models, which appear to have been dominant for some time before that. While the theme of satisfaction is often muted or minimized, it still plays at least a minor role in more recent expressions of the doctrine. Consider, for instance, this description from the article on purgatory in *New Catholic Encyclopedia*, in which the author contrasts modern accounts of the doctrine with earlier ones that construed the purpose of punishment primarily if not completely in terms of justice:

> It seems more in keeping with the holiness of God that He would progressively transform and perfect the soul until it was ready for heaven than that He would continue to punish a soul otherwise worthy of the beatific vision.... the image of God presented in Holy Scripture inclines modern authors to see the divine love, holiness, and justice combining to punish the soul still guilty of venial sins as the soul is transformed and cleansed.[64]

Notice that the divine justice remains part of the motivation for the punishment of purgatory, though it is a secondary emphasis. In the same vein, recall this passage from the documents of Vatican II, cited earlier in chapter 1:

> The doctrine of purgatory clearly demonstrates that even when the guilt of sin has been taken away, punishment for it or the consequences of it may remain to be expiated or cleansed. They often are. In fact, in purgatory, the souls of those "who died in the charity of God and truly repentant, but who had not made satisfaction with adequate penance for their sins and omissions" are cleansed after death with punishments designed to purge away their debt.[65]

Again, it is noteworthy that the document employs both language of expiation and cleansing, of both purging and debt. By retaining both types of language, the document is somewhat ambiguous, but appears to affirm a version of a satisfaction/sanctification account of purgatory. So let us turn now to assess these models.

ASSESSMENT OF SATISFACTION/SANCTIFICATION MODELS

First, as a model for ecumenical consideration, this account of purgatory will likely fare little better than the starkly satisfaction model we considered above. Protestants will view any talk of punishment in purgatory as necessary to satisfy a debt to divine justice, even if that talk is muted or minimized, as a compromise of their account of justification by faith, if not an insult to the work of Christ to save us. Versions of the model that place the predominant emphasis on satisfaction over sanctification are certain to draw the most insistent accusations of "works righteousness," but any claim that the remission of sin requires suffering or the willing acceptance of discipline is sure to be met by similar suspicions, as the comments by Bloesch at the beginning of this chapter attest.

Second, there are questions and potential problems concerning the relationship between satisfaction and sanctification in this model. It is altogether unclear, for instance, how a sentence to purgatory exactly proportioned to the demands of justice correlates with the notion that purgatory is simultaneously a process of spiritual improvement that lasts as "precisely" long as necessary to complete that process. Do the demands of justice in this respect always correspond precisely to the amount of time necessary to work a thorough moral and spiritual rehabilitation and transformation? The demands of justice, it seems, are a different sort of requirement than the necessities of character growth and spiritual healing. A person might undergo an appropriate punishment that would satisfy justice, but still have a significant way to go by way of rectifying his character flaws. On the other hand, his character flaws might be healed well before he has served a sentence sufficient to satisfy the requirements of justice.

Third, it might be suggested that the answer to the previous question lies in the willing embracing of punishment, and that is the essential correlation between the demands of justice and spiritual transformation. This suggestion, however, raises the question of whether embracing punishment as just is merely a necessary condition for sanctification, or a fully sufficient one. While it is plausible to think that it is necessary, it is much more dubious to think it is sufficient. Sinful habits and dispositions become rooted in our character, and can "adhere" to us rather tenaciously, as Aquinas observed. The layers of deception and complexity involved may require a very different sort of treatment than punishment in order to be adequately addressed and rectified. What may be needed is truth and insight, as well as new habits of thought and action.

Here it may be remarked that Dante's appeal to justice with respect to gluttony is relevant, for justice can be understood more broadly than in a merely legal or punitive sense. Understood as rightly ordered desires, and proportionate loves, the embracing of justice may address the complicated twists and distortions in our characters, and point the way to untangle the knots and straighten out what is crooked. The learning involved in embracing justice in this sense is more than a matter of accepting pain and punishment, it is also a matter of gaining a proper view of reality, of the relative value of things, and learning to shape our thinking and behavior accordingly.

Fourth, there are problems raised for the sanctification side of this model if the pain of purgatory is as intense as claimed by many adherents of this view. I am thinking here particularly of Augustine's claim, endorsed by Aquinas and many others, that any pain of purgatory is worse than any pain or suffering of this life. Now the question is whether such intense pain would not be so overwhelming as to rule out any meaningful sense of a free response to it that could be morally significant. It seems that would be the case, for certainly the most intense pain of this world is terrible enough to compel all but the most resilient to submit to whatever demands may be made by the one imposing the pain. Such a compelled response to torturous pain does not qualify as a rationally, morally free action that leads to genuine personal transformation. So again, there is a tension, if not outright conflict, between at least certain forms of punishment and the goal of satisfaction. It does not matter whether the pain is thought to include the pains of sense or whether it is thought to be "merely" psychological and spiritual. If the pain is said to be more intense than any pain of this life, it is hard to see how it serves some of the crucial aspects of sanctification.[66]

Fifth, it is unclear how indulgences function in this model. Recall Jugie's comment that it would be "incomprehensible" how offering the Mass or indulgences could be effective if purgatory is understood as a matter of gradual cleansing or purification. If, however, it is an objective debt to be paid, it makes sense, he argued, that living believers can draw on the treasury of merit in order to shorten the punishment of purgatory. Recall, too, Sayers's observation that since the punishment in ante-purgatory is purely penal, it can be remitted by a "simple act of Grace on God's part" in response to the prayers of the devout. However, if the punishment is not of the "bookkeeping" variety, but is specifically and precisely designed for the purpose of spiritual improvement, then it is more difficult to see how it can be remitted by way of indulgences, or similar interventions by living believers. If such improvement and transformation is really necessary for a person to be in the presence of God and fully enjoy a relationship with him, then it cannot simply be forgone or remitted.

In response to this, the defender of indulgences might appeal to the notion ascribed to Suarez by Egan, cited above. That is, God could choose instantly to heal the soul of a person who receives a plenary indulgence in a number of ways that do not require any sort of longer term process. God could instantaneously instill the appropriate virtues, withdraw the conserving influence from faulty habits, or simply admit the soul into glory where all defects immediately disappear.

This response, however, raises more problems than it answers. If the process of freely embracing discipline and otherwise freely cooperating in the process of transformation is not essential to sanctification, one wonders why God does not immediately perfect all souls when they die. The third option above is particularly troubling because a crucial part of the rationale for purgatory is that souls with stains and blemishes cannot, as a matter of moral or spiritual necessity, enter the full presence of God and take pleasure in doing so. If the entrance into glory is not only fully possible, but provides the immediate cleansing and perfection necessary to enjoy the beatific vision, then the rationale for purgatory is effectively undercut.

CAN'T GET NO SANCTIFICATION?

Let us turn now to consider sanctification models of purgatory. A good place to start here is with John Henry Newman, who, as noted in the Introduction, at least brushed up against purgatory in his reflections on the necessity of holiness if we are to see God. In one of his sermons he expressly repudiates the Roman doctrine of purgatory, but offers some speculations on the intermediate state that provide material for a sanctification model of the doctrine that many Protestants might find acceptable. As he describes the intermediate state, it is a disembodied state of rest in which believers remain at a distance from heaven as they await the consummation of God's kingdom and the resurrection of their bodies. It is the "paradise" Christ promised the dying thief on the cross, but not heaven proper, as believers remain "incomplete" in various ways. In view of the incomplete nature of this state, Newman ventures the speculation that it would not be "surprising if, in God's gracious providence, the very purpose of their remaining thus for a season at a distance from heaven, were, that they may have time for growing in all holy things, and perfecting the inward development of the good seed sown in their hearts."[67] Newman goes on to reflect on various classes of persons who may have genuine faith, but for different reasons are such that the fruit of grace has "but partly formed in them in this life," and again suggests that it seems likely that the intermediate state may provide time for this fruit to grow to maturity. "Such, surely, is the force of the Apostle's words, that 'He that hath begun a good work in us, will perform it *until* the day of Jesus Christ,' *until*, not *at*, not stopping it with death, but carrying it on to the Resurrection."[68]

There is no hint here of suffering to pay a moral debt, or the need to complete penance in order to satisfy divine justice. Newman's suggestion that the intermediate state might be a time for the good seed in the hearts of believers to grow to perfection is not in any way incompatible with Protestant accounts of justification by faith.

Here it is worth noting that Justin Bernard's distinctively Protestant account of purgatory is not premised on a transformational view of soteriology. To the contrary, he emphasizes that his project is also aimed at those "for whom salvation is principally a matter of forensic or legal justification."[69] Indeed, a driving motivation for his article is his contention that the traditional Protestant view that the possession of saving faith is sufficient for making it to heaven generates what he calls the "dilemma of sanctification." The dilemma arises from the belief that heaven is essentially morally perfect, along with the typical Protestant belief that having saving faith alone does not entail having a sanctified nature. Given these two beliefs, he points out that "it would seem that either heaven is not essentially morally perfect or saving faith is not a sufficient condition for eternal union and fellowship with God."[70]

Bernard explicates this dilemma by providing a rigorous account of the sort of sanctified nature that would be necessary to guarantee that heaven is essentially sinless. He thinks that the best way to construe this is in terms of causal or nomological necessity. That is, the human inhabitants of heaven do not avoid sin merely because they are lucky, or by virtue of the fact that they are no longer faced with temptation. Nor is it the case that it is metaphysically impossible for them to sin, or that there are no conceivable circumstances in which they might sin. Rather, they are sinless by virtue of having achieved an entirely settled virtuous character, so that the following counterfactual is true: "For any person x, if x were in circumstances C, x would not sin." The particular circumstances here are those appropriate to the nature of x. So again, there might be circumstances in which x might sin, such as circumstances in which the Holy Spirit is not present, but these would not be circumstances that apply to x. Bernard's account can be summed up in his claim that such persons "are those who could not sin in the sense that they would not sin under circumstances in which they ought properly to be expected not to sin."[71]

Bernard's defense of a Protestant account of purgatory is precisely due to the need for the human inhabitants of heaven to acquire such a nature. Without such a nature, again, the dilemma of sanctification arises. He believes that purgatory is the best solution to this dilemma. Of course, this means that he rejects the typical Protestant answers, which we examined in the previous chapter. I will not go into his reasons for doing so here, but for present purposes, the point I emphasize is that the sanctification model he defends is entirely concerned with acquiring the settled virtuous character necessary for heaven to be essentially sinless. Purgatory is thus understood as a temporary state after death in which the disposition to sin is purged so that the "lapsable" are transformed into the sanctified. It is not in any way a matter of making satisfaction for sins or meeting a demand for divine justice. Its sole purpose is to allow the sanctification process "to come to completion on the basis of its own internal momentum."[72]

Now this notion of "internal momentum" is a suggestive one, but Bernard doesn't give us much to explicate it, nor does he provide much detail as to how he thinks sanctification is achieved after death. In this connection, it is worth pointing out that the sanctification model can be construed in different ways, starting with whether or not it involves punishment or discipline of some sort. These are not automatically ruled out if the punishment or discipline has as its sole purpose the purging of the disposition to sin, rather than to pay a debt of justice or make satisfaction for sin. The punishment could be educational in some sense, in that it could bring home to us the destructive or hurtful nature of sin, and thereby strengthen our resolve to avoid it. This would especially be so if the punishment were an intrinsic consequence of the sin. To recall again Griffiths's example of gastronomic indulgence, the natural consequence would be a certain weakness of will and disposition, as well as impairment of physical health. The discipline involved might require a series of difficult choices to undo the damage and restore one's health. Such discipline would provide the momentum to carry the sanctification process to completion.

Another way to generate and sustain momentum would be through the power of newly grasped truth and insight. Richard Purtill offers this suggestion to explain how postmortem transformation might occur, particularly by coming to see our hurtful actions in their true light. Instead of seeing purgatory as a chamber of suffering, he proposes thinking of it in terms of reliving our evil through the eyes our victims, which he suggests would enable us to "fully realize and fully reject the evil." He goes on to apply the same point to our more personal sins that may not hurt anyone else, at least in any obvious sense. These may be purged by coming to see them as God sees them, so that we would thereby view them "in their full squalor and meanness and nastiness." Many of these sins, he notes, are such that we would be horrified if they were known to fellow human beings whom we love and respect. Purgatory would require us to "face up to the fact that God knew these sins in their full despicableness, and we too would see them so."[73]

To get a better understanding of how this might work, let us consider a famous literary example of transformation, namely, the notorious Ebenezer Scrooge from Charles Dickens's classic, *A Christmas Carol*. Early in the book, Dickens gives numerous indications of Scrooge's character, showing especially how self-centered he is and how isolated from his fellow human beings, including those with whom he interacts in his day-to-day business as well as others who may incidentally cross his path. "Hard and sharp as flint, from which no steel had ever struck out generous fire; secret, and self-contained, and solitary as an oyster."[74] This vivid character sketch is filled out with more color in the conversation he has with the men who arrive at his office early in the story to ask him to contribute to the Christmas fund they are raising for the poor and destitute who lack even the necessities of life. Scrooge dismisses them with a flourish by referring to the prisons, workhouses, and other public facilities which he says he helps to support with his taxes. Those who are badly off, he casually observes, can go there. When the men object that some would rather die than resort to these institutions, Scrooge retorts with his memorable line that if so, "they had better do it, and decrease the surplus population." Dickens goes on a few lines later to write: "Scrooge resumed his labors with an improved opinion of himself, and in a more facetious temper than was usual with him."[75]

The lasting appeal of this story is due to Dickens's account of how this self-contained oyster of a creature is transformed into "as good a friend, as good a master, and as good a man as the good old city knew, or any other good old city, town, or borough, in the good old world."[76] This is accomplished, of course, by his encounter with three spirits whose forays into the past, present, and future enable Scrooge to see himself with searing clarity. As is fitting for a self-contained, self-satisfied person, this is achieved largely by helping him to see others in ways he had not been able to before. By seeing himself rightly in relation to others, he came not only to see them differently, but himself as well. Thereby he was drawn out of his insulated oyster existence, and became a loving, and beloved, member of society, connected by bonds of mutual affection and respect to those he previously disdained and knew only from a distance.

Dickens provides numerous clues and indications of Scrooge's gradual awakening and transformation, which there is not space to detail here. I will focus on just one of the most striking instances, the turning back on Scrooge of his own heartless words about the "surplus population" as he truly sees for the first time examples of persons he had categorized in that fashion. For our purposes, an especially pertinent instance is the one when he witnesses the Cratchit family Christmas dinner, courtesy of the Ghost of Christmas Present. As he observes the family of his struggling clerk and their meager resources, he is particularly concerned for Tiny Tim and his future prospects. "'Spirit,' said Scrooge with an interest he had never felt before, 'tell me if Tiny Tim will live.'" After the spirit quotes back to him his earlier words, Dickens writes that Scrooge "was overcome with penitence and grief."[77] His earlier self-satisfaction and facetiousness are well on the way to being purged at this point in the story.

Now, I do not mean to suggest that Dickens gives us the full makings of an account of purgatory, or that this was his intention, only that his story gives us a plausible picture to flesh out Purtill's account of how coming to see our sins in their true light could play a crucial role in purging our sinful dispositions. A fuller account of a sanctification model of purgatory must highlight how our sins have offended and disappointed God, and emphasize that our sanctification is ultimately the product of his gracious work in our life. Jesus prayed to the Father for the sanctification of his followers thus: "Sanctify them in the truth; your word is truth."[78] In view of this text, perhaps God's work of purging us could be understood as an extended examination of our lives in the searching light of his word. God, through his Holy Spirit, might take us on a review of our lives not unlike that of Scrooge, and we would see with full clarity not only how our sins have hurt others, but most importantly, how God sees them. Even more than the visits of the three spirits to Scrooge, such an extended encounter with truth through the Holy Spirit would alter us and heal our disposition to sin.

The same point can be made in more personal and relational terms by thinking of this encounter as a matter of seeing our sins in their full measure in light of God's perfect love for us and his desire that we obey him precisely because he desires our true flourishing and well-being. In this case, the encounter would be more like a deep sense of shame and regret because of how we had disappointed God's love. The truth encountered here would be the depth of God's love and how far short of it we have fallen, and how often we have let him down. Understanding this would motivate true repentance, a profound change of mind, and a resolution to want to please such a lover by returning the love he has generously given to us.

This encounter, however, could also be experienced in an even more positive way, not as producing a sense of shame, but rather as producing an enormous sense of gratitude for God's overwhelming love as displayed in the death of Christ. A growing sense of gratitude would counteract and dispel one of the deepest roots of sinfulness, namely, the failure to be thankful for God's goodness to us.[79] Or, in a similar vein, it might be suggested that a gradual revelation of truth, along with beauty and goodness, would transform us in way that would elicit the best in us, but without pain. To perceive the truth as beautiful as well as good would invite us to embrace the truth and to internalize it with gratitude as well as joy.

ANOTHER SANCTIFICATION MODEL

In connection with this suggestion, another variation on the sanctification model, namely, the "heavenly sanctification" account, has been proposed by David Vander Laan in response to Bernard's defense of purgatory. Vander Laan contends that Bernard's argument suffers from a modal flaw, which allows for the alternative he proposes. In particular, Vander Laan argues that it is a mistake to conclude that the "lapsable" cannot be in heaven since heaven is morally perfect. He points out that it is possible that the lapsable may not exercise their capacity to sin even though they still have that capacity, and have not yet gained the settled character of the sanctified that assures they will never sin.

This possibility could be achieved in at least a couple of ways. First, by assuming a Molinist account of middle knowledge, according to which God knows what all possible persons would do in all possible circumstances, he could arrange things in heaven so that the lapsable are never put in circumstances in which they would sin. A person prone to lying about her past, for instance, might be kept from situations in which she would give in to this temptation. "Instead, she would be placed in situations such that the free acts she would then perform helped to weaken and finally to eliminate her tendency to lie."[80] Moreover, she might have a growing knowledge of divine grace for her sins of the past that would strengthen her resolve to be truthful.

A second way in which God might achieve the same result is simply by relying on his knowledge of her character and dispositions (without middle knowledge) to steer her away from situations in which she might sin. If necessary, he could even provide "overriding grace" to keep those dispositions in check, and over a period of time, "in part because of the saved person's own actions, the problematic dispositions would dissolve."[81] The important point to stress is that Vander Laan thinks he has shown that morally imperfect persons of unsettled character can be in heaven, contrary to Bernard's claim. On either of the two scenarios above, the essential moral perfection of heaven is preserved "since, with a necessity grounded either in the divine will or in divine goodness, God in love protects each person in the heavenly state from sin."[82]

Vander Laan goes on to point out that the descriptions of the New Jerusalem in the book of Revelation contain images of sanctification. One such suggestive image is the tree of life "with its twelve kinds of fruit, producing its fruit each month; and the leaves of the tree are for the healing of the nations."[83] It is natural, he proposes, to think that this healing involves character growth. Moreover, heaven is pictured as a place where the Lamb will "guide them to the springs of the water of life, and God will wipe away every tear from their eyes."[84] Both of these images, he notes, are suggestive of the sanctifying work of the Holy Spirit, the latter perhaps including the cleansing of "the sorrow-producing effects of sin."[85]

ASSESSMENT OF SANCTIFICATION MODELS

Now, by way of assessment, these models, unlike the previous two, are perfectly compatible with Protestant theology. Purgatory on this account is not in any way about satisfying divine justice or paying a debt of punishment. It is entirely a matter of continuing and completing the process of sanctification, of making us truly holy so that we can be fully at home in the presence of God and enjoy his presence with no troubling shadows to darken our fellowship with him.

Critics of purgatory may point out that this model still allows for pain and suffering, particularly versions that involve some sort of punishment, a notion that they often find objectionable. Indeed, even models that do not include punishment proper, but that see purgatory as an encounter that allows us to see our evil in its true light, also involve elements of pain. Returning again to Scrooge, we can see this in the scene where the Ghost of Christmas Past shows him the episode in his life when his fiancée broke their engagement because she had discerned that an idol had taken her place in his heart. As Scrooge watches this scene and realizes what he had become because of his misguided loves, he pleads, "Show me no more! Conduct me home. Why do you delight to torture me?"[86] Scrooge's "torment" here is precisely that of seeing a pure heart of love, and recognizing the coldness of his own heart in response to that love. He is pained, as well as regretful, to see how little he valued such a beautiful and generous gift.

Despite his protest, however, the spirit proceeds, and we read that "the relentless Ghost pinioned him in both his arms, and forced him to observe what happened next."[87] That encounter too was a painful one, as Scrooge again illustrates the reality that when we are out of sorts with truth, when our loves are misguided, it can be a painful thing to absorb. Scrooge, moreover, was not in control of truth, and he was graciously shown it against his will. His freedom lay in his response to it, not in the choice to see it in the first place. But, little by little, the truth was working into his heart and changing him. As the Ghost of Christmas Present comes to visit him in the next "stave," he is in a more willing frame of mind to accept what he will see, painful though it will still be at points. " 'Spirit,' said Scrooge submissively, 'conduct me where you will. I went forth last night on compulsion, and I learnt a lesson which is working now. To-night, if you have aught to teach me, let me profit by it.' "[88]

Such profitable pain that is the natural result of absorbing truth that clashes with our selfish attitudes and other sinful dispositions should not be objectionable. While it may be possible to conceive of scenarios that transform us without pain, as noted above, the reality is that our encounters with God's holy love are often, if not typically, painful, as we discern the contrast between his truth, goodness, and beauty, and the deceit, evil, and ugliness in our hearts. Healing often requires painful operations to remove diseases that will destroy us if left unchecked, and such pain should be embraced with joy because of the outcome it produces.[89]

Recall from the beginning of this chapter Judisch's contention that the contemporary Roman Catholic account of purgatory is in fact equivalent to the sanctification model as espoused by Bernard, and not a competing model. His account of the contemporary view is based heavily on the *Catechism of the Catholic Church* and, in my judgment, he makes a generally persuasive case for this claim. If he is correct, moreover, Protestants who are amenable to purgatory may be able to find significant common ground on this doctrine.

On one point, however, I found Judisch's argument particularly unpersuasive, namely, his attempt to make sense of the theology of indulgences on a sanctification model of purgatory. As noted above, those who explain the rationale for purgatory in terms of a debt of punishment that needs to be paid contend that their account can readily make sense of the role of indulgences. But if purgatory is about effecting a real transformation in our character and spiritual dispositions, it is hard to see how this could be remitted, or even abbreviated, through indulgences. Judisch appeals to the fact that we pray for each other in this life, and believe that our prayers make a difference in the lives of others, that our prayers may assist in their growth and sanctification. He situates this appeal in the larger context of the doctrine of the communion of the saints, and the belief that prayers can still pass both ways between the living and the dead.

The appeal to prayer here is intelligible enough, and indeed, it is worth noting that Protestants who embrace a sanctification model of purgatory should have no objection to praying for the dead and their sanctification. However, recognizing the legitimacy and value of such prayer does little to illuminate how indulgences can have the dramatic benefits that have been claimed for them. While we cannot pretend to understand how our prayers may be used by God to influence others, it is reasonably clear that our prayers cannot be guaranteed to produce a given result, as indulgences, particularly plenary indulgences, have been thought to do. Quoting John Paul II, Judisch concedes that how indulgences work remains "unfathomably mysterious."[90] So the price to be paid for embracing an exclusively sanctification model of purgatory is that the doctrine of indulgences becomes utterly mysterious. Protestants sympathetic to purgatory will see this as a good reason for Roman Catholics to give up indulgences altogether, along with satisfaction accounts of the doctrine, which fostered the worst abuses in the history of the doctrine. Indeed, Roman Catholics who want to espouse a sanctification model have good reason to agree.[91]

Now, what about Vander Laan's proposal? It is ingenious and it may plausibly be taken as an alternative to the doctrine of purgatory, as well as a variation on the sanctification model of it. The notion that purgatory is simply a part of heaven, moreover, may make the doctrine more palatable to many Protestants. The passages he cites from Revelation are beautifully appealing images of what the work of purgatory may effect in our hearts and lives on the sanctification model.

However, I find unconvincing his claim that his account preserves the essential moral perfection of heaven. The basic reason is that moral perfection is far more than a matter of avoiding sinful actions. Moral perfection is very much a matter of character and disposition, perhaps even more fundamentally than overt action. So long as our dispositions are sinful and imperfect, we cannot fully love God or our neighbor as we should, and hence cannot fully experience the unclouded fellowship with God that is the essence of heaven. Indeed, it is precisely such dispositions that purgatory is traditionally thought to cleanse and purge. Many traditional theologians have held that there will be no further acts of sin in purgatory, and while that is necessary for moral perfection, it is hardly sufficient.

Vander Laan recognizes this potential difficulty for his proposal and acknowledges that heaven, strictly speaking, may be identified as "some particular kind or degree of communion with God."[92] On this understanding, any place or experience of cleansing or sanctification would not be a part of heaven, but preliminary to it. Vander Laan's proposal, by contrast, is that we should think of different stages or levels of heaven, with sanctification occurring in an earlier stage before full communion with God is achieved. In his view, it is merely a semantic difference if one prefers to designate that earlier stage purgatory rather than an initial segment of heaven.

In response to this, I would argue that it may be a semantic difference, but it is not *merely* one. The traditional view of heaven does include complete purity and sinlessness, so it is not simply arbitrary to prefer that understanding. Perhaps purgatory could be thought of as an outskirt to heaven, or perhaps an antechamber to heaven, but so long as sinful dispositions are present, whether to lie, lust, condescend, or envy, one cannot truly enjoy the sort of communion with God and other persons that heaven represents.

It is also worth noting that Vander Laan wants to minimize, if not eliminate, any role for pain in his model. As I have already argued, I think certain pains are a natural part of coming to terms with truth in the process of sanctification. The tears that heaven finally wipes away may include tears shed in purgatory from the sorrow produced as we fully come to see our sins and their effects in the growing light of God's holy love.

Before concluding, it worth commenting that these tears that attend transformation provide an answer to one of the most eloquent protests against the doctrine of heaven in literature, namely, that of Ivan Karamazov.[93] Ivan's protest against the presumed final harmony of heaven is motivated by certain acts of human cruelty that are so extreme that it seems psychologically impossible, if not morally outrageous, that the victims of such cruelty could ever forgive them. The mother of a child who has been savagely murdered, for instance, should never forgive the perpetrator of such a heartless act, Ivan insists.

Ivan's passionate protest, understandable though it is, does not take sufficiently into account the thorough moral and spiritual transformation that finally accompanies those who are truly forgiven. Such persons will have come to see their sins, as well as their victims, as Christ sees them. So transformed, they will despise their sins and repudiate them with a holy passion, even as they love their victims with pure love and profound humility. The "harmony" of heaven among all those who are united in Christ is a mutual embrace of persons who have become like Christ through his purifying love. It is this sort of transformation, encompassing truly repentant perpetrators and victims alike, that makes the harmony of heaven a thing profoundly to be hoped for, rather than an escapist fantasy that trivializes evil.[94]

CONCLUSION

We have been exploring different models of purgatory and assessing them not only for their coherence and plausibility, but also in terms of whether they are consistent with Protestant theology. We have seen that there are three distinct models, and variations of each of these, a considerably more complex picture than the simple contrast between the satisfaction and sanctification models we noted at the outset of the chapter. While our analysis has focused on the role of satisfaction and/or sanctification in each of the models, it is also worth noting that there are other points of comparison by which the models could be further distinguished and other variations recognized. For instance, while some theologians have held that the inhabitants of purgatory are protected from further sin, not all agree. For another instance, some have held that the inhabitants of purgatory are fully assured of salvation, but again, not all agree.

Clearly, given this diversity, it is no simple matter either to accept or to reject the doctrine of purgatory. While some accounts of the doctrine are at odds with, or flatly incompatible with, certain claims of Protestant theology, not all are. Protestants can affirm sanctification models of the doctrine without in any way contradicting their theology, and may find that it makes better sense of how the remains of sin are purged than the typical Protestant account that it happens instantly and immediately at or after death.

It is also worth highlighting again that the history of the doctrine in Roman Catholic theology is a highly complex matter that this chapter hardly begins to show. It appears that the doctrine has swung from one end to the other between the poles of satisfaction and sanctification, sometimes combining both elements somewhere in the middle. The earliest official statement of the doctrine is a somewhat ambiguous combination of both elements, with perhaps a stronger stress on sanctification by the time of Dante, but the element of satisfaction came to predominate shortly thereafter, and later still became the exclusive emphasis in much Roman Catholic theology. Sometime in the twentieth century, sanctification came again to the fore, and it is arguable that today, at least in official doctrinal standards, that it is the primary if not the sole emphasis. If so, there are good prospects for an ecumenical version of the doctrine that can be affirmed not only by Catholics, but many Protestants as well.

4

ᴏᴧᴐ

Personal Identity, Time,
and Purgatory

The process of purification is, on all its levels, an activity of reciprocal caring.... We are not just ourselves; or, more correctly, we are ourselves only as being in others, with others and through others.

—Joseph Ratzinger

One of the fascinating themes running through *The Divine Comedy* is the contrast between the body of Dante the pilgrim, who has not yet died, and that of the shades who already have. Dante employs several devices to highlight the difference and to express the surprise and puzzlement of the shades who are often amazed to see him in their world. Dante casts shadows, for instance, whereas they do not. And yet, despite the striking difference in their condition, they typically have little if any difficulty in recognizing each other or interacting, at least in significant ways.

A particularly memorable example of this occurs early in purgatory. Dante and Virgil, having emerged from hell, are now on the island of purgatory but have not yet begun their ascent of the mountain. Shortly thereafter, a boat piloted by an angel, and bearing some one hundred souls who have recently died, arrives at the island. When they encounter Virgil and Dante, they notice that the latter is breathing in such a way that shows he is still alive in a sense that they are not, and stunned to see an embodied person, they clamor around him to take in the unusual sight. As the scene unfolds, Dante describes this poignant encounter:

> And one I saw advance, all eagerness
> To clasp me in its arms, whose looks expressed
> Such love as moved me to a like embrace.
> O shades! vain visual shows no touch can test!

Three times I felt my hands behind it meet,
Three times they came back empty to my breast.
I think amazement in my face was writ
In changing colors, for the shade withdrew
Smiling, and I plunged forward after it.
Gently it bade me cease; at once I knew
What man it was, and begged him to bestow
One moment on me, and a word or two.
"As in my mortal bonds I loved thee, so
I love thee free; and therefore I will stay;
I stay," said he; "but wherefore dost thou go?"[1]

There are several things worth highlighting in this passage that are most pertinent to our concerns in this chapter. First, the contrast between Dante's embodied condition and that of the shade is memorably depicted in their futile attempt to embrace each other. Even though the shades have "bodies" made of air, as we shall see later, those bodies are not substantial enough to allow for this sort of physical interchange. Three times Dante tries in vain to embrace the shade, who is eager to do the same. His physicality, moreover, is further conveyed by the changing colors in his face, which register his amazement, as the shade realizes what is happening and gently withdraws.

Second, notice that Dante at this point recognizes this shade, who turns out to be his friend Casella, the musician. It is not clear how this recognition is achieved, whether through his "look" or the way he gently urged Dante to give up in his attempt to embrace him.

Third, there are significant non-physical markers of identity which show that the person is indeed his friend Casella, beginning with his love for Dante, which continues in purgatory. The continuity of this love, of course, implies the continuity of memory between his life in this world and his life in purgatory. This is further demonstrated later in the conversation when Dante asks him to sing, if it is permitted, one of the songs Casella used to sing to calm him down. Casella responds by singing a song that begins with a line from one of Dante's own poems, and sings it so sweetly that Dante says the memory of it remained with him thereafter.[2]

Thus, what began as an awkwardly ambiguous encounter with an unidentified shade whose expression conveyed such love that Dante wished to embrace him, turned out to be a warmly affectionate exchange with an old friend. Despite the limitations imposed by the fact that physical interaction is impossible, distinctively personal interaction still occurs. A personal relationship that already had a rich history is further developed as old memories are recalled, and new memories and bonds of affection are created through fresh interactions.

As a preliminary observation, then, I want to suggest that this scene not only illustrates many of the contemporary questions bearing on the issue of personal identity, but also provides working material for a satisfactory account of personal identity. Now the issue of personal identity is a vexed one that has been with us at least since Hume raised doubts as to whether there is any underlying self in addition to the series of conscious mental experiences we undergo. However, it is also worth noting that no such doubts likely occurred to generations of readers of Dante before the modern period, and those readers would have been confident that the figure Dante encountered was indeed Casella, the same person he had known before his death.

Indeed, there is good reason to believe that the modern problem of personal identity grows out of a sense that there is nothing to give our lives unity, or a sense of cohesiveness over time. And this may be due to a loss of any meaningful telos for human beings, along with the sort of moral framework that provides a sense of accountability for our choices and the direction and shape of our lives.[3] Dante, with his vision of hell, purgatory, and heaven, had no such problem. These doctrines represent a compelling account of the human telos, and provide a moral framework that is both clear and richly detailed. Dante vividly depicts the unity of our lives over time, and even eternity, whether for good or for ill, with dramatic psychological power as well as moral profundity.

Ironically, these traditional Christian doctrines are often thought to exacerbate the problem of personal identity, or at least to raise it in new forms. This is primarily due to the Christian doctrine of resurrection, which holds that at some time in the future, all persons who have died will be resurrected, and eventually live forever in bodily form either in heaven or in hell. The obvious question this raises is how the person who is resurrected at the future date, perhaps very far in the future, would be the same person as the one who lived a certain number of years on this earth and then died. By what criteria of identity would they be the same person? These issues have received considerable attention in contemporary philosophy of religion, and I have addressed them at some length in an earlier book on heaven and will not repeat that discussion here.[4]

In what follows, I will identify the distinctive identity issues raised by purgatory. Then I will examine and compare how different theories of human nature and personal identity fare with respect to the doctrine of purgatory: materialist, Thomist, and dualist. I will then turn to consider arguments that purgatory is needed to make sense of personal identity between death and heaven, particularly arguments that contend for the essential role of time in personal identity and character development.

PURGATORY'S DISTINCTIVE IDENTITY ISSUES

While there is some significant overlap, I want to emphasize that the issues posed by purgatory are distinctly different from those posed by resurrection. In particular, much of the recent discussion has been generated by a physicalist or materialist view of human nature that holds that when a human being dies, the whole person is destroyed. Although it is beyond dispute that dualist views of human nature—ranging from Cartesian dualism, to the Thomistic view that the soul is the form of the body—have been dominant in Western philosophy as well as theology for most of the first two millennia,[5] a materialist view of human nature has been on the ascendancy for generations now. The physicalist view of human nature has gained significant impetus from contemporary science, particularly neuroscience, which largely operates out of a naturalistic material view of reality, and has accordingly been inclined to reduce mind and soul to matter. In theological circles, in addition to the influence of contemporary science, it has been widely accepted that the Hebrew view of human nature is holistic in a way that rules out dualism. The dualism that has dominated Christian theology has thus been ascribed to Greek philosophy, an alien import that has corrupted biblical thinking—though this claim has moderated somewhat recently. So a materialist or physicalist view of human nature has been adopted not only by many Christian philosophers, but also by biblical scholars and theologians, with the result that central Christian doctrines, including resurrection, have been rethought, and in some cases significantly revised.

On the materialist view of human nature, then, resurrection has been conceived as the restoration to life of a person who does not exist, at least in any sort of conscious form, between death and resurrection. So the debate has often centered on whether identity can hold across such gaps, and the sort of difficulties posed by such "gappy" existence. A notorious example of these difficulties is the so-called problem of re-duplication, which asks us to consider the scenario in which several persons might appear at the resurrection who look like Dante, who all claim to be the author of the *Divine Comedy*, who remember falling in love with Beatrice, and so on. Suppose these persons are indistinguishable in terms of appearance, memories, personality, and so on. Would any of them have a clear claim to be identical with Dante the famous poet that would distinguish him from the competing claimants?

While I am not sympathetic to the materialist account of the person, I do not think these sorts of difficulties pose insurmountable problems for personal identity, as I argued in my earlier work. I think Christian theism has more than adequate resources to make sense of how personal identity can be sustained across such gaps in existence. But here is where purgatory poses distinctive issues, for the doctrine (at least as traditionally understood) posits, by definition, the continued survival of the person in the intermediate stage between death and resurrection, and thus rules out the sort of "gappy" existence that some materialists defend.[6] Moreover, purgatory involves some rather distinctive claims about the sort of things persons undergo in this intermediate stage. As we saw in the last chapter, the purpose of purgatory is punishment, or sanctification, or some combination of the two. So for the doctrine to make sense, the beings who are subjected to purgatory must be the sort of beings for whom punishment is appropriate, and/or they must also be capable of growing morally and spiritually in the manner presumed.

The broadly traditional account of purgatory in Roman Catholic theology has held that the separated soul is the subject that undergoes purgatory, and in view of this, it has been suggested that Catholic theology is essentially dualist in its view of human beings. Now, strictly speaking, the doctrine of purgatory does not entail dualism, for it could be postulated that persons who die instantly receive bodies after death, a "purgatorial body" that would maintain continuity and identity of the person between death and resurrection.[7] To spell out this proposal in metaphysical detail would require an account of how this "purgatorial body" is related to one's body in this life, as well as how it is related to one's resurrection body. So let us turn now to consider such accounts.

POSTMORTEM PHYSICAL IDENTITY

One recent proposal that might answer this need has been developed by Kevin Corcoran, who offers a theory of how persons as essentially physical objects might survive death, even on the assumption that "gappy" existence is impossible. While he is not certain whether or not such "gappy" existence is actually possible, the appeal of his position is that it is an option for those who are convinced it is not. Corcoran's account of this is based on his view of the necessary and sufficient condition for the persistence of a human body. Before stating this, however, he offers a more general account of the necessary and sufficient condition for the persistence of an organism, an account that emphasizes the crucial role of causation that holds between different stages of an organism. He argues that causation is the crucial factor for persistence, and that this factor takes us beyond mere spatiotemporal continuity, which, he contends, is merely a consequence of continuity but not its ground. For instance, the body at point A on the racetrack at 6:35 is in spatiotemporal continuity with the body that is at point B at 6:37, but this spatiotemporal continuity is not enough to make them the same body without the right sort of causation between points A and B. Here is Corcoran's principle stating the necessary and sufficient condition for the persistence of an organism:

> If an organism O at t2 is the same as an organism P that exists at t1 (where t1 < t2), then the (set of) simples that compose P at t1 must be causally related in the life preserving way to the (set of) simples that compose O at t2.[8]

Corcoran goes on to dub this the "life-preserving condition," for it maintains that the persistence of an organism depends on "immanent causal relations" holding between different stages of its overall life. Building on this principle, he goes on to propose the following as a necessary and sufficient condition for the persistence of a human body:

> A human body B that exists at t2 is the same as a human body A that exists at t1 just in case the temporal stages leading up to B at t2 are immanent-causally connected to the temporal stage of A at t1.[9]

Corcoran spells out the specifics of his proposal in terms of a divinely directed process of fission. More particularly, he suggests that God could cause the simples that make up a human body to fission in such a way that they would be causally related to two distinct, spatially separated sets of simples. "One of the two sets of simples would immediately cease to constitute a life and come instead to compose a corpse, while the other would either continue to constitute a body in heaven or continue to constitute a body in some intermediate state."[10] What he has in mind here is an "all-at-once" replacement of simples so that a new body, in continuity with the old one, is constituted. The simples along the first branching path (the old body) would no longer be capable of subserving consciousness, and would thus no longer perpetuate a life, whereas those along the latter branch would.

This proposal is particularly interesting for our purposes because Corcoran suggests that it would explain what would constitute a body "in some intermediate state" as well as in heaven. What is less clear is whether he believes there would be a difference between such a body in an intermediate state, and one in heaven. His account is offered as an account of resurrection, so taken at face value, it appears he believes that a body produced in this fashion in some intermediate state would be a resurrected body. Now this poses theological problems, as we shall see a bit later, because the New Testament appears to teach that the resurrection is a future event, not something that happens immediately upon death. Resurrection bodies, moreover, are depicted in the New Testament as having powers that our present bodies do not. Taking Jesus' resurrection body as a model, such bodies are raised immortal, and are not subject to the same sort of limitations as our current bodies. It is not clear whether Corcoran believes that these new bodies are resurrected in that fashion, or if these bodies are more like our present bodies. At any rate, his theory provides the conceptual resources to fashion an account of personal identity for persons in an intermediate state, even if human beings are essentially physical beings. The bodies in this intermediate state could be produced by fission in such a way that they would be in continuity with our present bodies, but only intermediary in the sense that they would not yet be fully resurrected and made immortal in the sense depicted in the New Testament.

Corcoran acknowledges that critics of his view have suggested that his view is actually at odds with the doctrine of resurrection, for, according to his position, no one really dies, since fission at the instant of death entails they continue immediately alive in their bodies. Corcoran replies that this consequence is not unique to his view. Cartesian dualists, for instance, who hold that a person is essentially an immaterial soul, likewise believe the soul persists after death, in uninterrupted existence. To be sure, one's body dies on the Cartesian view, but Corcoran points out that something also dies on his view, namely, the cellular tissue that once constituted his body.[11] Whether his view is acceptable on theological grounds is debatable, but as a philosophical account of personal identity beyond death, it appears to be a promising option for those who hold that human beings are essentially physical objects, but reject the possibility of "gappy" existence.

THE POPE WEIGHS IN

Let us turn now to consider another physicalist view of human beings that poses difficulties for the doctrine of purgatory, and perhaps is incompatible with it. This view has gained considerable currency with some prominent theologians, but has also come under fire for its theological implications. I will examine an assessment of this view by Joseph Ratzinger, now Pope Benedict XVI.

The essence of this view is that resurrection takes place immediately after death, thus avoiding the problems associated with "gappy existence." In this sense, it is similar to the one we just examined, except that it is not motivated by the concern to insist that the resurrection body is the same as this body, nor with providing a particular metaphysical account of how this could be the case. The main motivation for this view is to highlight the fact that the Christian hope for life after death is resurrection, as opposed to the immortality of the soul. In fact, those who take this view think that it is a Greek corruption of biblical teaching to hold that the soul survives between death and resurrection.

What is perhaps most interesting and distinctive about this view, however, is what it claims about the relationship between historical time and eternity. In particular, it holds that there is a complete incommensurability between time and eternity, and accordingly, that persons who die step out of time and immediately into eternity. Those who have died have actually entered the end of the world, which is no longer understood as the final day of the cosmic calendar. Advocates of this account claim, moreover, that it illuminates the early Christian expectation that the return of Christ and the end of the world were imminent. Ratzinger spells out the implications of this view as follows:

> This starting point is then utilized to explain resurrection: when a person, by his dying, enters into non-time, into the end of the world, he also enters, by the same token, into Christ's return and the resurrection of the dead. There is, therefore, no "intermediate state." We have no need of the soul in order to preserve the identity of the human being. "Being with the Lord" and resurrection from the dead are the same thing. A solution of striking simplicity has been found: resurrection happens in death.[12]

It is worth emphasizing that this passage appears at the end of his book in an appendix entitled "Between Death and Resurrection: Some Further Reflections." Particularly significant is the fact that he begins these reflections by citing an official 1979 "Letter on Certain Questions in Eschatology" addressed to all bishops and episcopal Conferences, and made public by the Holy See's Congregation for the Doctrine of the Faith. What Ratzinger makes emphatically clear in these further reflections is that the recent debates are not merely scholarly controversies, but rather, impinge on the very core of the Christian faith.

In the main body of his original book, Ratzinger had already expressed fundamental misgivings about these recent proposals. In the first place, he suggested that these views represented a "camouflaged" version of the doctrine of immortality on more philosophically adventurous assumptions. Resurrection is instantly claimed for a body on its deathbed or on the way to its grave. "The indivisibility of man and his boundness to the body, even when dead, suddenly seems to play no further role, even though it was the point of departure for this whole conversation."[13]

Second, Ratzinger raised questions about the philosophy of time and of history, which, he contends, is the "true lever" that motivates this position. Is it even possible, he wonders, to conceive of human beings, whose lives are decisively achieved in the temporal realm, simply being transposed somehow into eternity? Moreover, is it coherent to suppose that an eternity that has this sort of beginning for those who enter it is really even eternity? Perhaps even more fundamentally perplexing here is how we are supposed to conceive of the relationship between temporal history and eternity. While history appears to be ongoing from the standpoint of our experience, according to this view it is already complete on the other side of death. "History is viewed as simultaneously completed and still continuing."[14] His overall assessment of this view is summed up when he describes it as "a quirky theological patchwork, full of logical leaps and ruptures" and goes on to recommend that we should as quickly as possible "bid farewell to this way of thinking."[15]

Ratzinger's positive prescription is a return to taking seriously the traditional view that resurrection is a future reality that awaits all of us, including those who have already died. He contends, moreover, that, paradoxical as it may seem, the doctrine of resurrection is actually bolstered by the traditional view of the immortality of the soul, rather than undermined or displaced by it. "As this debate proceeds, it becomes clearer that the true function of the idea of the soul's immortality is to preserve a real hold on that of the resurrection of the flesh. The thesis of resurrection in death dematerializes the resurrection. It entails that real matter has no part in the event of the consummation."[16] As he sees it then, this novel proposal allegedly motivated by a desire to affirm resurrection, as opposed to the Greek doctrine of immortality, has had the ironic effect of obscuring the robust biblical doctrine of resurrection. By contrast, the affirmation that the soul continues to survive apart from the body highlights the biblical hope of a real resurrection of the flesh that will occur only when history has run its providentially directed course.

ASSESSING PHYSICALIST VIEWS OF SURVIVAL

Now, by way of assessment, it is worth asking whether the sort of view Corcoran defends might be defensible against some of these fundamental criticisms. With respect to the first, a good case can be made that his view does indeed preserve "the indivisibility of man and his boundness to the body." For on that view, the body produced by fission of a man who dies is numerically the same as that man's body in this life, even though the cellular mass that has died is no longer his body. The body produced by fission is the one that supports his consciousness and mental activity and thereby his "boundness" to his body is preserved.

It is also at least arguable that the fission view may be on equal footing with the traditional view of the survival of the soul, followed by a future resurrection, with respect to preserving "a real hold on the resurrection of the flesh." The fission view hardly falls prey to the criticism of "dematerializing" the resurrection, or "entailing that real matter has no part in the consummation." The fact that a real material body is held to exist in the intermediate period, a body that is numerically the same as one's body in this life, as well as with one's later resurrection body, affirms rather than denies that real matter is included in the final consummation. Again, the threat to the doctrine of resurrection comes not from the claim that we might exist physically in the intermediate period, but rather, from the suggestion that there is no qualitative difference between one's intermediate body and one's resurrection body. Even if one's resurrection body is the same numerically as one's body in the intermediate period, for resurrection to maintain its meaning and theological significance, that body must be raised and made immortal, like Christ's body. Otherwise, resurrection does not involve raising our bodies in any sense that was not already true in the intermediate period, and the doctrine is accordingly trivialized or made superfluous.

The real problem with the immediate resurrection view, then, lies not in the claim that we might still have our physical bodies the moment we die, but rather in the claim that these bodies would be our resurrection bodies. So long as these bodies are understood to be "intermediate" bodies, they do not pose a problem for the distinctiveness of the resurrection. What this points up is that the deeper problem with this view is indeed its view of time, a view that holds that the resurrection has already occurred for those who have died, and stepped out of time and into eternity.

Our primary concern here is to determine which views of personal identity are compatible with the doctrine of purgatory, and I have argued so far that physicalist views of human nature are not inherently incompatible with purgatory. However, any view that denies an intermediate stage in which persons who die are still in time, and await the final resurrection, is at odds with the doctrine of purgatory. I want to underscore that Ratzinger's primary concern in insisting on an intermediate state is not with defending the doctrine of purgatory. This is not to say, however, that the doctrine is irrelevant to his concern. He notes, for instance, that the doctrine of immediate resurrection into eternity is at odds with the practice of praying for the dead,[17] one of the most ancient practices that led to the doctrine of purgatory. His primary concern is first and foremost to maintain a robust doctrine of resurrection, and the biblical realism that supports it.

Here let us compare a noted Protestant theologian who has similar concerns, namely, the New Testament scholar N. T. Wright. He has observed that many contemporary Christians have a sentimental view of heaven and the afterlife that does justice neither to the savage reality of death, nor to Christian hope of a future redemption that will include the renewal of all of creation from the effects of the fall. The Christian hope is not to be delivered from this world, but that God's kingdom will come here, and his will shall be done on earth as it is in heaven. The resurrection of our bodies is a vital component, but not the entirety of the final salvation of God's world for which we hope. Wright is emphatic about the nature of the resurrection hope. "It wasn't a way of talking about life after death. It was a way of talking about a new bodily life *after* whatever state of existence one might enter immediately upon death. It was, in other words, life *after* life after death."[18]

Wright has no stake in defending purgatory; indeed, he is a critic of the doctrine as noted in an earlier chapter, and he explicitly rejects the doctrine in the work just cited. The point I want to emphasize is that Wright is no less insistent than Ratzinger about the importance of holding to resurrection as a future hope that will be part of God's larger work of redemption and salvation for our fallen world. He is likewise clear that "life after death" in the intermediate state is a reality, but not the consummation for which Christians hope. Although he is somewhat vague about exactly what survives between death and resurrection, and shies away from talk of souls, he is clear in his conviction that conscious survival in the intermediate state is an important component of resurrection faith. In explaining what the Apostle Paul meant when he said that Christians sleep until the resurrection, he writes that " *sleep* here means that the *body* is 'asleep' in the sense of 'dead,' while the real person— however we want to describe him or her—continues."[19]

Now then, to summarize this discussion, we have seen that the doctrine of purgatory requires the continuing existence of its subjects after death, and is thus incompatible with any view that holds that death is the complete destruction of the person. To the contrary, purgatory requires subjects that retain not only consciousness, but are also able to undergo punishment, discipline, moral and spiritual growth, and the like, depending on how one conceives the doctrine. Purgatory is compatible with a physicalist or materialist view of human persons so long as the persons involved are presumed to persist in time, since purgatory is an intermediary experience preceding the final resurrection and consummation. Although a "purgatorial" body may be understood to be numerically one with a previous earthly body, as well as the resurrection body to come, it must not be understood as a resurrected body that is immortal, like Christ's resurrected body. Resurrection is a central component of the larger consummation and redemption of the world that Christians hope for, one that is yet to come for all of us.

ANY SELF-IDENTIFIED THOMIST SURVIVORS?

Let us turn now to consider views of human nature and personal identity that posit a non-physical source of continuity in the intermediate state between death and resurrection. As we do so, let us begin by further examining the view that Ratzinger commends in place of the immediate resurrection view, which he roundly rejects.

It is significant, and telling, that he added an "afterword" to the English edition of his book in which he begins by noting that since the original publication of his book in 1977 "the discussion it aroused has focussed almost entirely on the problem of the body-soul relationship, and the question of the soul's immortality."[20] He went on to observe that the 1979 document published by the Roman Congregation for the Doctrine of the Faith "regarded the idea of the soul as indispensable for the discourse and thinking that belong with faith."

In his original book, as well as his aforementioned "Supplementary Reflections," he had expressed astonishment that a word and concept as pervasive and deeply rooted in traditional theology and liturgy as the "soul" had been so widely abandoned in such a short amount of time. He analyzed the widespread antipathy in theology to anything Greek as stemming not only from a general skepticism about ontology in much contemporary thought, but also from "the fear, reaching almost panic proportions, of any accusation of dualism."[21] Ratzinger diagnoses this panic as an enormous overreaction, not the least because, as he demonstrates, Greek thought is much more diverse and complicated than popular pictures suggest, even with respect to the dreaded specter of dualism. Moreover, he insists that the Christian concept of the soul was not a case of simple borrowing from philosophical thought. While the concept of soul undeniably has philosophical and ontological content, in a theological context it is first and foremost a profoundly Christological concept, tied inextricably to the conviction that a life that is connected to Christ by faith cannot be destroyed even by death. As Saint Paul famously put it, when contemplating the prospect of departing this life and leaving his body behind, he was confident that if he were to do so, he would be "with Christ" in a sense that he positively anticipates.[22]

The soul accordingly can be defined in theological terms as "the bearer of existence with Christ," as Ratzinger puts it. In view of this fundamental conviction, he goes on to state that what the Church had to maintain was "on the one hand, the central certainty of a life with Christ that not even death can destroy, and on the other hand, the incompleteness of that life in the time before the definitive 'resurrection of the flesh.' "[23]

The view that best meets these desiderata, Ratzinger suggests, is a novel intellectual construct that shows that Christian theology did not simply take over the concept of the soul from philosophical sources. This construct is Aquinas's view that the soul is the form of the body, a position that "transcends both monism and dualism."[24]

Aquinas's position is notoriously difficult, but it has gained considerable attention and support in contemporary philosophy of religion. A large part of the appeal, no doubt, is the promise that it offers of a viable alternative to both monism and dualism. While it shares certain similarities with dualism, it should not be conflated with either the Platonic or Cartesian position. Indeed, it promises to provide a much more positive account of the relationship between soul and body, and of the essential value of the body, one that can avoid some of the major pitfalls that have plagued dualism.

To assess the appeal of this position, let us consider a recent account of it by Christina Van Dyke. Part of what makes her exposition and defense of Aquinas interesting is that she takes as her starting point an influential attempt to appropriate his views by noted evangelical Protestant philosopher J. P. Moreland, who has been critical of materialistic accounts of the human person. Moreland, along with Scott Rae, has recently developed a position they have labeled "Thomistic Substance Dualism," a view they find attractive not only for philosophical and theological reasons, but also because it appears helpful for a number of current ethical debates, particularly in the field of medicine.[25] While their aim is not simply to reiterate the Thomistic view, they do intend to remain faithful to the spirit of Aquinas's position, and to a significant extent, its letter. Their position can be summed up in two central theses. First, they hold that the rational soul is an immaterial substance. Unlike more traditional versions of dualism, however, they do not hold that the body is a distinct substance. So there is only one substance on their view, the soul. The body is an ensouled physical structure that does not exist as a body, strictly speaking, without the soul. The second thesis is that human persons are in fact identical with the immaterial substance specified in the first thesis, the rational soul.[26]

The bulk of Van Dyke's article is devoted to showing that Aquinas affirms neither of these theses, but rather, something subtly but significantly different in each case. With respect to the first thesis, that the rational soul is a substance, she points out that Aquinas was concerned that if the soul were acknowledged as a substance in its own right, it would not really need the body, which would raise questions about God's wisdom in his design plan that joins souls with bodies. Moreover, he worried that the essential unity of the human person would be compromised if both soul and body were independent substances. So, while it is true that a human being is composed of just one substance, that substance is not a rational soul, but rather a rather a living body. It is a composite of form and matter, and has both physical and mental properties.[27]

But the story, of course, is more complicated, and when the complications are taken into account, we can readily see why Aquinas's position has been understood as a variation on dualism, and why it seems easy enough to modify it in the sort of way that Moreland and Rae have done. In particular, Aquinas held that the soul, the form of the body, continues to exist between the death of the soul-body composite, and the resurrection. It continues to exist in conscious form and to retain its ability to engage in intellectual activity. Now, given that it can exist independently of the body, it might appear that it should qualify as a substance. However, Aquinas rejected this conclusion, on the grounds that independent existence is only one of two conditions that must be met for something to qualify as an individual substance. The second condition is that a thing must also be a member of a particular species and genus, and thus exist as a whole thing. A disembodied soul is not a proper member of the human species, but rather, is only one part of a human being.[28]

Now, with respect to the second thesis of "Thomistic Substance Dualism," Van Dyke argues that it fares no better than the first. Not only is it not the case according to Aquinas that the rational soul is not a substance, and therefore not properly a human being, it is also not a person. Again, there are complexities, but they need not detain us, for the fundamental point is similar to the one we have already examined. Since a soul is only part of the human species, it does not constitute a person by itself.[29]

For our purposes, the claim that the separated soul is neither a human being nor a person is a significant one. As Van Dyke puts it in very concrete terms, "David will *not* exist, in essence, when his soul separates from his body at death. Rather, death causes a rupture in human identity that only the bodily resurrection can repair."[30] This certainly raises interesting questions about purgatory if it is only David's soul that goes there, but not David himself. Earlier in her essay, Van Dyke noted Aquinas's view that sins as well as virtuous actions are committed by the composite person made up of both form and matter, and not merely by the soul. This, she notes, is the basis of one of Aquinas's arguments for the necessity of the resurrection: "Because it was the composite human being who sinned or acted well, corresponding punishment or reward would be incomplete if it involved the soul alone."[31]

VARIATIONS ON THOMISM

Dante offers a fascinating variation on Aquinas's view of the disembodied soul precisely in order to make sense of certain pains in purgatory. The matter comes up after the famous passage we examined in an earlier chapter that describes the punishment of the gluttons, who suffer from hunger and emaciation in purgatory. In particular, Dante is perplexed as to how the shades can suffer physically, how they can experience the pain of emaciation in a place where food is superfluous. To answer this question, Virgil yields to Statius, the Christian poet, who responds with a rather complex account of how the body is formed, along with the soul and its various powers. For our concerns, the most interesting part of the explanation pertains to what happens to the soul at the point of death. Statius explains as follows:

> When Lachesis has no more flax to twine
> It quits the flesh, but bears essentially
> Away with it the human and divine—
> Each lower power in dumb passivity,
> But memory, intelligence, and will
> Active, and keener than they used to be.[32]

Notice, the separated soul retains the powers of memory, intelligence, and will, not only as active, but even keener than before. However, the lower faculties of the soul, such as the capacity to feel physical sensation, remain "in dumb passivity." In Aquinas's view, these lower powers will not be reactivated until the resurrection, when the form-matter composite is restored. Dante, however, departs from Aquinas on this score, and holds that the soul is enabled to express its lower powers as well as its rational ones in purgatory.

He accounts for this is in terms of the famous bodies of air that I mentioned in the beginning of this chapter. Statius explains that departed souls find themselves either in hell or purgatory, and once there, the form radiates and forms a body out of air, in a fashion similar to what occurs when air is soaked by heavy rain, and refracts the rays of the sun in such a way that a rainbow appears. These bodies, he says, even form organs of sense that allow the souls to experience sensations of pain as well as emotions:

> And thence its semblance, which we therefore call
> A *shade*, derives henceforward; thence 'twill make
> For every sense an organ—sight and all;
> Thence do we speak and thence we laugh, thence take
> Wherewith to fashion forth the tears and sighs
> Thou'st heard, belike, from all the mountain break.
> Even as desires and other feelings rise
> To vex us, so the shade takes form, and there's
> The reason of what caused thee such surprise.[33]

Notice again, Statius's account is intended to explain to Dante what he had found perplexing in the suffering of the gluttons. Their bodies of air explain how desires for food can arise, and how those desires when frustrated can be painful, physically as well as emotionally.[34]

Indeed, it worth underscoring that the primary purpose of the bodies of air appears to be to make sense of corporeal punishment in purgatory (and hell) before the resurrection.[35] While these bodies contribute to the personality of the characters and give them a sense of humanity—even if they cannot engage in physical activities like embracing—that does not seem to be their main significance. Rather, personal identity lies in the continuity of memory, intelligence, and will that the soul, the form of the body, carries into the next life, and which will be communicated through the medium of the aerial bodies. While these bodies provide a certain epistemic identity, as when Dante recognizes his friend Casella, the essential identity arguably resides in the memories he has, his thoughts and will as expressed to Dante, and the like.

Before turning to look at substance dualism, let us consider briefly another variation on Aquinas's theory, this time a contemporary example from the physicist turned theologian John Polkinghorne. In his attempt to define the soul, or the carrier of the "continuity of living personhood," he rejects both the idea that the carrier is "a separate spiritual component" as well as the notion that it is "merely material."[36] His preferred alternative is that the soul is the "information-bearing pattern" that organizes the matter in our bodies and that is "modified as we acquire new experiences, insights and memories, in accordance with the dynamic of our living history."[37] While it appears that this "information-bearing pattern" will be dissolved when our bodies decay, Polkinghorne proposes that it is coherent to hope that God might preserve these patterns in his memory, and then re-embody them at the resurrection.

Now at first glance, it might be supposed that preservation in the mind of God between death and resurrection would be a purely objective sort of survival, with no subjective consciousness sustained. However, Polkinghorne suggests otherwise in a passage that sounds as if the "information-bearing patterns" undergo something like purgatory as they await the resurrection:

> We do not need to suppose that being held in the mind of God is a purely passive kind of preservation. We may expect that God's love will be at work, through the respectful but powerful operation of divine grace, purifying and transforming the souls awaiting resurrection in ways that respect their integrity.[38]

What Polkinghorne says here is not altogether clear, but he suggests that these souls are interacting with God in personal ways, ways that respect their freedom and agency even as they purify and transform. Presumably, these information-bearing patterns must retain memory, intelligence, and will, even if they are, as Polkinghorne says, "less than fully human."[39] The similarity here with the Thomist view is obvious.

THE SURVIVAL OF SUBSTANCE DUALISM

Let us turn now to consider full-blooded substance dualism, a view that readily lends itself to providing an account of postmortem identity. The classic expression of this, of course, is Cartesian dualism, which is construed, appropriately enough, in two distinctly different ways. On one interpretation, we are wholly immaterial beings, namely, souls. While we *have* bodies obviously enough, and are intimately related to them, and interact with the world through them, they are not part of us. When our bodies die, we continue to exist with our personal identity fully intact. The second interpretation holds that we are composed of two parts, soul and body, a view that is called "compound dualism." For our concerns, the differences between these two interpretations are relatively unimportant, for they essentially agree about the status of the soul after death.[40]

I will now examine an example of substance dualism to see how it accounts for personal identity after death, namely, that of Richard Swinburne, which is a version of compound dualism, for he holds that persons consist of two parts, bodies and souls, with souls being the essential part. He argues that it is possible that persons can continue to exist when their bodies are destroyed, so given his view, the continuing existence of the soul would count as the continuing existence of the person.[41]

For our particular purposes, his account of what he calls "the structure of the soul" is especially interesting. What he means by this phrase "is very roughly that the determinants of change of belief and desire are in part soul-states, not mere brain states; and that if body and soul were separated, some character would remain with the soul."[42] Since belief and desire are not merely brain states, and can continue after body and soul separate, according to dualism, the character that one has formed by way of these beliefs and desires will continue as well.

A person's character, Swinburne holds, is essentially a matter of his beliefs about what is important and how central those beliefs are, as well as his intrinsic desires, which are those desires he gladly owns and welcomes. Extrinsic desires, by contrast, are those desires one does not welcome because they are at odds with one's central beliefs and long-term intrinsic desires, so to indulge them would be a bad thing overall. For instance, suppose (to use a purely hypothetical example) I very much believe it would be a good thing to finish my book on purgatory, and I accordingly desire to spend all day Saturday working on it. This is important to me, so I welcome the desire to work on it. Suppose, however, that I am somewhat distracted by thoughts of all the big football games on TV, their implications for the national championship, and so on, and I consequently also desire to watch several of those games. To do so would be at odds with my deeply rooted and long-term desire to finish the book, so it would be bad overall to indulge my desire to watch football for ten hours.

Now the recognition that some beliefs are more central than others, and that some desires are intrinsic, while others are extrinsic, points to what Swinburne means when he says that the soul has a structure. Some beliefs and desires are more central and deeply rooted, whereas others are more peripheral, tentative, or fleeting.

Moreover, there are structural relationships among our beliefs and desires. Our beliefs may be more or less consistent with each other, and the same is true of our desires. Furthermore, not only are there structural relationships in how beliefs are related to beliefs, and desires related to desires, but there are also relationships between beliefs and desires. For instance, long-term desires depend on certain beliefs in order to be sustained. That is, an agent must believe that a thing has significant value or worth in order to sustain a deeply rooted, long-term desire for it. (I must really believe it is important to finish my book in order to maintain the desire to do so, and to resist competing desires.) An agent has a well-integrated and structured soul to the degree that his beliefs and desires are mutually consistent and supportive.

We will come back to Swinburne's view in the next section, but for now the important point is that, on his view, the soul has a structure that survives death, and that this structure is formed, and can be re-formed, by our continuing beliefs and desires and their mutual interaction. The deeply rooted beliefs and desires that we have make up our character, and this provides an intelligible account of how the survival of the soul is the survival of the person.

Before moving on, it is worth pausing to reflect on the common ground shared by the Thomist view, the revision of Thomism designated as TSD, and Cartesian-styled substance dualism. What is striking at one level is the agreement between all of these positions about what we might broadly call the ontology of what survives between death and resurrection. All of them agree that the rational soul retains consciousness, memory, and will. They disagree to be sure, on the more precise metaphysical issue of whether the entity that survives is a substance, or properly speaking a person, but there is still significant agreement that the separated soul retains psychological properties that allow for such activities as thought, communication, choice, and the like.

PURGATORY AND OUR SURVIVAL OPTIONS

Let us turn now to consider the question of how these different accounts of personal identity, both physicalist and dualist, fare with respect to the doctrine of purgatory. Recall that the doctrine of purgatory requires an account of personal identity that continues during the period between death and resurrection, ruling out "gappy" existence. Moreover, the account of personal identity must be adequate to make sense of whatever one believes happens during purgatory, whether that is some sort of punishment, spiritual discipline, or other forms of sanctification and moral formation.

I think it is clear that the first view we considered, namely, the view of immediate bodily replacement by a process of fission, provides an account of personal identity that not only sustains continuity, but would be sufficient to underwrite any of the models of purgatory that we considered in the previous chapter. The satisfaction model that we considered understood the punishment of purgatory as the delay of the beatific vision, but other accounts of the punishments of purgatory have emphasized its corporeal dimensions. Obviously, an account of personal identity that holds not only to continuity of memory, character, personality, and the like, as well as bodily continuity, is well situated to make sense of physical punishment as well as the psychological and emotional punishment involved in the delay of the beatific vision. Moreover, just as clearly, this account is equipped to make sense of purgatory as a further process of sanctification and spiritual growth, even if that does not involve any sort of physical discipline.

A potential pitfall for this view, as noted above, concerns the relationship between this intermediate body and the resurrection body. In order to maintain that the intermediate state is not the fullness of eternal life for which Christians hope, the distinctiveness of the resurrection as a future hope must be maintained. It is also doubtful that the notion of embodied life in the intermediate state is taught in scripture. If scholars such as N. T. Wright are correct in their interpretation of the New Testament, the life after death that precedes the life *after* life after death is likely a disembodied state, though he is prepared to say that it is "the real person" that continues in existence. John Cooper has also argued that the intermediate state of disembodied existence is the only position definitely attested in the New Testament, and is compatible with all relevant texts, whereas other positions conflict with some texts.[43] Those with a physicalist view of human persons contest this claim, but for their position to be convincing to the larger community of orthodox Christians, they have the burden of proof in showing that their interpretation of the New Testament is to be preferred to the interpretation that has been a matter of broad consensus in the history of theology.

When we turn to the various dualist views, it is clear enough that they provide accounts of the persistence of consciousness, memory, and will that account for how there could be psychological continuity between death and resurrection. Whether this is enough for an account of personal identity depends on how a person is defined, and as we have seen, Aquinas did not think that the separated soul is properly a person. Now this raises interesting implications with respect to purgatory. If the separated soul that survives the death of David is not David, then it is not David who goes to purgatory. It is not David who is punished for David's sins, on the satisfaction model, nor is it David who would grow spiritually and undergo the completion of the sanctification process, but rather, only David's soul. These are curious consequences of the Thomistic view, to put it mildly.

Although Aquinas may not consider the separated soul a person, he nevertheless makes some very strong statements about what the soul is capable of experiencing, and how it is liable to punishment or reward. He does not shrink from insisting that separated souls immediately experience either the pain of hell, which includes punishment by fire, or the delights of heaven. "Straightway, therefore, when the holy soul is separated from the body, it sees God by sight. And this is the ultimate beatitude."[44] Indeed, he even goes so far as to suggest that separation from the body makes beatitude possible. "For the separation of the soul from the body makes it capable of the divine vision, and it was unable to arrive at this so long as it was united to the corruptible body."[45]

Of course, there are exceptions to immediate entrance to either the misery of hell, or the "ultimate beatitude," namely, those souls who are good, but still require purification before they can enjoy the beatific vision. And it is in the same chapter in *Summa Contra Gentiles* from which I just quoted that Aquinas gives us his concise explanation for why he holds that there is a purgatory, a passage I quoted in the previous chapter. His basic explanation is that if souls do not perfect their purification in this life, they must undergo the appropriate punishment in the next life.

Now it is most interesting to note that earlier in this same chapter, he gives his explanation for why he thinks it is appropriate for the separated soul to be the subject of punishment or reward:

> But merit and fault are fitted to the body only through the soul, since there is essentially
> no merit or demerit except so far as a thing is voluntary. Therefore, both reward and pun-
> ishment flow suitably from the soul to the body, but it does not belong to the soul by

reason of the body. There is, therefore, no reason in the infliction of punishment or bestowal of reward why the souls should wait for the resumption of their bodies; rather, it seems more fitting that, since the souls had priority in the fault or merit, they have priority also in being rewarded or punished.[46]

It is important to recognize that in an earlier chapter of this book, Aquinas insisted that the soul separated from the body is imperfect, and will find its ultimate happiness only when body and soul are reunited in resurrection. In this same chapter, Aquinas also pointed out that our actions, both sinful and righteous, are done by a composite of soul and body, which means that both deserve punishment or reward. As Van Dyke observed, this provided the basis for one of his arguments for the necessity of a bodily resurrection.[47]

My purpose here is not to work out the details of Aquinas's views in systematic fashion. While he held that our actions are done by a composite of body and soul, and that both accordingly deserve blame or credit, he also made the remarkable claim that it is fitting for the separated soul to be punished or to be rewarded in the intermediate period prior to the resurrection, and offers suggestive reasons for thinking this is true. Notice, punishment flows suitably from the soul to the body, but it does not belong to the soul because of the body. The soul, it seems, is the source of free choice, and deserves credit or blame in a way the body does not, so much so that it is fitting for the separated soul to be rewarded or punished, to an extremely high degree, before the resurrection occurs.

And yet, as much as he gives priority to the soul in this regard, the soul is severely limited in another respect when it leaves the body. In particular, Aquinas holds that the soul is in a mutable state as long as it is united to the body, but once it is separated, it is immutable. The body, he says, was given to the soul for the purpose of moving the soul toward its perfection. But once separated from the body, it is no longer in a state of movement, but will be fixed in the end it has chosen, either good or evil. "Therefore, there is not in the separated soul a will changeable from good to evil, although it is changeable from this object of will to that so long as the order to the same ultimate end is preserved."[48] While the fundamental change from good to evil is impossible (or from evil to good), there is a range of free choice that remains for the separated soul that has chosen good, so long as the ultimate end is preserved.

Again, my purpose here is not a systematic exposition of Aquinas's views, but rather to identify and consider issues of personal identity suggested by his views as they bear on the doctrine of purgatory. And while there is something undeniably counterintuitive about the notion that the separated soul is liable to punishment and reward even though it is not properly a person, Aquinas makes strong enough claims about the power of the soul both in this life, as well as the next, to make sense of that claim.[49] The soul, again, is the primary agent of voluntary choice, and retains memory of those choices and awareness that they were freely chosen. And a soul that has chosen the good for its ultimate end, but needs further purification, retains not only rationality, but also the ability to make further choices in keeping with that end.

To explore this further, let us come back to the version of substance dualism represented by Swinburne to how it can help us make sense of what the soul undergoes in purgatory. Recall that on his view, beliefs and desires may be mutually consistent and supportive, but they may also be at odds with each other. For instance, Swinburne points out that "agents may desire much less that which they believe to have most worth, and in particular that which they believe to have moral worth. There is a conflict between what they desire to pursue and what they think worth pursuing."[50]

Now then, I propose that purgatory can be understood in this light as the process of changing the structure of a soul in a positive fashion by resolving the inconsistencies that remain. In particular, this would involve altering an agent's peripheral beliefs and desires in such a way that they become fully compatible with his central beliefs and desires, which would be true beliefs about God and that which is truly good, and corresponding desires to know and love God and to do his will. What is particularly significant here is that this sort of change of structure is perfectly intelligible given what dualists, both of the Thomist and broadly Cartesian varieties, believe is true about the powers of the separated soul.

One of the principal ways that Swinburne thinks such change occurs is through reflection, including reflection on new experiences and insights. Agents are often little aware of the inconsistencies among their beliefs and desires, and as long as this is true, those inconsistencies may remain undisturbed. Reflection, however, can bring them to light and provide an impetus to change. As Swinburne puts it, "[a]gents can attempt to make their belief-desire systems more integrated by testing the coherence of their beliefs and desires with each other . . . thinking through their consequences and facing up to their conflicts."[51] Separated souls in purgatory, we may assume, are not simply left to their own initiative in doing the appropriate reflection. Rather, we may assume that God is actively involved in guiding and provoking the sort of reflection best suited to expose inconsistencies and resolve them in a positive character-forming fashion.

Recall the example of Scrooge from the previous chapter. It is easy enough, on dualist assumptions, to imagine his experience as a separated soul. As the story goes, the experiences come through dreams. When Scrooge revisits the various scenes and observes them, he is there invisibly and cannot interact with the persons involved, as the ghosts have to remind him from time to time. So we might alter the story and retell it with Scrooge as a separated soul after his death. Moreover, let us assume that he is not simply a hardened sinner, but rather, a man who was converted late in life but still has an undue love for money, and insufficient love for his fellow human beings.

We can now think of the guided tour he took to Christmases past, present, and future as guided reflection that made him face up to conflicts and inconsistencies in his beliefs and desires. Thereby he would be pushed to reassess his beliefs about money and its true value in light of his belief that God is the ultimate good and the true source of all real happiness and fulfillment. Likewise, and more importantly, he would be moved to reevaluate other people and his relationship with them in light of Christian truth. Consider in this light the forceful words of the Ghost of Christmas Present as he and Scrooge observe the Cratchit family Christmas dinner, and Scrooge begins to have feelings of concern for Tiny Tim. The Ghost ruthlessly exposes the profound inconsistency between his humane reaction and his attitude as reflected in the heartless comment about the "surplus population" he had made earlier:

> "Man," said the Ghost, "if man you be in heart, not adamant, forbear that wicked cant until you have discovered What the surplus is, and Where it is. Will you decide what men shall live, what men shall die? It may be, that in the sight of Heaven, you are more worthless and less fit to live than millions like this poor man's child."[52]

We may easily imagine our converted Scrooge will eliminate the inconsistencies in his thoughts and desires as he is faced with them, and examines his life and values "in the sight of heaven." The structure of his soul, under the pressure of reflection, will become thoroughly consistent and solidified in goodness as beliefs and desires at odds with his central beliefs and desires are altered and adjusted so that they align with those core commitments.

Now all of this, I reiterate, is perfectly intelligible if separated souls have the sort of powers that dualists believe they do. A sanctification model of purgatory is coherent on a dualist account of human nature and personal identity. It is also worth noting that the sort of satisfaction model we noted in the previous chapter is perfectly compatible with dualism. Recall that the punishment of purgatory on that model is the delay of the beatific vision, and a separated soul could certainly undergo this sort of punishment, with its attendant regret, longing, and the like.

Dualism does, however, face a potential problem if purgatory is thought to include physical discipline, whether that is understood in terms of satisfaction or sanctification. In the discussion of Scrooge as a separated soul, his sins consisted of wrong beliefs, attitudes, evaluations, and desires that stemmed from those. His disordered desire for money, for instance, was due to his misguided belief that money made him more important, enhanced his power, status, and the like. His sins, accordingly, could be purged by changing his beliefs and desires to bring them in line with true beliefs about God, the value of other persons, his true status, and so on. "In the sight of heaven" he comes to see that the value of things, particularly people, is not measured in terms of money and status.

Consider, by contrast, sins that involve the body much more directly, such as Dante's examples of lust and gluttony. Recall that the explanation of aerial bodies comes in response to his question about how the shades who were guilty of gluttony can experience the pain of hunger and famishment. The aerial bodies, we are informed, were given precisely to make possible corporeal punishment. Now given that sins are performed by a composite person, and that the consequent habits, dispositions, and character belong to a composite person, it is not always easy to see how those habits, dispositions, and so on could be rectified without the involvement of the body. This seems especially so when the sins in question involve the body so directly, and affect the body so significantly, as in the case of gluttony. There is something intuitively as well as experientially right about Dante's notion that such disordered loves require for their healing that the agent must undergo a process of learning to restrain his bodily urges. Without such discipline of the body, it is hard to see how a glutton, or one given to lust, could truly change his habits, dispositions, and thereby reform his character.

Dualists may reply that even with sins such as lust and gluttony, it is possible to undergo the necessary moral and spiritual transformation through a process of reflectively assessing one's beliefs and desires. Perhaps the lustful person needs to be made more aware of how his lust disrespects God, other persons, and even himself, and is deeply incompatible with his core convictions and values. If this inconsistency is brought sufficiently to light, the soul may experience the requisite repentance, or change of mind, that would repair the disorder and weakness in its character. The soul would regret lustful or gluttonous acts and desires deeply enough that its dispositions would be corrected, and its structure would be modified in such a way that core convictions and values would hold sway over all beliefs and desires.

We have been examining both physicalist and dualist views of the human person and personal identity, and I have argued that both sorts of position can make sense of what subjects of purgatory are supposed to undergo and experience. While each position faces potential pitfalls or problems, there are no decisive objections to any of them with respect to their compatibility with the doctrine of purgatory.

TIME, CHARACTER, AND IDENTITY

Now I want to turn to consider another argument involving personal identity and purgatory from a very different direction. Until now, the basic issue has been whether the various accounts of personal identity are sufficient to make sense of the doctrine of purgatory. Now we want to examine an argument that says we need purgatory to make sense of personal identity between death and heaven. So here the claim is that the doctrine of purgatory actually provides essential resources to resolve an issue pertaining to personal identity in Christian eschatology.

I will begin with a version of the argument developed by David Brown several years ago as one of a series of three related arguments he offered for a defense of a broadly traditional account of purgatory. The first he called the "temporal" argument and the third the "self-acceptance" argument. The essence of the first argument is that there is no way to make conceivable the abrupt transition of a morally imperfect being into a morally perfect one. Since all or most persons who die are morally imperfect, purgatory is needed as an intermediate state in which this transition can occur in a fashion that fits our condition as essentially temporal beings. The self-acceptance argument turns on the claim that God desires our free cooperation in his relationship with us, so he will respect that reality and work with us in such a way that we freely endorse each aspect and step of our moral and spiritual transformation.

Nestled between these two arguments is the identity argument, which starts with the assumption that we can know and identify ourselves "only through continuity with our past." The key premise is the second one, which is as follows: "Therefore, the more dramatic the contrast in character between a person A at time x and person B at a subsequent time y, the more likely is the latter individual B to doubt whether he could in fact be the same person as person A at time x."[53] In order to save the coherence of heaven, Brown argues that we must postulate an intermediate stage in which persons can be morally transformed in such a way that will allow them to preserve sufficient continuity with their past. Only then will they be able to recognize themselves and be certain of their personal identity through the changes that take place in their character.

This argument, it should be noted, is epistemic in nature. That is, the issue is not stated in terms of what constitutes personal identity as a matter of ontology or essence. Rather, the issue concerns the grounds one rationally has for recognizing or believing oneself to be the same person at two different times.

Brown defends the central point of his argument by appeal to a thought experiment. He asks us to imagine someone waking up in your bed who looks like you and has your present "memories" but is different from you in the very significant sense that he is morally perfect. Brown thinks that this person would not be inclined to see himself as you, but rather, as a different person who has somehow mysteriously been substituted in your body. He would think this because he would have no idea how he became such a radically different person. For example, he may remember strong desires he had only yesterday that have simply and unaccountably disappeared. He may likewise remember finding a certain person very irritating, but now he can be in the presence of that person with no irritation whatever. A person who died far from perfect, but found himself in heaven with a perfect character, would have the same sort of reason to doubt he was the same person.

Brown considers the objection that the connection between person A and person B could be secured in some other way than through gradual character development. In particular, perhaps God could close the character gap by providing an explanation in terms of his own activity. That is, God could simply decree that all this person's character defects were instantly rectified and healed, and could inform the person of that fact. While Brown does not doubt that God has the power to perform such an action and to make such an announcement, he still does not find this account of character development sufficient to maintain personal identity. He thinks it would be hard to see how one could personally identify with such an explanation for why much of what one did not even regard as wrong is now viewed as reprehensible. "If it is to be part of one's identity, it surely has to be in some sense a personal discovery, and that takes time."[54]

Brown's intuition about the essential role of time in character formation as a component of personal identity is an intuition shared by a number of philosophers and theologians. Another philosopher who has articulated a conception of personal identity that takes temporal considerations as essential is Charles Taylor. He develops this account in describing what he believes to be an essential link between one's identity and one's orientation in what he calls "moral space." To know who you are, you must gain orientation in moral space in such a way that you know what is good and bad, what is important to you, what is trivial, and so on.[55] The process of gaining this orientation is like a journey. It requires knowing not only our direction, and where we are headed, but also knowing how we have gotten to where we are, and knowing what we have become. Orientation in moral space is like orientation in physical space in all these respects. We can only know where we are by recognizing relevant landmarks, and knowing the way we have traveled to arrive at our current location. Taylor gives the example of a person who walked out of a drugstore in Montreal and turned the corner to see the Taj Mahal staring him in the face. In such a scenario he would be more likely to think the movie industry was on location shooting a film than to think he had instantaneously appeared in India. "Part of my sense of its genuineness will turn on how I got there."[56]

Likewise, to have a sense that one's character is genuine, one will have to know how he "got there." As beings whose characters are growing and becoming, we can no more arrive at our destination in an instant than a person can walk out of the drugstore in Montreal and turn the corner to arrive at the real Taj Mahal.

> It is not only that I need time and many incidents to sort out what is relatively fixed and stable in my character, temperament, and desires from what is variable and changing, though that is true. It is also that as a being who grows and becomes I can only know myself through the history of my maturations and regressions, overcomings and defeats. My self-understanding necessarily has temporal depth and incorporates narrative.[57]

Again, as with Brown, Taylor is concerned primarily with epistemological issues, particularly our self-knowledge and self-understanding, an understanding that requires a certain sort of temporal narrative in order to be genuine.

For one more example of this line of thought, let us turn back to Ratzinger. Recall that he rejects the idea that people are immediately resurrected and enter eternity when they die, and argues instead that biblical realism and theological coherence require us to take the flow of time seriously with respect to cosmic history. In view of this, it is not at all surprising that he insists that "time belongs to man precisely as man."[58] He goes on to make clear that this is not true simply by virtue of the fact that we are embodied and therefore share in time as measured by the velocity of bodies in motion. We are temporal beings also as spiritual beings, and indeed, in an even deeper sense.

Man is temporal as a traveler along the way of knowing and loving, of decaying and maturing. His specific temporality also derives from his relationality—from the fact that he becomes himself only in being with others and being toward others. Entering upon love, or indeed refusing love, binds one to another person and so to the temporality of that person, his "before" and "after." The fabric of shared humanity is the fabric of shared temporality.[59]

Notice particularly the emphasis on the connection between relationality and temporality. We are not mere isolated units who can achieve our full identity flying solo. Rather, it is only in our relationships with others, particularly relationships of giving or refusing love, that our identity is fully forged. And this includes not only our relationships with our fellow human beings, but most significantly with the ultimate Lover and Source of Love, God himself, who demonstrated his love most fully by entering the world of human relationships in the incarnation.

This shared temporality does not end at death, according to Ratzinger. Although in one sense we step beyond history when we die, we do not lose our relationship to history, precisely because human relationality is essential to human nature. So we remain in relationship to other persons, including persons who remain in the flow of history in this world.

Now it is very significant for our purposes that Ratzinger explicitly applies this insight to explicate the doctrine of purgatory, as well as heaven in the intermediate state. He broaches purgatory when he raises the question of whether anyone can reach his fulfillment so long as people on earth continue to suffer because of him, and his guilt still brings pain to others. This guilt persists as part of who we are as persons in relationship with others who share together in the fabric of temporality. The essence of purgatory, then, is unresolved guilt as it continues to be felt in suffering we have caused to other persons. "Purgatory means, then, suffering to the end what one has left behind on earth—in the certainty of being definitively accepted, yet having to bear the infinite burden of the withdrawn presence of the Beloved."[60] Notice, this is not guilt simply in the legal sense that requires forgiveness. Rather, it is the natural suffering that attends broken and damaged relationships.

This suggestive proposal raises the prospect that purgatory could last a substantial amount of time. The suffering one causes may pass down to more than one generation, and if one has caused significant suffering to a number of people, the ripple effects could be felt for many years to come. If Ratzinger means that one must literally "suffer to the end what one has left behind on earth," the prospect of prolonged suffering looms large. As we shall see from his comments below on the nature of time in purgatory, it is doubtful that he means this in a straightforwardly literal sense.

Now, it is noteworthy that later in Ratzinger's book he has a section explicitly devoted to purgatory, and that the comments just above are not from that section. Moreover, on the face of it, there is a tension between these comments and his more developed statement of the doctrine of purgatory. In the latter, he aims to state the "authentic heart" of the doctrine that is of permanent significance. He takes as his starting point the Pauline text from I Corinthians 3 that describes those who build with wood, hay, or stubble, and are saved "as through fire," one of the central texts traditionally cited in favor of the doctrine of purgatory. Following J. Gnilka, he gives this text a distinctively Christological twist by interpreting the fire as an eschatological encounter with Christ that will transform us and conform us to his own glorified body. The Christianizing of the Jewish notion of a purging fire leads us to understand that fire as "the transforming power of the Lord himself, whose burning flame cuts free our closed-off heart, melting it, and pouring it into a new mold to make it fit for the living organism of his body."[61]

Ratzinger's views here have received some ironic criticism from N. T. Wright, who suggests that the pope has downsized, if not vaporized, the doctrine of purgatory with his recent proposals. He remarks that on this view, purgatory is not a "long, drawn out process" but something that happens "in the moment of final judgment itself." He claims, moreover, that Ratzinger has "detached the doctrine of purgatory from the concept of an intermediate state" and has offered us something that is "quite a radical climb-down from Aquinas, Dante, Newman, and all that went in between."[62]

Now these are understandable criticisms, but I think they are misleading and wide of the mark. Four points are relevant here. First, it is clear from his book as a whole that he takes the intermediate state very seriously, a state of disembodied existence as we await the final resurrection. Moreover, it is clear from the preceding discussion that the intermediate stage is a time of purgatory, though there is no reason to assume that it lasts throughout this period for all persons. Second, while he repudiates the notion of purgatory as a "supra-worldly concentration camp where man is forced to undergo punishment in a more or less arbitrary fashion," he continues to affirm that it is "the inwardly necessary process of transformation" we need in order to be capable of unity with God, as well as the communion of saints.[63] The emphasis on the "process of transformation" that he goes on to elaborate shows that he does not understand the "moment" of transformation as a simple instant of time. Full transformation requires the full assent of faith, which may be buried under many layers of wood, hay, and straw, and it may require time to burn these away so that faith shines forth with complete purity. Third, this point is further clarified when he insists that the "transforming moment" cannot be quantified in earthly time measurements. While it is a transition, to be sure, "trying to qualify it as of 'short' or 'long' duration on the basis of temporal measurements derived from physics would be naïve and unproductive."[64]

Fourth, and finally, Ratzinger explores the traditional idea of prayer for the dead in light of his account of purgatory. The point of such prayers, he suggests, is not to remit punishment, as it has often been construed. Rather, he proposes that we think about how our prayers might enter into the highly personal encounter with Christ that transforms, an encounter that makes clear that the heart of the matter is about "being," not remission of punishment. In developing this suggestion, he returns to the point he made earlier, that we do not enjoy our full human existence as isolated monads. "We are not just ourselves; or, more correctly, we are ourselves only as being in others, with others and through others."[65] It was his emphasis on human interdependence, recall, which provided the grist for his argument that we often leave unfinished business in this world when we die. Our guilt from pain that we have caused remains, and requires time to be resolved before we can embrace the fullness of joy. This, he suggested, is the essential meaning of purgatory.

BUT CAN'T WE JUST DISPENSE WITH THE CLOCK?

Now then, let us sum up and assess the argument of the preceding section. We have been examining the argument that purgatory is needed to maintain personal identity between this life and heaven. Without an intermediate stage that allows for gradual moral and spiritual growth that keeps pace with our ability to recognize and own truth in a correspondingly progressive fashion, there would not be sufficient continuity between our past and present to maintain our personal identity. The argument is primarily cast as an epistemic one to the effect that we would not recognize ourselves if we underwent such radical and abrupt moral transformation. In a slightly different but related vein, the argument turns on intuitions about what counts as "genuine" moral transformation and character development, and the role of time and narrative in such change. Moreover, it also includes elements of a relational notion of identity, insofar as it highlights our relationships with other people in the shared fabric of time as essential to who we are.

This argument is primarily advanced, notice, by thought experiments that aim to elicit the relevant intuitions about what sort of change is too abrupt, what sort of change could be owned as authentic, and so on. Such thought experiments, of course, are seldom if ever conclusive, and sometimes are only suggestive at best. Critics of the argument may not share the intuition and may find little problem with the idea that personal identity can be sustained through rather dramatic and abrupt moral and spiritual changes. Consider in this light Brown's argument against the suggestion that God could close the character gap by explaining the transformation in terms of his own action. Brown is dubious of this suggestion, and thinks that any genuine character development that one could own as part of his identity must be a matter of personal discovery over a suitable period of time.

Now let's alter the scenario slightly, and suppose that a believer, who is on his deathbed, but is far from perfect, sincerely asks God to perfect his character. (We might even assume he is a deathbed convert.) He dies an hour later, and wakes up in heaven with a flawless character, filled with perfect love for God and his fellow human beings. All his various sins and moral and spiritual defects that he remembers as he lay dying have completely vanished, and have been replaced by corresponding virtues and spiritual graces. He remembers his deathbed prayer, and believes with gratitude that it has been answered, and thinks this explains the remarkable change in character he has undergone. In this case, the radical transformation due to God's action may seem not only to be a perfectly intelligible explanation for closing the character gap, but also the sort of change that retains sufficient continuity to preserve identity. For the dramatic change can be understood as the fulfillment of the man's honest wishes and desires as expressed in his prayer, and the outworking of all that is implicit in that prayer.

This line of argument certainly has some plausibility, but is also open to criticism. Perhaps the real issue raised by this scenario is whether such a broad prayer for perfection can be answered while maintaining personal continuity and identity, and effecting what would be recognized as genuine transformation. To see what is at stake here, consider how deeply rooted sinful habits and dispositions may be rooted in a person's character, and how little aware he may be of its various dimensions. This point is emphasized in the article on purgatory in the *New Catholic Encyclopedia*. The author points to this reality in explaining why recent theological speculation on the doctrine tends to see purgatory as a gradual process, instead of instantaneous perfection, as has sometimes been held. "There must be quite literally a process, a purification that lays bare, so to speak, the successive layers of the personality and exposes to view the faults buried in the depths of the nature."[66]

So the question is whether a "blanket prayer" for perfection can cover all these layers of which the person may not even be aware. Can a person's prayers meaningfully address layers of sin and deeply buried faults of which he may not have even the faintest suspicion? Or is it the case that moral and spiritual growth and character development must work through these layers successively so that one acknowledges each of them and embraces the truth and repentance necessary as ever deeper insight is gained? Is such growth and character development an incremental, progressive matter that cannot be short-circuited or achieved by short cuts that slice through the various layers all at once?

The difficulty in cutting through all the layers at once is further highlighted if we take into account the relational dimensions of our identity, noted by both Taylor and Ratzinger. What needs to be rectified and healed here are not merely our own personal sins and character defects, but also our relationships with various people, some of whom we have hurt, and others who have hurt us. What is needed for such deep and thorough healing is the acknowledgement of wrong and the willingness to extend and accept forgiveness. Again, the question is whether this sort of healing can be accomplished in a way that bypasses the free cooperation of the persons involved. They must own the hurt and the broken and damaged relationships, they must acknowledge the role their actions have played in causing the hurt and damage. And they must be prepared to change their attitudes and actions to restore those broken relationships in light of the truth they have come to see.

Again, seeing and owning this truth arguably takes time, and cannot happen by fiat, not even by divine fiat. Let us recall Scrooge again, and his progressive moral enlightenment as he started at the beginning of his life and reflected on his own broken relationships and the various failures of love, both in giving and receiving, that were involved in his personal history. When he is first informed by Marley that he will be visited by three ghosts, Scrooge is less than enthusiastic about the prospect, and when told that it is his only hope to escape Marley's fate, he proposes an abbreviated version of the cure. " 'Couldn't I take 'em all at once, and have it over, Jacob?' hinted Scrooge."[67] The rest of the story can be taken as a narrative argument that moral and character transformation cannot happen all at once, but happens incrementally and progressively as truth is discerned, acknowledged, and elicits the appropriate change in attitude, values, and behavior. The same point, of course, is portrayed in Dante's depiction of purgatory as a mountain with seven cornices, on each of which a separate vice is purged away, allowing him to gain strength and speed the farther he climbs.[68]

Again, narrative arguments, like thought experiments, are suggestive but hardly definitive. At the end of the day, the appeal of the argument proposed by Brown may come down to one's intuitions about the nature of moral transformation, and what is required for it to be genuine—in particular, to what degree such transformation requires our free cooperation. Before concluding this chapter, I want to consider another argument that bears on this issue. This argument is developed at some length by Justin Bernard as a reason to favor the doctrine of purgatory over the characteristic Protestant view that God unilaterally transforms us at death.

Bernard's argument is that the Protestant view poses a version of the evidential problem of evil. Here is the essence of the argument. If God can unilaterally perfect persons at death who have saving faith, then he could do so now. So if God does not perfect those persons now, then he is responsible for whatever evil they commit, for such evil would be properly eliminable, since he could eliminate it without sacrificing any greater goods, or causing greater evils. So there is good reason to think that God cannot unilaterally perfect persons now, and if so, then he cannot do so at death either.[69]

Now as Bernard points out, the obvious strategy for responding to this argument is to give some explanation for why God cannot perfect persons now that would not hold for persons at death. I will not take the space to review all the suggestions he considers, but one is particularly relevant to our concerns. It might be objected that the sanctification process is an intrinsic good that should be completed under its own internal momentum, and if God were to unilaterally perfect persons now, it would sacrifice the greater good of the sanctification process. But if the objector takes this line, notice what it seems to imply: if the sanctification process is a sufficient good that it should not be short-circuited in this life, then the same seems to hold true after death.

The upshot is that this argument gives us another reason to think that God takes our freedom most seriously, as well as our cooperation in the sanctification process. He chooses to let our free choices play out rather than determine our choices, or unilaterally perfect us, even at the cost of considerable evil. While we may not think our freedom is worth this price, the stark and persistent reality of evil is significant evidence that God thinks otherwise. The evil that remains in the lives of believers, and the often inconsistent moral progress they make, if not the baffling lack of progress they show, is striking evidence that God not only takes our freedom seriously, but also that it takes time to move through the layers of sin and illusion that must be removed before we can achieve the fullness of faith to claim the perfection he desires for us. Time is the space in which free choices are made, and the more we are inclined to think our free choices are necessary for genuine moral transformation and character development, the more we will be inclined to think that time is essential for these choices.

To conclude, let us draw this discussion to a close by connecting these thoughts with Ratzinger's defense of the soul's persistence in the intermediate state. Recall his insistence that the separated soul maintains continuity of personal identity between death and resurrection. In a highly suggestive line, he writes: "Soul is nothing other than man's capacity for relatedness to truth, with love eternal."[70] This line underscores that personal identity is more than a matter of substance, or ontology, or memory, or consciousness. It is also a matter of relationship, not only to other finite persons, but also to the ultimate relationship, the perfect love that exists in the Trinity between Father, Son, and Holy Spirit. Coming to embrace this love, is, among other things, coming to own and internalize the truth, not only about ourselves, but more importantly about God. Owning the truth, like learning to love, is an essentially temporal process for finite beings, and this is why it seems likely that our identity is forged in time, both here and in the hereafter.

5

❦

Purgatory and Theories
of a "Second Chance"

Jesus comes as the light of absolute love.... The question, to which no final answer is given or can be given, is this: Will he who refuses it now refuse it to the last?
———Hans Urs von Balthasar

" Purgatory is hope." These three words encapsulate what Jacques Le Goff takes to be "Purgatory's essential function in the early thirteenth century."[1] He offers this assessment after relating a few anecdotes involving purgatory that were part of larger collection entitled *Dialogue on Miracles,* compiled between 1219 and 1223 by a Cistercian monk, the purpose of which were to inspire and edify the reader.

The story Le Goff had recapitulated right before his summary comment concerned a nun who had been seduced by a priest and later died in childbirth after entrusting herself to the care of her family, including her parents and two married sisters. Her family, despairing of any hope of her salvation, did not bother with performing any suffrages on her behalf. The soul of the dead woman, however, seeks out a Cistercian abbot, and shamefacedly requests "at least a psalter and a few masses," but without identifying herself fully or disclosing the nature of her sin. The abbot is surprised by this apparition since he does not know the woman, but eventually he encounters an aunt of the dead woman, who is a Cistercian nun, and the aunt fills in the details of the story for him. The family is then informed of the news, and their desperation and despair give way to hope. All of the monks and nuns of the province are mobilized in behalf of seeking her salvation, and it turns out that the rekindled hope was not disappointed as the fallen nun presumed eternally lost was quickly saved.

Another story from the same collection is equally fascinating as well as revealing. The hero of this one is a usurer who had died but was denied burial in hallowed ground. Usurers were typically considered hopelessly lost because their work involved handling money in a way that was held in contempt. Despite this, however, his devout wife appealed to the pope on the basis of the Pauline doctrine that husband and wife are one, and that an unbelieving husband might be saved by his believing wife. The pope yielded to her pleas, and allowed the man to be buried in the cemetery, after which she prayed for seven years for his salvation, and also performed other suffrages such as the giving of alms, fasting, and vigils. At the end of those seven years, he appeared to her and said: "May God reward you, for, thanks to your trials, I have been plucked from the depths of Hell and the most terrible punishments. If you render me further services of this kind for seven years, I shall be completely delivered."[2] She did so, and at the end of those seven additional years, he appeared to her to announce that he had been set completely free. The question naturally was raised how he could be set free from hell, a place from which it is not possible to be redeemed. The explanation given was that "the depths of hell" actually means the harshness of purgatory. It was disclosed, moreover, that the usurer had repented in the end, and that if he had not done so, he could not have been saved. So again, the notion that "purgatory is hope" is affirmed, while maintaining the orthodox doctrine that there is no escape from hell. His last-minute contrition allowed him to enter purgatory rather than the hopeless fate of eternal hell.

These vignettes from the thirteenth century resonate very much with the role that purgatory played centuries earlier when it arguably first took the form of an orthodox doctrine of the Church. Recall from chapter 1 that Isabel Moreira makes the case that the Venerable Bede is the figure who first situated purgatory theologically as a matter of orthodox belief. For our present concerns, it is even more noteworthy that his account of purgatory aims to sustain the orthodox conviction that those consigned to hell are eternally lost, while also casting a wider net for who can hope to be saved. Bede held out hope even to serious sinners, so long as they repented at the end, even on their deathbed. Indeed, Moreira suggests that Bede's theology of purgatory represents something of a combination of Augustine's orthodoxy together with Origen's more generous view of final salvation that can be described as "an orthodox variation on universalism."[3]

Moreover, the conviction that "purgatory is hope" is not confined to medieval times, whether the very early or later part of that era. Rather, purgatory has been defended in other times, including modern, as a theologically grounded basis for extending hope where otherwise it may appear to be lost.[4] Indeed, it is arguable that the doctrine at its best has always been motivated by a desire to do full justice to the mercy and grace of God, and the full range of hope flowing from this grace that otherwise hopeless sinners may cling to as their only hedge against despair.

In the pages that follow, I want to continue to pursue this matter in a somewhat different direction by examining whether, and in what sense, purgatory may be thought of as a second chance for salvation. My argument to this point has worked with an account of purgatory that is broadly traditional in its main contours. So understood, I have contended that purgatory is not ruled out by scripture,[5] but more positively, is implied by things clearly taught in scripture, along with what seems obvious from empirical observation, namely, that many people die far short of perfect holiness. The sanctification account of the doctrine I have defended is arguably not only the dominant view of Roman Catholics today, but also the real heart of the doctrine in much of the tradition.

In this chapter, however, I shall argue for a significant modification of the traditional view of purgatory, namely, that it should allow for postmortem conversion. I shall suggest, moreover, that this modification is not only true to the original impetus for the doctrine, but also a consistent outworking of this impetus that resolves certain tensions that appear in classic accounts of purgatory. I will illustrate this by looking in some detail at these tensions as they emerge in Dante's fascinating treatment of some key characters in his narrative.

Next, I will turn to sketch the views of several proponents of the idea that purgatory provides postmortem opportunity to repent and be saved, which will show that the modification I defend is hardly without precedent, in Roman Catholic theology as well as Protestant. I will then assess these theories and draw on this material to articulate my view of how the traditional doctrine of purgatory should be modified to allow for postmortem conversion.

IS PURGATORY A SECOND CHANCE?

In the early pages of his book, Le Goff provides a summary account of the basic logic of the doctrine, as follows: "Belief in Purgatory implies, in the first instance, belief in immortality and resurrection, since something new may happen to a human being between his death and resurrection. It offers a second chance to attain eternal life."[6] The notion that "something new may happen" between a person's death and resurrection is connected to the idea that there are two judgments: one at the time of death and a second final judgment at the end of time. In the time between death and resurrection, a person may be subject to a judgment in the sense of undergoing certain penalties and possibly also having his sentence shortened by various factors. What I want to emphasize about this quote, however, is that Le Goff characterizes the doctrine of purgatory as a "second chance" to attain eternal life, the opportunity for which is closely related to the epigraphic observation that "purgatory is hope." The notion that significant things happen between death and resurrection, before the final judgment, provides warrant for hoping that persons may be saved in the end, persons who may otherwise appear hopelessly to be lost.

Now let us turn to another account of purgatory that appears at first glance to be at odds with this claim. In the Introduction to her translation of Dante's *Purgatory*, Dorothy L. Sayers spells out six claims to capture the essence of the doctrine "as generally held by Catholics" in order to "clear up a number of widely current perplexities and misunderstandings about Purgatory."[7] For our purposes, the second and third of these are particularly interesting:

(2) Purgatory is *not* a "second chance" for those who die obstinately unrepentant. The soul's own choice between God and self, made in the moment of death, is final. (This moment of final choice is known as the 'Particular Judgement'.)

(3) Repentance in the moment of death (*in articulo mortis*) is *always* accepted. If the movement of the soul is, however feebly, away from self and towards God, its act of confession and contrition is complete, whether or not it is accompanied by formal confession and absolution; and the soul enters Purgatory.[8]

Now her denial that purgatory represents a second chance is especially interesting, particularly given her concern to clear up misconceptions about the doctrine. Certainly, as Sayers's emphatic denial attests, it is often popularly conceived as providing a second chance, and even someone as well informed as Le Goff employs that language to describe the essential logic of the doctrine. It is easy to see, however, that Sayers's rejection of the notion that purgatory represents a second chance is not at odds with Le Goff's affirmation that it does, given how he uses the term.

In particular, Sayers is concerned to deny that purgatory provides a postmortem opportunity to repent for those who have spurned God's grace in this life. Sayers balances this denial, however, with a warm insistence that God accepts any repentance in this life, however late, and however feeble it may be. So the stern temporal limit on the chance to repent as defined by the moment of death is counterbalanced by the generous claim that God is always willing to accept any motion toward repentance before that fatal line is crossed. To be sure, Sayers goes on to highlight the point that deathbed penitents have not beat the system, and their entrance to purgatory is hardly to be viewed as an unqualified pleasure. Rather, the soul is now required "with prolonged labour and pains" to achieve "the entire process of satisfaction and purification, the greater part of which should have been carried out on earth."[9] Still, however strenuous or unpleasant this process might be, it is immeasurably to be preferred to the alternative of eternal damnation.

So while purgatory might not represent a second chance in the sense of a postmortem opportunity to repent, it does offer a second chance for repentance to go deep, and to transform our character thoroughly, if that did not happen in this life. And indeed, this seems to be the sense in which Le Goff is using the term when he affirms that "purgatory offers a second chance to attain eternal life."[10] This is indicated by the example of the usurer cited above, whose admission to purgatory was only secured because he repented at the end. Having a second chance to attain eternal life is more than merely a chance for initial repentance and "feebly" turning to God. "Eternal life" is apparently understood to mean a fuller relationship with God, a relationship that is only possible if one has been more deeply transformed so that he truly loves God with his whole being and is accordingly united to him with bonds of genuine affection. Purgatory is the second chance to attain this sort of relationship for those persons who were tardy in repentance, or complacent, or who pursued this relationship only halfheartedly in this life.

WHEN SECONDS MATTER

But even if purgatory is understood as a "second chance" only in this more limited sense, there are a number of interesting issues here. For a start, why is it thought so objectionable that there should be a chance to repent after death, especially if God welcomes any repentance before death, no matter how minimal or how much postponed? Why is death viewed as such an absolute limit on the opportunity to repent? Many people apparently have multiple opportunities to repent in this life, many of which they may spurn, before they finally repent. So why should there be no further chance to repent after death, if numerous opportunities are extended before death, and indeed right up to the very point of death itself?

Look again at Sayers's two paragraphs above. She says there is no second chance for those who die "obstinately unrepentant." But here the obvious question is whether there might be persons who die without even "feebly" repenting, but who are not "obstinately unrepentant." Consider, for instance, a young person who dies suddenly in a car accident, or perhaps in a random drive-by shooting. Suppose this person has not yet repented, but like most young persons, is far from set in her character or spiritual commitments. Is it not possible that even though she failed to repent in even a minimal sense, that she could not be characterized as hardened in her sin? Suppose, moreover, that she has had relatively few opportunities to repent, especially compared to a person who has had many such chances and only repents at the very end of his life with his final breath. We might even push this question further and ask whether she might have repented later in life had she not died in the car accident.

Let's explore this suggestion further by considering a more detailed story. Suppose the car accident involved two college-aged young women, identical twins named Rapunzel and Gretel, both of whom had starting attending church occasionally and had heard the gospel several times, and felt some attraction to it, but had thus far resisted accepting it. Furthermore, they were not only twin sisters, but close friends who had very similar background experiences, interests, and convictions. Suppose, moreover, that while Rapunzel dies in the crash, Gretal lives and experiences the accident and death of her sister as a "wake-up call" that moves her to reflect more seriously on ultimate issues. She begins to attend church more regularly and to consider the gospel even more seriously than she had before. A few weeks after the accident, Gretel attends an Easter service and senses God's grace powerfully inclining her to accept the gospel, and she does so. She goes on to become a devout believer for the rest of her life.

Now it is only natural to wonder whether Rapunzel would have followed a similar course had she survived the accident, particularly since she was similar in so many ways to her surviving twin. Indeed, we might even think this is fairly probable, without engaging in undue presumption. Moreover, given God's perfect knowledge of her, he might know the exact probability that she would also have repented had she lived and perhaps even know it to be highly probable.

Indeed, on certain theories of divine knowledge, God could know for certain whether Rapunzel would have repented had she lived. I have in mind, of course, the Molinist view that God has "middle knowledge," which is, roughly, his knowledge of what all possible free creatures would do in all possible circumstances, situations, or states of affairs in which they remain free. Particularly interesting for our purposes is his knowledge of what free creatures would freely do in various circumstances. These propositions, which are commonly called counterfactuals of creaturely freedom, have the general form: if person P were in situation S at time t, he would freely do action A. To be more precise, it is important to specify that the circumstances or situations referenced in such counterfactuals are complete ones. This means that God knows in exhaustive detail all the factors affecting the person in the situation, factors which influence but do not determine his choice, leaving it truly free. These factors include the choices and activity of God himself.[11]

So let us make the counterfactual complete by thinking of a possible world with the same history of the actual world almost up to the moment of the accident, but in this world, Rapunzel swerves two seconds earlier, and although she still has an accident, both she and Gretel survive. Moreover, the subsequent history of the world is much the same as the actual world, leading up to the Easter service in which Gretel accepted the gospel. In this world, Rapunzel also becomes more serious about ultimate issues, and attends the same service, hears same sermon, and so on. Moreover, God moves on her heart as well as that of Gretel, inclining them both to accept the gospel. Let us further assume that God knows that if Rapunzel were in these circumstances, she too would have heartily accepted the gospel and become a devout believer.

Now then, if God knows it is highly probable that Rapunzel would have repented if she had lived, or better yet, if he knows for certain that she would have in a feasible world very similar to the actual world, then I want to suggest that this has significant implications for the actual world. In particular, it is plausible that she could be moved to repentance and faith, since it seems apparent that she has not rejected God decisively. To be more specific, it is reasonable to suppose that in the afterlife, if she were presented with the gospel in ways similar to the ways she would have heard it had she lived, that she would accept it.

Now it might be doubted that the gospel could be presented to Rapunzel after death in any way similar to how it would have been presented had she lived. Life after death in the intermediate state before resurrection, after all, is presumably very different from life on this earth, particularly if that life is disembodied. We can grant this, however, and still contend that it is plausible to think that the gospel could be presented to her in a way that she could freely accept. The key point is that if she has not rejected the gospel decisively, then it is reasonable to think it could be presented to her in a fashion that she would find compelling, just as she would have had she not died in the car accident. If she is still a rational agent, capable of discerning truth and responding to it, this seems like a plausible enough assumption.

So let us for the moment assume God could find a way to present the gospel to Rapunzel after she has died. The deeper question, perhaps, is whether God *would* do this even if he could. To raise this question is to go to the heart of our conception of the character of God. It is to ask whether God truly loves all persons, and is truly willing to save them. How far is he willing to go to save persons? There are, of course, some Christian traditions that hold that God has unconditionally elected to save some persons, and has chosen to pass over the rest, leaving them to eternal damnation. But even if this view is rejected, the question remains of how God distributes his grace to the lost. Does he give everyone some chance, but not an equal chance? Do some have much better opportunity to achieve eternal salvation than others, who may have few chances, and not very good ones at that? Or does God love all persons fully and sincerely in such a way that he makes his grace equally available to all?

Before pursuing these questions more extensively, let us pause for a moment to specify what we mean when we say that God makes his grace equally available to all. Elsewhere, I have explored this matter in some detail by proposing that God gives to all persons what I called "optimal grace."[12] Now this does not mean that there is some quantity or measure of grace that God simply pours out or bestows on all persons in a mechanical, cookie-cutter fashion. Rather, such grace is deeply personal and individual in the sense that God knows how best to elicit a positive response from each person, without destroying or overriding their freedom. What would be highly effective in converting one person might make another more resistant. The notion of optimal grace assumes that God knows and loves each of us as individuals as well as members of the larger human race, and values each of us as unique persons.

Optimal grace, moreover, implies that God is not content with merely giving everyone some chance for salvation, but desires to give everyone every opportunity as made possible by the death and resurrection of Christ, and all that flows from those events. God truly desires to save all persons, and does not extend the offer of grace merely in a cursory fashion so that everyone has some minimal chance, in order to establish God's justice in damning them if they reject it.[13] The sort of genuine chance I have in mind requires that the offer of grace is communicated clearly and lovingly, so that both the substance and the spirit of the gospel are faithfully represented. Patience and care must be taken to make sure that honest misunderstanding is cleared up so that the response that is elicited is actually to the gospel, and not a distortion or caricature of the gospel.

Now, given that God bestows abundant grace on all persons in this fashion, damnation only results from the persistent choice to reject optimal grace. Damnation is the decisive choice of evil by a person who has been given every opportunity to repent and has rejected optimal grace.[14]

DANTE, DAMNATION, AND DIVINE LOVE

Now let us turn to explore more fully the question of how God distributes his grace by returning to Sayers, who offers a defense of Dante's accounts of hell and purgatory against the common criticism that they are cruel. Recall from chapter 3 her point that the fundamental difference between hell and purgatory, where the punishments often seem superficially similar, lies in the attitudes of those who receive those punishments. Whereas those in hell refuse to accept the judgment that their sins deserve, those in purgatory do so, with the result that those punishments are experienced as remedial and transforming. Underlying this observation is a more fundamental point about the freedom of will that Dante repeatedly emphasizes at various points in the *Comedy*. As Sayers sees it, this freedom is such that each of the figures in the *Comedy* are getting exactly what they want. Those in hell want to have their own way, and they are getting it, painful as it is. Those in purgatory want the will of God, and they embrace the punishment and pain they experience as means to help them along to heaven. She sums up what she takes to be Dante's picture as follows: "When every allowance is made (and Dante makes generous allowance), when mercy and pity and grace have done all they can, the consequences of sin are the sinner's—to be borne, at his own choice, in a spirit of sullen rebellion or ready acquiescence."[15]

I particularly want to highlight from this quote the strong claim that Sayers makes about Dante's view of how far God is willing to go in offering grace to save sinners, how extensive and exhaustive is his effort to save them. Sayers claims that "every allowance is made" and "mercy and pity and grace have done all they can" to redeem lost sinners. Only their free choices prevent them from being saved, in particular, the consequences of their own sins and their "sullen rebellion" that keeps them separated from God. Put in terms of the definition I introduced above, Sayers seems to be suggesting that God does indeed provide optimal grace, and it is only the decisive choice of evil that keeps anyone in hell.

Now, is it in fact Dante's view that all those who are excluded from heaven are excluded by their own choice, and their own obstinate refusal to repent? And is it the case that divine mercy has made every allowance and done all that could be done to reach all persons with the grace that God has provided through the incarnation, death, and resurrection of Christ? It is my contention that Dante does not in fact display such a generous view of divine grace, nor does he persuasively show that all those in hell are getting what they truly want.

The tensions in Dante on this matter begin to appear in the very first Canto of his *Purgatory* when Dante and Virgil emerge from hell and find themselves on the island of purgatory. There they encounter Cato, the guardian of the mountain that the inhabitants of purgatory must climb to enter heaven. Cato's presence is significant because he was regarded both by the Romans as well as the Middle Ages as the ideal exemplar of the natural moral virtues. As Sayers comments in her notes on this Canto, there are some puzzling features of Dante's treatment of Cato. Although he has been removed from Limbo and set on Christian territory, as it were, there is no suggestion that he himself will ever climb the mountain that he guards. There seems to be no hope for him that he will receive the grace to purify and perfect the natural virtues that he embodied, and finally enter the joy of heaven.[16]

It is important to underline here the broadly Catholic view that grace perfects nature. That is to say, there is continuity between natural virtue and the perfection of character in the redeemed, just as there is continuity between natural reason and revealed truth. Natural revelation and virtue are not sufficient to save or to perfect us in themselves, but this does not mean that grace is at odds with nature. Rather, grace purifies and perfects nature, and brings it fully to the ends for which God created and designed it. So it might be thought more than likely that Cato would be a "natural" candidate to receive the grace to ascend the mountain that he guards and to eventually share the joy of other travelers who undertake the climb. This provides us with some of the initial pieces of the puzzle, a puzzle that only grows more difficult to solve as the story unfolds.

The puzzle surfaces again in Canto three, where Virgil lectures Dante on the limits of human reason, and the need for divine revelation.

> "Content you with the *quia*, sons of Eve:
> For had you the power to see the whole truth plain
> No need had been for Mary to conceive;
>   And you have seen such great souls thirst in vain
> As else had stilled that thirst in quietness
> Which now is given them for eternal pain;
>   I speak of Plato, Aristotle—yes,
> And many others." Here he bent his head
> And moved on, silent, with a troubled face.[17]

Quia is knowledge *that* a thing is, and is obtained by arguing a posteriori, from effect to cause, as opposed to knowledge of *why* it is as it is, which is a priori knowledge, obtained by arguing from cause to effect. This distinction of Aristotle's, as adopted by medieval theologians, was employed to show that finite minds in this life cannot know God as he is in himself, but only by his effects. Thus, virtuous pagans, even those as eminent as Plato and Aristotle, are consigned to Limbo, since they had only natural knowledge of God and lacked the knowledge of God given by special revelation.

Limbo, of course, is the most pleasant part of hell, and its pain consists "only" in the longing to know God that will never be satisfied. The poignancy of this eternal thirst as experienced by Plato, Aristotle, and Virgil himself understandably causes the latter to bend his head and move on with a troubled face as he navigates his way up the mountain with Dante. The poignancy of virtuous pagans forever consigned to Limbo is brought into sharper relief later in the Canto when it details cases of last-minute repentance of souls who made it to purgatory. A most notable example is that of Manfred, son of Emperor Frederick II and a notorious sinner who repented only when he had been mortally wounded:

> When I had suffered two strokes, mortal both,
> I sighed my soul out weeping unto Him

Whose sole delight is always to have ruth.
　My sins were horrible in the extreme,
Yet such the infinite mercy's wide embrace,
Its arms go out to all who turn to them.[18]

The depth of the mercy shown to Manfred is further detailed in the following lines, which describe how his body was exhumed at the order of the bishop, and cast out of the kingdom as an unholy object, since he had been excommunicated. The mercy of God, however, overrides decrees of excommunication by ecclesiastical authority:

Their curse cannot so damn a man for ever
That the eternal love may not return
While one green hope puts forth the feeblest sliver.[19]

Notice: all it takes for a notorious sinner, even one who has been excommunicated, to be saved from hell at the last moment of his life, is "one green hope" that "puts forth the feeblest sliver."

The glaring contrast between such a notorious sinner receiving "the eternal love" in the last moment of his life, whereas virtuous pagans such as Plato and Aristotle are consigned to "the eternal pain" of fruitlessly thirsting for God in Limbo, is striking indeed. Now it might be suggested that this contrast serves to highlight the mercy and grace of God, and shows that divine grace runs counter to our evaluations and assessments. Grace is a divinely bestowed favor, it might be argued, and does not in any way depend upon or reward human effort, goodness, or virtue. The fact that a character like Manfred is finally saved, whereas Plato is not, only goes to show that grace exceeds our grasp, just as divine revelation surpasses what human reason can manufacture or construct on its own.

While there is a sound point somewhere in the neighborhood of these claims, they do little to relieve the perplexity that concerns us here. Grace does indeed display the mercy of God in a way that surpasses and unsettles our assessments. The claim that a sinner like Manfred can receive the eternal love is enough to establish this point in vivid fashion. However, the claim that virtuous pagans are consigned to eternal pain does nothing to enhance divine grace, but only increases our perplexity, particularly if there is indeed continuity between the so-called natural virtues and redeeming grace. For such natural virtue is in fact also a gift of God, and not merely a product of human effort. Both "natural" virtue and supernatural grace come ultimately from God and reflect his love and goodness.

So the question remains of why such virtuous pagans must remain in Limbo. Is there some reason that they cannot be given supernatural grace? Or is there some reason to think that they would not receive supernatural grace and revelation even if it were offered to them? This seems unlikely, again, precisely because of the continuity between natural revelation and virtue, and supernatural revelation and grace. If one has responded to the natural in a positive fashion, it seems he would welcome the fuller and deeper truth and virtue of supernatural grace that purifies and perfects the natural. Or has God simply chosen not to make it available to them, so they must settle for the least of hell's pains rather than enjoy the delights that come from full knowledge of God? If the latter claim is made, then it is certainly not the case, as Sayers claims, that divine mercy and pity and grace have done all they can to save all persons.

The poignancy of the notion that virtuous pagans are consigned to Limbo comes into even sharper focus in Canto seven, where Virgil himself comes under the microscope when the troubadour Sordello asks him his identity. "Virgil I am," he answers, and then goes on to say, "and I came short of Heaven for no default, save that I had not faith."[20] Sordello then bows in admiration to clasp his knees, and asks if he is from hell, and if so, what cloister. Virgil explains his mission with respect to Dante and goes on to explain his eternal fate:

> Not what I did, but what I did not do,
> Lost me the sight of that high Sun, the prize
> Thou seekest, whom too late I learned to know.

He continues by describing Limbo as a place where "no shrieks resound, but only sighs," a place inhabited by unbaptized infants as well as virtuous pagans:

> And there dwell I, with those who ne'er put on
> The three celestial virtues, yet, unsinning,
> Knew all the rest and practiced every one.[21]

Virgil's fate, it appears, is solely due to the contingency of when he was born. The only thing keeping him out of heaven is a lack of faith, a lack he could not possibly make good since he was born and died without ever hearing of Christ and the gospel. Now, however, he seems to be fully apprised "of that high Sun, the prize" that is sought by all the inhabitants of purgatory. His problem now is not ignorance, apparently, nor unbelief nor obstinacy. He seems simply to have come to know this truth too late, through no fault of his own. Like other virtuous pagans who "practiced every one" of the virtues they knew, his shortcoming consists in never having "put on the three celestial virtues," a failure he could not have avoided due to lack of opportunity. So now all he can do is walk with face downcast in eternal longing for what he can never know.

The tensions in this scenario are further exposed in Cantos twenty-one and twenty-two in the account of the poet Statius and his encounter with Virgil. As the conversation unfolds, it becomes clear that Virgil was not only a powerful influence on Statius as a poet, but also played a key role in his conversion to Christianity. Sayers remarks that his significance in the imagery of the *Comedy* has been controversial, but in her view, "it seems likely that Dante wished to show the soul as being accompanied and helped on its journey, not only by Old Rome (natural Humanism) but also by the New (Christian) Rome (redeemed Humanism)."[22] In terms discussed above, Statius illustrates the continuity between natural revelation and virtue, and the supernatural which purifies and completes the natural.

In a most interesting passage, Statius offers a rather ironic description of how Virgil provided the initial light that led him to God:

> Thou wast as one who, traveling, bears by night
> A lantern at his back, which cannot leaven
> His darkness, yet he gives his followers light.[23]

The notion that Virgil could provide the light that led Statius to God, but could not himself similarly benefit from that light, is more than a little perplexing. Again, if he understood, embodied, and gave powerful articulation to the very truths that were instrumental in converting Statius, it is reasonable to think it likely that he would also have converted to Christianity if given the opportunity before he died. And of course, the regret that Dante depicts him as expressing—because he learned this truth too late—only confirms this sense. If Dante does intend Statius to image the notion that New Rome represents the ultimate fulfillment of and completion of the truths of Old Rome, then the notion that such an exemplary source of the truths of Old Rome as Virgil should be precluded from any chance to experience that fulfillment is extremely odd.

As fascinating, and in some ways puzzling, as these passages are, the most interesting passage concerning the eternal fate of pagans occurs late in the third part of the *Comedy*, namely, in *Paradise*. There we encounter the remarkable accounts of the Roman emperor Trajan, and Rhipeus, a Trojan hero, who are included along with King David, Hezekiah, Constantine, and William of Sicily II as outstanding examples of justice on earth. Dante is clearly surprised to see these pagans in heaven, and wonders how they got there.

Let us focus especially on Trajan, who is most interesting for our concerns. We first encounter him in *Purgatory*, where he is presented as an example of great humility by means of stone carvings that depict his story. In particular, those carvings picture the time he was setting out for war, and was stopped by a poor distressed widow, who requested justice for the murder of her son. Despite the pressing demands upon him, he responded favorably to her persistence, and granted her request before he departed. The story as recounted by Dante also alludes to the legend that Saint Gregory prayed for Trajan so powerfully that he was brought back from hell, and baptized.

> And there in stone narrated was the glory
> Of the great Roman prince, whose virtues wooed
> Gregory to conquer Heaven with oratory.[24]

Before he ever became pope, Gregory was deeply disturbed by the thought that virtuous pagans should be lost and consigned to hell without ever hearing the name of Christ. Apparently, he was especially bothered by the case of Trajan, whose statue he constantly saw on his walks through Rome, and this led him to pray in Saint Peter's Church that he might still be saved.[25]

What Dante has given us in his treatment of Trajan is as dramatic an example of a "second chance" as could be imagined. In response to Dante's surprise at seeing the

Roman emperor in heaven, it is explained that for a short time he resumed his body, thereby empowering his will to choose the good in a way that spirits in hell cannot. With the power to choose so restored, he exercised saving faith and became worthy to join the luminous figures with which he was numbered in heaven.[26] The significance of this extraordinary second chance is underscored by the following lines, which draw a vivid contrast between the sadness of hell (Limbo) and the joy of heaven:

> And now he knows how dear they pay for it
> Who serve not Christ, by his experience
> Of this sweet life and of the opposite.[27]

Having experienced the delights of heaven, he now fully understands the true nature of the low-grade misery of those in Limbo, who are consigned to an eternal fate of longing for what they can never enjoy. This is the price they pay for not serving Christ, inevitable though it was that they did not, just as it was for Trajan until he was given his remarkable opportunity to have saving faith.

Significantly, similar issues are addressed not only in this immediate context, but in the larger context of the Cantos before and after the one just cited. In the previous Canto, Dante the Pilgrim overtly raises the question, which has been troubling him, of why virtuous pagans are excluded from heaven, and the apparent injustice of condemning them for the unbelief which seems not in any way to be their fault.[28] I want to highlight two lines of response that are given to Dante in order to address his perplexity. The first of these appears when he cannot contain his surprise at seeing Trajan and Rhipeus in heaven and cries out for an explanation. In the lines preceding the description of how Trajan resumed his body and was given the chance to attain faith, we read this striking account of the deeper issue, namely, the nature of divine love that led to their salvation:

> *Regnum coelorum* suffereth violence
> From ardent love and living hope, which still
> Conquer God's will and beat down His defence—
>   Not as man beats down man; Himself doth will
> To suffer conquest, who by His own love
> Conquered, comes conquering and unconquerable.[29]

Particularly striking here is the paradoxical description of how the will of the unconquerable God is conquered. This happens only because He wishes to be conquered, and it is his own love that leads the conquest. This phenomenon is illustrated by God's response to the ardent love of Gregory the Great as expressed in his fervent prayers for Trajan, love inspired by God himself.

This is a beautiful picture of divine love, a love that so delights to give and to be received that it takes pleasure in honoring the extraordinary petition of Gregory. However, this very picture of divine love also raises difficult questions. If God would grant such an opportunity to Trajan, why would he not do the same for other inhabitants of Limbo? Indeed, why would he not do it for other inhabitants of hell?

Here we come to the second line of response to Dante's perplexity, a line that recurs in all three of the Cantos we are currently considering, namely, an appeal to the unfathomable mystery of divine predestination and justice. For instance, after the account of how Trajan and Rhipeus came to faith, the following caution is issued:

> Predestination! what far depths conceal
> From feeble sight, unable to detect
> The First Cause whole, thy root of woe and weal!
>   And, mortals, keep your judgment straitly checked
> For here we see God face to face, and still
> We know not all the roll of the elect.[30]

Now the reminder that "we know not all the roll of the elect" is clearly an important one that we need to heed, and it underscores the wonders of grace and the reality that God can make his grace available to people in ways we could never guess or anticipate. It is only fitting that Dante's bewilderment that Trajan and Rhipeus were recipients of saving grace is met by accounts that show that the ways of grace surpass our imaginations.

The mystery of grace in this sense is surely a thing to celebrate and acknowledge with grateful humility. However, Dante's appeal to mystery also leaves us with questions that are troubling in a much more negative sense. Does God extend special favors of saving grace, like the one to Trajan, in an arbitrary fashion? Or does he do so only in response to fervent acts of intercession, as in the legend of Saint Gregory? If so, while we may marvel at the divine resources in finding a way to reach Trajan with his saving grace, we are left wondering why he would not do something similar for Virgil and Plato, just for a start.[31]

Before moving on from Dante, let us attempt to situate his position relative to other options. On one end of the spectrum is the view that God unconditionally elects some people for salvation, and passes over others, for reasons that are inscrutable to us. On the other end is the view that God truly loves and desires to save all persons, and gives to all optimal grace, so if any are lost, it is due to their own persistent choice to resist grace and to choose evil decisively. Earlier in this chapter, I suggested that Sayers claims that Dante holds a view essentially like this.

I have argued, however, that Dante does not in fact espouse this view. While he does indeed emphasize human freedom and holds that sinners are responsible for their fate, he does not consistently depict God as doing all he can to extend his grace to lost persons. Rather, he holds that for reasons utterly beyond us, God makes his grace available to some persons in special ways that are not available to other persons in comparable circumstances or situations. Moreover, it seems likely that many of these others would respond favorably to God and be saved if they were given optimal grace. While I have focused on the instances of virtuous pagans to make this case, a similar line of argument might be developed for other sinners in hell. Dante speaks, for instance, of those who repent too late, and one wonders if such persons would repent if given more opportunity to do so.[32]

If God is willing to accept any repentance in this life, no matter how late, and however feeble, one wonders why he would not accept sincere repentance after death, if indeed, he truly desires to save all persons. For someone who truly repents in hell is not getting what they really want, as Sayers claims is true for everyone. Dante's position, then, represents a sort of uneasy combination of conflicting views, and places him somewhere in the middle between the more consistent views on either end of the spectrum.

PURGATORY AS POSTMORTEM PROBATION

So let us turn to consider the possibility that persons might have the chance to repent after death. In this section I will survey some interesting examples of theologians who have put forward this proposal, particularly in connection with purgatory. In chapter 2, I cited a number of Protestant theologians who have floated this suggestion, so this section will augment that earlier discussion with further detail that will provide fodder for critical analysis. The proposal that purgatory might be understood as an opportunity for postmortem repentance differs, of course, from the Roman view that it is strictly for those who have accepted grace before they die, so it represents a modification or revision of the traditional account of the doctrine.

Let us begin with the views of Olin Alfred Curtis, an American theologian of the early twentieth century who offered some fairly developed speculations about the nature and purpose of the intermediate state. Although he does not describe his position as a version of purgatory, it is amenable to such a construction. Like the traditional view of the doctrine, he insists that the intermediate state is not a second or continued probation, contending that such a view trivializes this life as something that could be dispensed with. Despite this denial, however, he affirms the essential sentiments of those who defend such a continued probation on the grounds of "equity" and "the moral sense of fair play."[33] In his view, these concerns can be met by a proper understanding of our probation in this life. He summed up what he believed is the true Christian view in four claims. First, personal salvation is based entirely on the atonement of Christ. Second, the fullness of distinctively Christian experience involves correct belief and the right mental attitude toward the person and work of Christ. Third, final salvation depends on one's personal moral bearing as shown in "repentance and faith under a supreme moral ideal."[34] Fourth, "every person with a conscience has in this life a fair, full probation; for he has a fair full test of moral intention."[35]

Curtis's position is interesting for our purposes, for while he insists that full Christian experience requires true beliefs about Christ and explicit faith in him, he also holds that final salvation does not. That is, a person can be saved by exercising the necessary repentance and faith "under a supreme moral ideal," even if that person has never heard of Christ in this life. That is, a person can appropriate God's grace whether or not he has any theologically informed understanding of that grace simply by recognizing that he is morally accountable, repenting of moral failures, and aspiring to goodness. A person who has come to a spirit of repentance and faith in this fashion, Curtis suggests, is "longing for all Christ Jesus is, although he has never known him."[36]

The purpose of the intermediate state then, is not a second chance to choose the good, for everyone makes that choice in this life. Rather, the intermediate state is a time to adjust one's mental life to one's moral intentions and aspirations. The longing for Christ that is implicit in moral aspiration will no longer be frustrated by false or distorted opinions or beliefs. Instead, that longing will be completely fulfilled by coming to know the reality of Christ and his saving work for us. Curtis sums up this view in one sentence: "In the intermediate state every man must see Jesus Christ as he really is; and seeing him as he is, every man who is in harmony with Christ's nature will accept him; while every man who is not in harmony with Christ's nature will reject him."[37]

Curtis's theory faces an apparently obvious counterexample in infants and children who die before they reach moral awareness or responsibility. He addresses this objection on the assumption that all such children are saved, which he takes to be a matter of Christian consensus. He recognizes that as an Arminian, he cannot simply take this for granted. Whereas Calvinists may hold that all such children are unconditionally elected for salvation by God, a consistent Arminian must provide some account of how they freely accept Christ. He takes up this challenge by arguing that in the intermediate state, all these children will grow into moral awareness and will achieve full personal experience, as surely as children do in this life. As they grow to feel the force of moral motives, moreover, they will freely accept Christ, "and, in companionship with him, they achieve, in the intermediate state, the full equivalent of a perfect Christian experience."[38] What these persons experience apparently, according to Curtis, is an abbreviated probation in which their moral awareness is more or less simultaneous with their free decision to accept Christ.

It is also interesting for our purposes that Curtis offers a conjecture as to why certain persons are treated in this special manner that allows them to be saved without the same sort of probation that occurs in the normal course of this life. Here is his suggestion:

> They are exceptional persons who have no need of a prolonged probation to fix their moral destiny; and their death is so entangled with the probation, or with the development, of other persons as to be of more providential worth than is their continued life in this world. That is, they die not to get advantage but to give service.[39]

This is an intriguing proposal that perhaps raises as many questions as it does provide solutions, but we shall defer them for now. It is, however, worth remarking that this proposal may rely implicitly on something like the Molinist picture of middle knowledge and providence. Otherwise, it may be hard to make sense of how God could know these persons would freely choose Christ without a longer probation, not to mention how he could know that their early death would be of greater providential worth than their continued life.

Let us turn now to a contemporary of Curtis, namely, P. T. Forsyth, a leading British theologian of the late nineteenth and early twentieth centuries, whose views we briefly noted in chapter 2. Forsyth's speculations on purgatory arose in a pastoral context, in a fashion reminiscent of the way that the doctrine first began to take shape among some of the early Church fathers. In his context, the pressing issue was the eternal fate of the many young soldiers who had died in World War I, men whose piety or religious commitments may have been in doubt, but who made the ultimate sacrifice of love for their fellow man. Grieving loved ones were seeking assurance and reason to hope that these young men were not forever lost.

Forsyth appealed to a version of purgatory to provide a theologically grounded hope for these bereaved persons. In particular, he saw the sacrificial deaths of these war heroes as grounds to hope for their final salvation. At first blush, such a suggestion might appear to be, however, nobly motivated, a version of a doctrine of salvation by good works or self-atonement. Forsyth makes clear that he is advocating no such thing, but rather suggesting that such heroism is a sign of saving grace in the one who displays it. Here is the larger context of the passage I quoted from him in chapter 3:

> It [a heroic death] does not save. Yet it may be the moment of his conversion. It may open his moral eyes. It may begin his godly sorrow. It may be the first step in a new life, the beginning of repentance in a new life which advances faster there than here. We threw away too much when we threw purgatory clean out of doors. We threw out the baby with the dirty water of its bath. There are more conversions on the other side than on this, if the crisis of death opens the eyes as I have said.... If a man does not at once receive the prodigal's robe, at least he has the entrée to the father's domain.[40]

Now there is an ambiguity here as to when Forsyth believes that conversion occurs. Initially, he suggests that the act of dying sacrificially is the moment of conversion. In a slightly different vein, he also states that it may be "the beginning of repentance," which would not be conversion properly speaking, but only a crucial "first step" in that direction. Later still in the quote, he suggests that conversion proper takes place on the other side, with the crisis of death opening the eyes. At any rate, what is clear is that he sees his proposal as a way to recover the truth in the doctrine of purgatory, stripped of accretions and distortions.

Forsyth goes on for the next several pages to defend the practice of praying for the dead as a natural extension of this line of thought, and indeed, as a natural practice for all those who take seriously the biblical admonition that we should pray for all non-trivial matters. Again, he argues that the practice of praying for the dead would never have been lost among Protestants had it not been for the abuses of the doctrine of purgatory and the magical mind-set often associated with it. But a doctrine of purgatory stripped of such abuses and accretions is a valuable pastoral and theological resource, as well as a spur to devotion and prayer that strengthens the communion of the saints.[41]

Let us turn now to a contemporary representative of the view that purgatory can underwrite postmortem repentance and salvation. William H. Willimon, a United Methodist bishop, appeals to the doctrine not only in behalf of this claim, but also in support of the possibility of universal salvation. His discussion of "who will be saved" is premised upon the frequently recurring biblical theme that God's love is far more expansive and abundant than we are inclined to think or imagine. Whereas we are often all too willing to draw lines and emphasize limits, many of Jesus' parables push us in the complete opposite direction. As Willimon notes, God is pictured as "the searching shepherd, the careless farmer, the undiscerning fisherman, the reckless woman, the extravagant father, the prodigal Samaritan. Jesus thus reveals a God who is no discreet minimalist."[42]

While Willimon does not go so far as to affirm that universal salvation is true, he does follow Karl Barth and others in arguing that it is a possibility that we should hope and pray for. Recognizing that salvation takes time, and that many persons not only need more time to experience the personal transformation that is at the heart of salvation, while others need more time to respond to the gospel in the first place, he urges that Protestants need a version of purgatory to make theological sense of these claims. "If judgment is to be made to stare in the fierce, merciful mirror of truth, and if we turn away from that truth, might God allow us yet more time to turn around and look in the mirror?"[43] He notes that in Jesus' parable of the lost sheep, the shepherd seeks the lost until he finds it. The word "until" is one of the most comforting in scripture, particularly in light of the fact that God is eternal and has forever to find the lost. "The idea of purgatory is an affirmation of the possibility that Jesus seeks us in order to save us, seeking us as long as it takes, seeking us not only in life but also in death."[44]

Now it may have been noticed that the thinkers I have cited in this section are all Protestants. This is perhaps not surprising, since the Roman Catholic account of the doctrine explicitly rules out the idea that purgatory is a second chance to repent or accept salvation. It is exclusively for those who die in a state of grace, even if that grace was only achieved at the last minute of life. Despite this official teaching, however, some Roman Catholic theologians have recently proposed variations of the doctrine that open the door to the possibility of postmortem conversion.

One prominent example is Karl Rahner, a leading voice in twentieth-century Roman Catholic theology, who broached this idea in an essay on purgatory, written in dialogue form as a conversation between two unnamed theologians. While the form of this essay requires us to be cautious in identifying either theologian as exactly expressing Rahner's own views, one can nevertheless reasonably assume that the overall trajectory of the dialogue is an accurate reflection of his thought.

For our purposes, the last few pages of the dialogue are most interesting. There, the second theologian proposes that the Roman Catholic view of purgatory might be modified by taking into account the traditions of other world religions that allow for more fundamental postmortem decisions than traditional Roman theology has recognized. In particular, he appears to be suggesting that the fundamental decision either to accept or reject God might be made for some persons in the afterlife. This is made explicit when he goes on to observe that at least some persons have not had the opportunity in this life to make a definitive decision on this matter. Perhaps, he suggests, the traditional view that one's eternal fate is sealed at death should not be applied to all persons, but only to those who have enjoyed a full "history of free-dom" and have settled their choice in this life. In view of this possibility, he thinks it is reasonable to "imagine that it [purgatory] might offer opportunities and scope for a postmortal history of freedom to someone who had been denied such a his-tory in his earthly life."[45] Rahner's suggestion of a modified account of purgatory that allows for postmortem conversion is particularly interesting in light of the fact that he has argued that Christians should at least hope for the final salvation of all persons.[46] We shall come back to this point in the next section, but for now it is enough to note that the hope of universal salvation may require some such notion of postmortem freedom and the continued opportunity to choose God.

Before concluding this section, it is worth underscoring that Rahner is hardly alone among Roman Catholic theologians in hoping for universal salvation. Indeed, formerly Cardinal Ratzinger, now Pope Bendict XVI, has been counted among this number, and it is most interesting for our purposes that he does so in the context of discussing purgatory. In chapter 4, I examined his views on the interdependence of humanity, of how we are related to each other in such ways that our very identity is at least partly constituted by our shared temporality. In this connection, he defined the essence of purgatory as "suffering to the end what one has left behind on earth." In this passage, he had in mind our guilt, particularly insofar as we have hurt other persons and left behind a trail of damage and destruction. However, he also pointed out the other side of the same truth, namely, that it is not only our guilt that we leave behind that prevents us from reclining at the eschatological banquet with unalloyed joy, but also our love. For love at its best cannot close itself off from others as long as time and suffering remain.

In explicating this point, Ratzinger appealed to Therese of Lisieux, who insisted that a mother could not be completely happy so long as even one of her children was suffering. He goes on to cite, in the same vein, the Buddhist "idea of the Bodhisattva, who refuses to enter Nirvana so long as one human being remains in hell. By such waiting, he empties hell, accepting the salvation which is his due only when hell has become uninhabited."[47] Ratzinger at least gestures in the direction of universalism when he makes explicit the comparison with Christ, who he claims is the true Bodhisattva and the ultimate fulfillment of this idea.[48]

Again, my aim in this section has only been to show that a number of theolo-gians, both Protestant and Roman, have deployed the doctrine of purgatory to pro-vide a theological grounding for the idea of postmortem conversion and a "second chance" for salvation. The examples I have cited are of course merely representative, and not exhaustive, but they provide sufficient evidence to show that the doctrine of purgatory is easily merged with the notion of a "second chance" and why the two claims are often identified with each other.[49] Let us turn now to provide a more critical and constructive analysis of the relationship between these two ideas and how it may bear on a convincing and theologically coherent account of purgatory.

PURGATORY AS POSTMORTEM PROBATION: A CRITICAL ANALYSIS

I will begin by returning to a question that I raised earlier in this chapter: How extensive and expansive do we believe God's love to be? Does he truly love all persons, and is he sincerely willing to save all of them? As noted above, there is a range of positions on this question in Christian theology. On one end of the spectrum are those who hold that God unconditionally elects some for salvation, while passing over the rest, who are inevitably damned. On the other end are those who hold that God does everything he can, short of overriding human freedom, to make the grace of Christ available to all persons and elicit a response of saving faith from them.

The first claim I want to make by way of constructive statement is that both the doctrine of purgatory as well as second-chance theories of salvation are positions on the spectrum that affirm an expansive view of God's love and grace. Indeed, it is the conviction that God's love is overwhelmingly generous that motivates both of these views and perhaps also explains why the two view are often identified with each other, or in some cases confused with each other. Recall the beautiful line from Dante above that describes God as one who "Himself doth will to suffer conquest, who by His own love conquered, comes conquered and unconquerable." It is this stunning vision of an unconquerable God who is willingly conquered by love that Christians not only dare to hope is true, but have been given reason to believe God himself has revealed to be true. This is the love they believe was displayed most dramatically in the cross and resurrection of Christ, a kind of love that is so powerful and all embracing that even the chief of sinners may be saved. Because of the conquering power of this love, there are pagans in heaven whom Dante had assumed could not be saved. Because of the lengths and heights and depths and breadths this love is willing to go, many Christians resonate deeply with Sayers when she says that God's mercy does all it can to save sinners, so those in hell are getting what they want, not what God wants.

The fundamental claim I want to advance in this section is that any satisfactory doctrine of purgatory (or any other Christian doctrine for that matter) must do justice to this picture of God's love. Accounts of purgatory, such as Dante's, that aspire to be true to this vision of God's love, but fail to do so, are deeply inconsistent and require modification. The same is true of versions of purgatory that affirm further opportunities for salvation, but qualify this claim in such a way that they still fall short of this target.

Let us reflect on this further by considering the notion, which many Christians would affirm, that God gives everyone at least one opportunity to be saved, an opportunity that would suffice to enable each person to exercise saving faith. Now if it possible that God can assure this, it is hard to see why it should be a stretch to think that God could give everyone further chances if necessary. Indeed, there seems to be no reason that he could not give everyone optimal grace. While optimal grace may be more complicated, and may require more time, it is hard to imagine that God could not achieve this, especially if he can extend grace beyond death and continue to find ways to reach out to lost persons and draw them to himself.

There is one traditional argument against even the possibility of postmortem repentance that we should note at this point, since it is alluded to in the account of Trajan above. Aquinas held that a separated soul cannot change its fundamental dispositions without the body and therefore cannot repent after death. His reasons for arguing this are metaphysical in nature and will only have force for those who accept his claims about the nature of human persons and the limited powers of the separated soul. The argument, consequently, will have little force for dualists who believe that the soul retains the power to will and choose and make morally significant choices.[50] But even if he is correct in his claims about the metaphysical limitations of the separated soul, the possibility of postmortem repentance is not ruled out altogether, as the legend of Trajan shows. If necessary, God could restore a person's body, or give one some sort of "purgatory body" that would empower one to repent and accept the gospel. In any case, it is hard to take seriously that there are any obstacles of a metaphysical variety that would prevent God from granting postmortem repentance if he were willing to do so.

The more typical reasons for denying postmortem repentance are in the vein that God *would* not grant such repentance after death, rather than that he *could* not. The reasons given are usually broadly moral in nature, to the effect that this life would be drained of its seriousness if we could repent after death. This sort of reason is presumably not taken to be a strict entailment of perfect justice such that God would be less than morally perfect were he to grant postmortem repentance. If that were the claim, then again, God *could* not offer postmortem repentance for it would be incompatible with his perfect nature. Rather, I take the claim to be that God has imposed this sort of limit for the purpose of reinforcing the seriousness of our moral probation in this life.

The obvious difficulty with the notion that God would impose such a limit, of course, as Rahner and many others have noted, is that many people do not seem to have a full history of freedom, and thus do not have a full and fair moral probation. And certainly, many never hear the gospel or have any real opportunity to exercise faith in Christ in this life. Curtis, recall, acknowledges this, but differs from Rahner in insisting that everyone has a full probation and makes their moral intentions clear in this life, and can thereby gain final salvation. All persons are treated equitably, so no one is at a disadvantage so far as eternal salvation is concerned.

Now if Curtis is correct that all have a full probation in this life, then at least the issue of a fair opportunity for all is addressed, and the seeming problem identified by Rahner and others is an illusory one. However, it seems highly unlikely that

Curtis is correct on this score, and much more probable that his optimism is unwarranted. Admittedly, judgments of probability or plausibility in such matters are somewhat subjective to say the least, and there is surely no way to show or demonstrate that Curtis is wrong. But if our empirical observations are broadly reliable, it appears that many people die well before their characters are formed or their moral commitments are clarified. It usually takes some degree of maturity for moral intentions to emerge in any sort of definitive shape, and indeed, people who are morally confused and even irresponsible early in life often come to have strong moral convictions and commitments later on. It is hard to deny that many die before their character has taken anything like definitive shape.

Indeed, Curtis's claim that all have a full probation in this life appears to be motivated by his twofold commitment, first to the moral conviction that God treats all persons fairly and equitably, and second, to his belief that probation does not continue into the next life. Given these commitments, he really has no option but to insist that everyone has a full and fair probation in this life, as implausible as it may appear from our actual experience and observations of people.

Moreover, Curtis's account of infant salvation suffers from the same sort of implausibility. In particular, his view is driven by his assumption that all infants who die are saved, along with his non-negotiable conviction that all persons must freely choose the good, and exercise faith in Christ. This leads him to speculate that all such infants require only a brief probation, and to make the theologically and pastorally dubious claim that their early death was willed by God because it serves some good providential purpose for other persons. In short then, Curtis can only maintain his essential theological conviction that God is equitable and fair to all persons in giving all a full probation by holding claims that are highly implausible from both an empirical and a theological standpoint.

Here it may prove illuminating to compare another view that is similar to Curtis's, namely, the view that those who have not had a chance to decide for Christ in this life will encounter him in the moment of death and either accept or reject him then. For a contemporary example of this position, let us consider the Reformed theologian Terrance L. Tiessen. Like Curtis, he wants to insist that his view is not a theory of postmortem probation or a second chance for salvation for those who did not respond positively to God's grace in this life. Rather, his theory pertains to people who have responded to *God* in faith, but have not yet heard of *Christ* and the full truth of the gospel message. It is his contention "that the response one makes to Christ at the moment of death will be *consistent* with the response one has been making to God in whatever form God has been revealing himself *prior* to death."[51] Unlike Curtis, he does not think that these persons learn of Christ in the intermediate stage after death, and thereby adjust their intellectual beliefs to their moral meaning. Rather, Tiessen wants to show that all persons who are saved respond to God in faith before death, and come to explicit faith in Christ no later than the moment of death.[52]

Indeed, so intent is Tiessen on denying postmortem conversion that he even insists, again unlike Curtis, that infants who are saved make a response of faith before they die. While they too may meet Christ at the moment of death (like unevangelized adults), if they are saved, it will be because they have already responded in faith to God. As Tiessen puts it, his proposal is "that God reveals himself to infants (and the unborn) during their brief lives, and that their salvation can, therefore, take place before death, but that it does not occur without an act of personal faith."[53] Tiessen realizes that it may seem implausible to think that infants are capable of any sort of response to God, but he appeals to mind-body dualism to defend his theory. What he calls "personal ability," cannot be reduced to physical ability, he suggests, so even though infants cannot communicate with us, we should not presume they lack the ability to communicate with God.[54]

Now, substance dualism is a defensible theory of the nature of human persons, and has natural affinities with traditional Christian belief, as argued in a previous chapter, but it is much more dubious that dualism provides good grounds for Tiessen's theory. While mind and brain may be distinct, it is much more doubtful that the development of the mind outstrips the development of the brain in the way he seems to be assuming. At any rate, like Curtis, he is forced to rely on highly speculative assumptions to avoid postmortem conversion. Indeed, the notion that all persons encounter Christ at the moment of death is itself a speculation that goes beyond what scripture teaches, as Tiessen recognizes.[55] The same is true, of course, of the theory of postmortem conversion, but the point is that it is no more speculative than Tiessen's own proposals.

Now, it is interesting to note that Tiessen admits his attraction to the idea of postmortem conversion. "It would be wonderful if people did, indeed, have opportunity after death to reverse decisions they have made during their lives," he writes.[56] He does not find the notion morally or theologically objectionable apparently, but he believes the possibility is precluded by scripture, so we must reject it, regardless of however appealing it may seem to us. In particular, he cites Hebrews 9:27–28, which teaches that judgment follows death, and Jesus' parable in Luke 13:23–30, which depicts the owner of a house shutting the door once and for all, which suggests that people cannot reverse decisions that were once available to them.

I believe that Tiessen is reading far more from these texts than they actually say. The text from Hebrews is often cited to disprove both purgatory and the theory of postmortem conversion, but this claim purports to extract far more juice from a handful of grapes than they contain. While the text clearly teaches that we die only once, and that there is judgment after death, it does not specify exactly when after death the judgment occurs, nor whether the judgment is a preliminary one or a final one. Indeed, given that the final judgment is an event at the end of the world, it seems unlikely that the text teaches that the final judgment occurs immediately after death.[57] Recall the observation at the beginning of this chapter that the doctrine of purgatory implies that something significant may happen between one's death and resurrection, and how this is connected to the idea of two judgments. In particular, there is a judgment immediately after death in which one faces the consequences of his sins with the possibility of having them forgiven and cleansed, to be followed later by a final judgment. This scenario is perfectly compatible with the text from Hebrews.

Likewise, Jesus' parable in Luke does not rule out postmortem conversion. At best, it would rule out postmortem conversion for those who had opportunity to know Christ in this life, but did not truly come do so, except in an entirely superficial manner. The text warns against evildoers who imagine they will be saved simply because they "ate and drank" with Jesus or heard his teaching. Such evildoers are depicted in the parable as regretful but not truly repentant. The text does not describe true penitents and gives us no indication of how genuine repentance would be received by God. It is, moreover, notoriously unwise to press all details of parables as if each has a parallel spiritual meaning or significance. Unlike allegories, parables typically have one central point, and it is far from clear that the central point of this parable is to rule out postmortem repentance and conversion.

Now if scripture does not rule out postmortem conversion, and it would be wonderful if people could repent after death, as Tiessen acknowledges, is there any good reason to believe that a God of perfect love would not welcome such repentance? If God's mercy endures forever, as the Psalms insist, and if his very nature is love, and if he is more prodigal in his grace than we are with our sin, would he not always welcome home his erring children who sincerely repent? Evangelical theologian Donald Bloesch suggests that scripture gives us positive reason to think so:

> The unbridgeable gap spoken of in Luke 16:26 is between hades and paradise, and it is a
> gap only in the sense that unrepentant sin constitutes a formidable barrier to salvation.
> The gates of the holy city are depicted as being open day and night (Is 60:11; Rev 21:25),
> which means that access to the throne of grace is a continuing possibility. . . . even when
> we find ourselves prisoners in the inner darkness that we have created, Jesus Christ has
> the keys to this hell and can reach out to us by his grace (Rev 1:18). Even when one is in
> hell, one can be forgiven.[58]

Indeed, if this is true, there is no good reason to think that Rahner is correct in the strictures he places on the hope of postmortem conversion. Recall that he seems to hold that such repentance would only be available to people who had not had the chance to make a fully formed free choice in this life either for or against God, but not to those who had already had this opportunity. Morwenna Ludlow presses the obvious question for Rahner's view of purgatory when she remarks that "it is difficult to see why it should be a possibility for some people and not for others. Could it provide the opportunity for repentance for those who had previously rejected God?"[59]

She goes on to note, moreover, that the question becomes more urgent in view of the fact that Rahner expresses the hope for universal salvation. Now, if universal salvation is even a possibility that Christians can hope and pray for, then either it must be possible that all persons, appearances much to the contrary, have actually responded in faith in some fashion before they died, or that all persons who have not done so will have the opportunity to repent and respond in faith after death. Without one of these possibilities, the hope for universal salvation is an incoherent one.[60] The same point applies, obviously, to Ratzinger's apparent hope for universal salvation. Either the traditional Roman view that only those who die in grace can be saved must be modified, or it must be held that it is possible that all in fact die in grace, or the hope of universal salvation must be rejected as impossible.

THREE UNAVOIDABLE QUESTIONS

Now if it is possible in the afterlife to reverse decisions we have made in this life, three questions immediately arise. The first, already mentioned, is whether this does not trivialize this life and make it insignificant. I would argue that it does not, for the fact remains that every decision we make affects us and has consequences for our character and the shape of our lives. While the choice of sin does not necessarily damn us, as countless redeemed sinners can attest, it does always harm our soul and our relationship with God and other persons. So the more we sin and persist in our rebellion, the more complicated will be our repentance and subsequent transformation. Repentance means that we can reverse bad decisions, but this requires us to turn around and change the direction of our lives, and the further we have walked away from God, the further we must walk back. It is precisely the logic of the doctrine of purgatory that it allows the hope of return but does not trivialize the time and process necessary to do so.

Moreover, if deathbed repentance is possible, it seems rather artificial to think that such late reversals do not trivialize this life, while repentance two minutes after death would. Of course, some have rejected deathbed repentance for just this reason, namely, that it seems to trivialize one's life and choices up to that point.[61] But those who hold, like Sayers (and Dante), that God is merciful right up to the point of death, and will accept any repentance, however feeble, seem to lack any principled reason for claiming that postmortem conversion would trivialize this life.

A second and more troublesome question is whether the possibility of postmortem repentance raises the specter that persons who have decided *for* God in this life might reverse their decision after death and turn away from him and be lost in the end. The traditional view, of course, is that this is impossible. But if we allow for people to turn to God after death, is there any good reason to think they cannot likewise turn away from him? Consider the case of a recently converted person who has just begun the road of Christian discipleship and has a long way to go in order to be fully transformed in the image of Christ. Is it possible, or perhaps even likely, that such a person might end up resisting the demand for sanctification and transformation in purgatory and turn away from God, as people often seem to do in this life?

How one answers this question will depend in part on whether one thinks it is ever possible for a person who was genuinely converted to turn away from God and be lost. This is a disputed issue within Christian theology, with some holding to "the perseverance of the saints," which is the view that the truly converted can never fully apostatize and be lost, and others holding that even the truly converted can fall away and be damned in the end. However, this does not settle the matter entirely, for one may think it is possible for a converted person to fall into sin and turn completely away from God in this life, while denying the same is true for the life to come. Aquinas, for instance, thought that true believers could fall from grace in this life and be lost, but denied that anyone who died in grace could be lost. This holds not only for those who go straight to heaven, but also for those who go to purgatory.[62]

Now, I am inclined to think it is possible but unlikely that persons who die in grace but need purgatory would turn completely away from God after death and be lost. The fundamental reason is because there are deep differences between the choice for God and the choice against him. There are far deeper and more intelligible motivations for choosing God than for choosing against him, and these make the former choice far more stable in the long run. Indeed, the radical asymmetries between the two choices are such that there is good reason to think the choice for God is not reversible in the same sense that the choice against him is.

Aquinas shows the profound difference between the two choices by developing a number of psychological reasons for why the saved in heaven cannot alter their decision and fall away. These reasons have to do with the fact that souls who enjoy the beatific vision are experiencing the fulfillment of all their desires, and all the happiness and satisfaction they naturally seek. Consequently, they simply have no motive to ever turn away from God or the perfect joy they know as they gaze on his beauty. "But a happy rational substance that sees God grasps Him as the best. Therefore it loves Him the most…. Therefore, the wills of those who see God cannot be rendered perverse."[63]

This explanation points up the profound asymmetry between the final state of the blessed and that of the lost. The blessed are settled in their choice and their final condition for reasons that have no parallel in the lost. The choice of God and the good is a settled choice that is irreversible because there is no intelligible reason to want to reverse it. The experience of the beatific vision is wonderful beyond compare, and satisfies beyond imagining every good desire of a rational soul. It fulfills our God-given nature completely, and answers fully to who we are at our deepest and best. By contrast, the choice of evil results in pain and unhappiness, and goes sharply against the grain of our truest nature.[64]

Now, of course, those in purgatory do not yet experience the complete fulfillment of their desires or the consummate joy of those who partake of the beatific vision, so the reasons for their inability to fall away from God are not altogether the same as those in heaven, and certainly they do not hold to the same degree. Nevertheless, Aquinas holds that their fundamental orientation to God and the good assures that their will, too, is immutable and not vulnerable to perversion. If we believe, moreover, that purgatory is an experience of growing knowledge and awareness of God, it is reasonable to think that those who have already shown an attraction and love for God by their initial choice will continue to grow in that love and gain ever deeper satisfaction from it. And the more this is so, the less reason to think they would reverse their choice and fall away from God.

The asymmetry between choosing God and choosing evil has been developed at length in the contemporary literature by Thomas Talbott as an argument for universal salvation. Talbott's view also represents an interesting variation on "purgatory," and why none of its inhabitants will finally turn away from God and be lost. His argument for universal salvation hinges on a precise definition of what is involved in choosing an eternal destiny. The essence of what is required for this momentous choice is that it must be fully informed in such a way that once the person making it gets what he wants, he does not later regret the choice. To meet this condition, the choice must be free of illusion not only initially, but also in the long run. The one making the choice must fully understand what he has chosen and must freely persist in preferring what he has chosen.[65]

Now Talbott thinks it is clear that the asymmetry between the choice of eternal happiness in heaven on the one hand, and the choice of eternal misery in hell on the other, is so radical that, whereas the former is fully intelligible, the latter is not. It is understandable enough that free persons could choose evil in the short run, but since evil inevitably leads to greater and greater misery, no one could persist in choosing it forever, so the notion of choosing the eternal misery of damnation is simply incoherent. So some people go to hell on Talbott's view, but all eventually repent, because no one could persist in the choice to remain there forever. On his view then, hell actually plays the same sort of role that some of the thinkers we have noted have proposed for purgatory, since it is a place of postmortem repentance and conversion for its temporary inhabitants, all of whom will eventually make it to heaven.[66]

It is important to underscore that, on Talbott's view, persons in hell retain their agency and their essential humanity, unlike some views of hell that hold that the choice of evil has the ever-increasing effect of corrupting, and thereby diminishing, those who choose it. Indeed, on the latter view, the more persistently people choose evil, the more they lose their human capacities, perhaps even to the point of total annihilation.[67] By contrast, any view that takes universal salvation to be a reasonable likelihood, or even a plausible hope, let alone a certainty, must likewise hold that sinners retain their essential humanity so that they could be rehabilitated by grace and eventually come to love God and embrace the good.

Third, if it is possible to repent after death, and if Bloesch is correct that even people in hell can be forgiven, does this not rule out the traditional doctrine of the last judgment? Clearly, scripture teaches that there will be a judgment at the end of history in which all persons will give an account of their lives before God and be judged accordingly. This judgment will demonstrate for all to see God's ultimate triumph over evil, and the coming of his eternal kingdom, when his will shall be done on earth as it is in heaven. Some will gain entrance to heaven come to earth, and others will be consigned to hell. There is, however, no inconsistency in holding that even after this time, some may repent and receive forgiveness.[68] In this case, the lines between hell and purgatory again become blurry, but this does not entail a denial of the traditional doctrine of a last judgment. The verdict of the last judgment does not change that those who reject Christ are lost and excluded from heaven, while those who accept him are admitted to eternal joy. If any of those in hell repent, it is they who have changed, and not the reality or the terms of God's ultimate judgment on our lives.

All three of these questions we posed, then, have plausible answers, so none of them gives us convincing reason to think that persons could not reverse their decisions in the afterlife if they have rejected God in this life. It is not the case that our decisions here would be trivialized if it is possible to reverse our choices in the afterlife. Nor must we grant that if it is possible to turn back to God after resisting him in this life, that it is just as likely that persons who have made an initial decision for God might turn away from him and finally reject him in the afterlife.[69] Nor, finally, do we deny the last judgment if repentance is possible after death.

CONCLUSION

Now then, much more could be said about many of the issues I have raised, but for the sake of space, I want to conclude by stating in summary form how I believe the doctrine of purgatory should be modified to include the opportunity for post-mortem repentance and conversion. Any such proposals must, of course, be somewhat speculative, but as I have observed, the same is true of those positions that deny postmortem conversion. Scripture simply does not give us detailed information either way on this question, and the best we can do is lay out the view that seems most likely, given what we think scripture does clearly teach.

As I have indicated, the fundamental controlling conviction of this discussion is that God deeply loves all persons and truly desires to win a free response of faith and obedience from all of them. This conviction is not only deeply rooted in Scripture, but also readily attested by a wide range of Christian thinkers, as the examples cited above suggest. I have been pressing this claim to show where it leads if consistently applied. For a start, it implies that God is not concerned merely to give all persons one chance or some reasonable chance to be saved so that he will be fully vindicated in judging them and damning them. Rather, he who "by His own love conquered, comes conquering and unconquerable" takes full delight when we prevail on his mercy and grace, and sinners find their way back home.

If we take this picture of God's love as a serious truth claim, and not merely a piece of pious rhetoric, we have reason to accept a modified or expanded view of purgatory that grace is further extended not only to the converted who are partially transformed and imperfectly sanctified, but also to those persons who have not yet exercised any sort of saving faith. This latter group includes not only persons who have not had opportunity to respond to gospel because they live in parts of the world where it has not yet been clearly preached, but also infants and children who have died before responding to it. Moreover, it includes those whose mental capacities were impaired in this life to such a degree that they could not respond to the gospel. All such persons, it is reasonable to believe, will hear and understand the gospel in the life to come and have every opportunity to respond to it.

The issue of infant salvation has been much debated in the history of theology, and has also played a significant role recently in shaping the larger discussion of the possibility of postmortem conversion for those who have not had a chance to accept the gospel in this life.[70] Unfortunately, discussion of the issue has also often been driven more by sentimentalism than principled theological reasoning. On this score, neither Curtis nor Tiessen are convincing. Tiessen's appeal to infant faith preserves the notion that all who are saved must respond to God in faith in this life, but at the price of assuming a rather implausible claim about the mental powers of infants. This difficulty can be avoided by Curtis's proposal that infants and children will achieve maturity in the life to come, and will be presented with the gospel when they are capable of understanding it. Like others who have not heard it before, they too must respond freely in faith to the gospel to be saved. Given the conviction that God will give optimal grace to all persons, they will have neither a better nor a worse opportunity to be saved than anyone else, and we should not assume that all infants who die are saved, any more than we assume this of all adults. Curtis's speculation that God takes the lives of infants for providential purposes is theologically as well as pastorally highly dubious, and his widely shared assumption that all infants are saved has little to be said for it, beyond its sentimental appeal.

Given optimal grace, however, and God's infinite mercy, we may hope that many persons will respond to God in a saving way in the afterlife. Indeed, Forsyth may well be correct in thinking there are "more conversions on the other side than on this." The arguments of Aquinas and Talbott above give us profound theological reasons to hope that many will respond favorably to the gospel if given every opportunity to do so. The fact that we are created in God's image is a much deeper and more resilient truth about us than our sin and whatever damage we have done to ourselves. Since a loving relationship with God and other persons answers to our deepest needs and fulfills our natures like nothing else can, we may hope that purgatorial grace will shatter the illusions of sin for countless persons in the long run.

Indeed, does this not lead to univeralism?[71] If even those in hell can repent, as Bloesch says, will not all surely end up doing so? Is Talbott correct in thinking that universalism is not merely something fondly to be hoped for, but in fact the only possible outcome, given God's infinite love, and the fact that the choice of eternal misery is an irrational one? Here I demur. I have argued at length elsewhere that even with optimal grace, it is possible that some, perhaps many, persons will persist in choosing evil and remain forever separated from God, and I will not repeat those arguments here.[72]

Even if the notion of purgatory is expanded or modified in the directions I have been defending, and the gates of heaven remain open forever for any persons who may wish to enter, some, against all reason and their own deepest nature and true satisfaction, may decisively reject God's grace.[73] While it may remain true indefinitely that purgatory is hope, there may be those who choose to abandon hope and thereby make hell their eternal destiny. But for any who do so, it will not be because they were not given every opportunity and encouragement to leave purgatory behind and return to their true home.

6

⌒⋎⌒

C. S. Lewis and the Prospect
of Mere Purgatory

The point is not that God will refuse you admission to His eternal world if you have not
got certain qualities of character: the point is that if people have not got at least the
beginnings of those qualities inside them, then no possible external conditions could
make a "Heaven" for them—that is, could make them happy with the deep, strong,
unshakable kind of happiness God intends for us.
                                                                  —C. S. Lewis

In the preface to *Mere Christianity*, a book in which C. S. Lewis's avowed intent
was to avoid doctrines that divide believers, he expressed the altogether reasonable preference that he "should be very glad if people would not draw fanciful inferences from my silence on disputed matters."[1] Purgatory, apparently, is one of those
"disputed matters," since Lewis never mentions it, at least by name, in that book.
However, he made his opinions on the doctrine quite clear elsewhere, and even in
that book, there are sufficient clues that we need not resort to "fanciful inferences"
to get a pretty good idea what he thinks about it.

In this chapter, I want to look in some detail at his account of purgatory, and
explore how the doctrine relates to what he called "mere Christianity." In particular,
I want to examine his version of the doctrine for its ecumenical potential, as one
that may be acceptable to many Protestants as well as Catholics, Roman and otherwise. There are at least three reasons for thinking that his conception of purgatory
may have potential for this sort of broad appeal.

First, Lewis is widely considered the most influential Christian writer and apolo-
gist of the twentieth century, and his influence continues to loom large as we move
well into the twenty-first century. His extraordinary ability to expound the doctrinal
core that is common to all Christians, while playing down the differences that divide

denominations, has earned him an enormous readership across all branches of the Church. Second, Lewis gave significant attention to the Christian doctrine of the afterlife, commenting extensively about heaven and hell, so his comments on purgatory are part of a larger picture of the life to come that many contemporary believers have found both persuasive and appealing. Third, Lewis has achieved something of a status as an arbiter of orthodoxy, particularly among evangelical Protestantism, where his influence is perhaps especially strong. Ironically, not all of Lewis's views are readily amenable to evangelical theology, and indeed in some cases he held views that are at odds with typical evangelical orthodoxy.[2] Nevertheless, Lewis has been warmly embraced by evangelicals, even adopted by them, as is perhaps best symbolized by the fact that his writings are housed at the eminently evangelical school Wheaton College. Evangelical theologians not infrequently appeal to Lewis for support when they put forward proposals that might be viewed with suspicion by the larger Protestant and evangelical community. Lewis's imprimatur can break down defenses and raise the odds that controversial proposals will at least get a hearing.

This third point is especially relevant to the prospects for an ecumenical version of purgatory, since evangelicals by and large remain very dubious of the doctrine. While some evangelicals have expressed tentative openness to reassessing it, as pointed out in chapter 2, the general attitude remains negative if not hostile. All of this is well illustrated by an article on purgatory that appeared just as I began to write this chapter. The author, noted evangelical theologian Roger Olson, provocatively suggested that a number of Protestant heroes of the faith, including Luther, Calvin, and Zwingli, were considerably less than loving in the way they treated people, and might need some corrective measures before they would be fully ready for heaven. This, he proposed, might give us good reason to consider a Protestant version of purgatory.

For our purposes, it is revealing that the second paragraph of his article consists of a plea to his critics to be fair and not to misrepresent him. Noting that his views have in the past been misconstrued by his fellow Baptists, he takes pains to emphasize that he is simply offering a "hypothesis for discussion," not advocating any particular dogmatic version of the doctrine. For our concerns, it is even more interesting to point out that in his very first paragraph, he attempts to disarm his critics by observing that "C. S. Lewis held to a version of purgatory while rejecting the classical Roman Catholic view."[3]

So let us begin by establishing that Lewis, did, in fact believe in purgatory. Later, we shall examine just how he understood the doctrine, and how his view compares with the Roman view, and conclude by suggesting why his account has ecumenical promise.

LEWIS'S AFFIRMATION OF PURGATORY

As we shall see, Lewis explicitly referred to purgatory in a positive way several times in a number of his various writings, and alluded to it other times as well. However, his most direct and extensive statement on the doctrine occurs in the last book he wrote, namely, *Letters to Malcolm: Chiefly on Prayer*. The fact that Lewis discusses the doctrine in a book about prayer is another instance of a certain pattern we have observed with respect to purgatory, that it has often emerged in a pastoral context. And indeed, in the letter in question, Lewis begins by reporting that he had finally managed to forgive someone he had tried unsuccessfully for years to forgive. He went on to ponder whether the dead know it when this sort of thing happens and to express the opinion that it would be a pity if they do not. This was his entry point to answering the question which his (imaginary) friend had raised of whether Lewis prayed for the dead. Recall too that the early practice of praying for the dead was one of the significant factors that gave rise to the doctrine of purgatory, which further shows the doctrine is rooted in long-standing habits of piety and devotion. Here is his answer to the question:

> Of course I pray for the dead. The action is so spontaneous, so all but inevitable, that only the most compulsive theological case against it would deter me. And I hardly know how the rest of my prayers would survive if those for the dead were forbidden. At our age the majority of those we love best are dead. What sort of intercourse with God could I have if what I love best were unmentionable to Him?[4]

Lewis goes on to point out that on the traditional Protestant view, prayer for the dead is pointless, because all the dead are either fully saved by God or else hopelessly damned. Over against this assumption, prayer for the dead implies that some sort of further progress is possible on the other side of the grave, which raises the specter of whether he is affirming "something like Purgatory." Lewis does not shrink from this specter, but rather goes on as follows:

> Well, I suppose I am. Though even in Heaven some perpetual increase of beatitude, reached by a continually more ecstatic self-surrender, without the possibility of failure but not perhaps without its own ardours and exertions—for delight also has its severities and deep ascents, as lovers know—might be supposed. But I won't press, or guess, that side for the moment. I believe in Purgatory.[5]

Notice that Lewis here suggests that prayer for the dead might make sense even without assuming purgatory, for those in heaven may experience "perpetual increase in beatitude" and perhaps our prayers can assist them in this. However, he puts this speculation aside and concludes with the blunt assertion that he believes in purgatory.

Lewis goes on to explain more fully his rationale for believing in purgatory as well to make clear his conception of the doctrine, and we shall come back to this in due course. But for now let us look at another of his interesting affirmations of purgatory, one that appears in a highly personal, existential context. I refer to Lewis's well-known crisis of faith and his personal struggles in the wake of the death of his beloved wife, Joy, from cancer. She no doubt was one of the people he had in mind in the passage above, where he noted that most of the people he loved best were dead, and that he spontaneously prayed for them. After her death, Lewis recorded in a journal his sometimes angry and confused, as well as deeply insightful and moving thoughts, which were first published under a pseudonym. As he pondered the fate and whereabouts of his departed wife, he resisted the comforting thought that she was perfectly happy and at ease in heaven. In a self-conscious commitment to integrity and consistency, he did not flinch from his belief in purgatory and what this likely implied for Joy:

> How do I know that all her anguish is past? I never believed before—I thought it immensely improbable—that the faithfulest soul could leap straight into perfection and peace the moment death has rattled in the throat. It would be wishful thinking with a vengeance to take up that belief now. H. was a splendid thing; a soul straight, bright, and tempered like a sword. But not a perfected saint. A sinful woman married to a sinful man; two of God's patients not yet cured. I know there are not only tears to be dried but stains to be scoured. The sword will be made even brighter.
>
> But oh God, tenderly, tenderly.[6]

It is worth highlighting that Lewis's belief in purgatory does not appear to have the level of a dogma, but only a judgment he considers "immensely" probable. While he does not explicitly employ the term "purgatory" in this passage to express this conviction, he does so later in the book (in adjectival form) when he challenges the assumption that bereavement is experienced only by those left behind when someone dies. "If, as I can't help suspecting, the dead also feel the pains of separation (and this may be one of their purgatorial sufferings), then for both lovers, and for all pairs of lovers without exception, bereavement is a universal and integral part of our experience of love."[7]

It is clear, then, that Lewis believed in purgatory, and while this may make him something of an awkward fit in some Protestant circles, this was hardly an unusual view in his ecclesiastical and intellectual context. Purgatory was accepted not just among his Roman Catholic friends such as J. R. R. Tolkien, but also many of his Anglican friends such as Charles Williams and Dorothy L. Sayers, the latter of whose translation of Dante's *Comedy* I have been using in this book. That Lewis took belief in purgatory as rather commonplace among his fellow Anglicans is suggested by a remark in the introductory chapter of one of his lesser known books, *Reflections on the Psalms*. There, as in *Mere Christianity*, he notes that he writes as a member of the Church of England, while also aiming to avoid controversial matters as much as he can. He goes on to observe, however, that on a certain issue he addresses in his book, he differs from both Roman Catholics and "Fundamentalists." Despite this, he expresses his hope that both parties will extend to him their good will, realizing that at least some among them will likely refuse to do so. He concludes by recognizing that his critics may well be right, for he is not without his own flaws. "But then I dare say I am a much more annoying person than I know. (Shall we, perhaps, in Purgatory, see our own faces and hear our own voices as they really were?)"[8] This reference to purgatory is striking indeed, since it comes just a few lines after his stated intention to avoid controversial topics. Apparently he takes it for granted that believing in purgatory is par for the course among many Anglicans of his time.

That Lewis took the doctrine for granted in this way, and seemed to sense no special need to defend it, is also suggested by the fact that he refers to it almost casually in some of his correspondence. Here is a somewhat humorous example in a letter to a female American correspondent:

> I have often had the fancy that one stage in Purgatory might be a great big kitchen in which things are always going wrong—milk boiling over, crockery getting smashed, toast burning, animals stealing. The women have to learn to sit still and mind their own business: the men have to learn to jump up and do something about it. When both sexes have mastered this exercise, they go on to the next....[9]

There is ample evidence, then, that Lewis not only believed in purgatory but did not seem to see it as a particularly controversial doctrine, at least in the form he affirmed it.

While some Protestants, such as Olson, may welcome his support for a contemporary version of purgatory, others see his views on the matter as opening the door to unbiblical notions that will compromise the heart of Protestant theology. For those who generally admire Lewis and his work, criticizing him on a matter like this can be a bit dicey. One strategy is to downplay Lewis's belief in purgatory and to suggest that it is tangential to his overall theology. This sort of maneuver is deployed, for instance, by Wayne Martindale, a professor of English at the aforementioned Wheaton College, in a book dealing with Lewis's treatment of heaven and hell. He begins his own brief chapter on the doctrine by claiming that "Lewis didn't say much about Purgatory," and goes on to point out that Lewis gave it only scant attention, compared to his extensive treatment of heaven and hell.[10] Moreover, Martindale contends that Lewis believed in purgatory on the basis of tradition, and because it appealed to his imagination, rather than for sound biblical and theological reasons. Indeed, Martindale claims that he "appears to believe the necessity of Purgatory against his own logic."[11] Since Lewis believes that salvation is to be received as a total gift, he thinks Lewis is inconsistent to think that our final sanctification cannot be received as a gift without the sort of process he envisions in purgatory.

I want to argue, by contrast, that Lewis's belief in purgatory flows easily and consistently out of his theology, particularly his account of the nature of salvation. While his views on purgatory are clearly not as important or central to his thought as his beliefs about heaven and hell, they are not incidental either. Indeed, purgatory is very much a natural implication of Lewis's account of "mere Christianity," and as we shall see, he suggested as much in his most famous book of Christian apologetics.

LEWIS ON SALVATION

Let us begin our examination of Lewis's account of salvation by looking at his theory of the atonement, a doctrine that is obviously central to the Christian story of how God redeems us and saves us from our sins. It is not insignificant that Lewis gives his interpretation of this doctrine in the chapter of *Mere Christianity* that immediately follows what is probably the most famous passage in the book, namely, his "trilemma" argument for the deity of Christ.[12] The trilemma is generated by the extraordinary claims Christ made on his own behalf, one of the most striking of which was that he had the authority to forgive sins. Lewis's conclusion that Christ is indeed who he claimed to be, the Son of God who has the right to forgive sins, leads him to explore the question of just how his death and resurrection saves us.

While Lewis provides an answer to this question, it is important to emphasize that he offers his theory of the atonement as nothing more than that, a theory. He certainly recognizes that the atonement itself is essential to Christianity, but insists that a particular understanding of how it works is not. It is, however, noteworthy in this connection that he rejects the view that is probably the most popular among Protestant evangelicals, the "penal substitutionary" theory of atonement, which holds that Christ was punished in our place and thereby satisfied the justice and wrath of God, allowing us to be forgiven. He admits to finding this view morally implausible as well as "silly," though not as much so as he previously did.

Lewis's theory of atonement is colored, naturally, by his understanding of the human predicament, of how our sin has affected our relationship with God. He describes fallen human beings as having gotten themselves into a big hole and needing help to get out of it. The question is what sort of hole we are in. As Lewis sees it, we have dug ourselves in by going our own way and acting as if we are independent beings who belong to ourselves. As such, we need far more drastic measures than any sort of superficial treatment aimed merely at making us better than we are.

> In other words, fallen man is not simply an imperfect creature who needs improvement: he is a rebel who must lay down his arms. Laying down your arms, surrendering, saying you are sorry, realising that you have been on the wrong track and getting ready to start life over again from the ground floor—that is the only way out of our "hole." This process of surrender—this movement full speed astern—is what Christians call repentance.[13]

Lewis's conviction that the only way out of this hole is by way of radical repentance, "from the ground floor," is the key to understanding his view of the atonement.

In his view, the heart of the work of atonement is accomplished in the ironic role that he ascribes to Christ when he calls him the "perfect penitent." The irony lies in the fact that a perfect person does not need to repent, but only such a person could repent perfectly. Since none of us is perfect, no merely human being could successfully pull off this project. And since God in his nature never has to surrender, suffer, and die, he does not seem suited to the task. However, Lewis reasons, if God became man, if he took on human nature, the resulting person could achieve what is needed. "He could surrender His will, and suffer and die, because He was man; and he could do it perfectly because He was God. You and I can go through this process only if God does it in us; but God can do it only if He becomes man."[14]

In surrendering his will, even to the point of death, Christ offered to God the perfect repentance, the complete apology if you will, that none of us could offer, and he thereby made good our deficiency. "This is the sense in which he pays our debt, and suffers for us what He Himself need not suffer at all."[15] The atonement so understood is still "substitutionary" in some sense, though not in the penal sense of Christ taking our punishment. Rather, he is our substitute who surrenders his will completely to God on behalf of all of us who have not.[16]

However, it is very important to be clear that Lewis does not believe that Christ is our substitute in the sense that we are now exempt from perfect repentance since he did it on our behalf. Quite to the contrary—repentance is not an optional matter that God can dispense with, nor is it what God requires of us before he will take us back. Rather, "it is simply a description of what going back to Him is like. If you ask God to take you back without it, you are really asking Him to let you go back without going back. It cannot happen."[17] As Lewis sees it then, Christ's perfect penitence makes it possible for us to do what we must do in order to return to God, but could not do on our own. The radical repentance, from the ground floor up, which is necessary for us to be saved, must still be accomplished. The atonement means that what was previously impossible for us is now possible because he will accomplish it in us if we let him.

Lewis's emphasis on repentance as the very essence of what is necessary for us to be saved highlights another significant sense in which his account of salvation is at odds with many Protestant evangelicals. For many of them, the heart of the matter is justification by faith. In particular, justification is understood to be God's gift to those who have faith in Christ's atonement, typically understood in terms of penal substitution. For those so justified, Christ's righteousness is "imputed" to them so that God views them as righteous.[18]

By striking contrast, Lewis never once employs the term "justification" in *Mere Christianity*, nor does he ever suggest that faith is a matter of having the righteousness of Christ imputed to us. Accordingly, it is not the case that those who have trusted in Christ are viewed as righteous in such a way that all their sins, past, present, and future, are covered by his blood. While it is clear that he believes that Christians who put their faith in Christ are justified in the sense that they are forgiven and accepted by God, he does not subscribe to the notion of "justification by faith" as the term is used by many evangelicals.[19] Nor is it the case that the human race can be neatly divided into two groups: the justified, who are saved and completely assured of heaven, and the unjustified, who are not. Rather, given that repentance, and final salvation, is a "process," the true picture as Lewis sees it is considerably more complicated:

There are people (a great many of them) who are slowly ceasing to be Christians but who still call themselves by that name: some of them are clergymen. There are other people who are slowly becoming Christians though they do not yet call themselves so. There are people who do not accept the full Christian doctrine about Christ but who are so strongly attracted by Him that they are His in a much deeper sense than they themselves understand.[20]

Notice the adverb "slowly" in this passage. The response to God by way of faith and repentance which finally saves, or of unbelief and rebellion which finally leads to damnation, is not an all-at-once matter, but something that happens more gradually over time.

To put it another way, Lewis believes that we are being formed through our everyday choices into persons who have the sort of dispositions that will, at the end of the day, make us at home either in heaven or in hell:

And taking your life as a whole, with all your innumerable choices, all your life long you are slowly turning this central thing [the part of you that chooses] either into a heavenly creature or into a hellish creature: either into a creature that is in harmony with God, and with other creatures, and with itself, or else into one that is in a state of war and hatred with God, and with its fellow creatures, and with itself.[21]

There is nothing arbitrary or legalistic about who enters heaven and is finally saved, as Lewis sees it. We cannot enter heaven if heaven has not first entered us and formed us in its image.

Lewis spelled out his understanding of the relationship between this character formation and faith in a fair amount of detail in two chapters of *Mere Christianity*. There he distinguishes between two levels of faith, the first of which is simply a matter of taking as true the doctrines of Christianity. Faith so understood is a virtue, along with hope and love, because we are at times required to choose to continue to believe what our reason has told us is true despite wavering moods or desires. Developing the virtue of faith in this sense requires us to "train the habit of faith" so that it becomes a settled disposition that remains intact through the various circumstances that tempt us to unbelief.[22]

But Lewis also identifies a second level of faith that is higher than the first one. Faith in this sense, he says, cannot be exercised until someone has gone some distance down the road on their way back to God. Traveling this road is a matter of moral effort, he explains, but somewhat paradoxically, the effort we expend in this fashion will not get us to our goal. Rather, what this effort actually makes clear to us at the deep existential level of genuine experience is that we are incapable of living as God requires us to live. We cannot, however, genuinely arrive at this realization without serious and sustained effort. But when have come to this realization, we are properly prepared to exercise faith in the second and higher sense that Lewis distinguishes. That is, we have arrived at the place that we are truly aware of our inability and therefore ready to trust God to do in us what we cannot do for ourselves.

> The sense in which a Christian leaves it all to God is that he puts all his trust in Christ: trusts that Christ will somehow share with him the perfect human obedience which He carried out from His birth to His crucifixion: that Christ will make the man more like Himself and, in a sense, make good his deficiencies.[23]

Now taken alone, this passage might be taken to mean that Christ shares his perfect obedience with us in the sense that his righteousness is imputed to us. However, a more careful reading shows us that Lewis is saying that Christ is actually making us more like himself, and in that sense making good our deficiencies.

If Lewis's meaning is doubtful here, it is utterly clear later, particularly in book four of *Mere Christianity*, where he elaborates most explicitly on Christ's intentions for us once we open ourselves to him and allow him to have his way with us. Significantly, this final book is about the doctrine of the Trinity, and this is the ultimate theological setting for Lewis's extended reflections on the nature of salvation. For the essence of salvation is a loving relationship that draws us into the fellowship of the Three Persons of the Trinity in order to share the joys and delights of being children of God. Lewis depicts this stunning reality in vibrant terms that are deeply appealing. In Christianity, he points out, "God is not a static thing—not even a person—but a dynamic, pulsating activity, a life, almost a kind of drama. Almost, if you will not think me irreverent, a kind of dance."[24] So for us to participate in this relationship, we must join the drama and take our place in the dance. Therein lies our true happiness and fulfillment, and indeed, this is the only possible way we can hope to experience the joy and satisfaction for which we were created.

Lewis underscores this claim by insisting that the whole point of Christianity is that we become like Christ so that we can share in the eternal life of God. If we are willing to "let God have His way," we will share in the very life of Christ, and "we also shall be sons of God. We shall love the Father as He does and the Holy Ghost will arise in us." Notice again that his description of the essence of salvation is in Trinitarian terms that involve all three Persons of the Godhead. He concludes the chapter by reiterating again what he takes to be the very center of the Christian enterprise. "Every Christian is to become a little Christ. The whole purpose of becoming a Christian is simply nothing else."[25]

Now this extraordinary description of what God is up to can sound daunting and unrealistic. That each of us should become a "little Christ" who is so thoroughly transformed that we "love the Father as He does" may sound like a goal that is not only utterly out of reach for us, but also very much at odds with the reality of who we are as we struggle with various sins, defects, and embarrassing weaknesses. Lewis is mindful of this and offers an encouraging description of how God's purpose for us goes forward in a matter as simple as saying our prayers. The transformation that is taking place in such encounters is not accomplished by our own efforts, nor is it simply a matter of us finding inspiration in Christ and doing our best to follow his example and be like him. Rather, Christ himself is the agent of transformation who is remaking us in his image every time we engage him in prayer. Lewis reminds us in very strong terms that Christ remains very much a living man, as much so as any one of us, and still as much God as he was before the world began. It is the very Son of God who is steadily at work in our lives, putting our old self to death and replacing it with a self like his, however slow and sporadic the progress may sometimes appear to be.[26]

As this remarkable reality sinks in, it must be utterly clear, Lewis insists, that Christ is singularly committed to finishing the job. While we may be satisfied with much less than he has in mind, and gladly settle for something far short of what he is determined to accomplish in our lives, he never will be. If we have overcome our more obvious and demoralizing sins and have made decent moral progress, we may be content to stop there. However, we should be under no illusion that he will settle for anything short of making us completely like himself. Christ was not talking "vague, idealistic gas" when he called his disciples to perfection.[27] He meant exactly what he said.

> That is why He warned people to "count the cost" before becoming Christians. "Make no mistake," He says, "if you let me, I will make you perfect. The moment you put yourself in My hands, that is what you are in for. Nothing less, or other, than that. You have free will, and if you choose, you can push Me away. But if you do not push me away, understand that I am going to see the job through. Whatever suffering it may cost you in your early life, whatever inconceivable purification it may cost you after death, whatever it costs Me, I will never rest, nor let you rest, until you are literally perfect—until my Father can say without reservation that He is well pleased with you, as He said He was well pleased with me. This I can do and will do. But I will not do anything less."[28]

As committed as Christ is to our perfection, there is one possible obstacle that he may not be able to overcome, namely, our freedom. While we do not have the ability to transform ourselves, or to become perfect by our own power, we do have the ability to prevent him from making us so. We cannot bargain for less than perfection or call the shots if we want him to remain in our lives, but we can push him away and refuse to allow him to finish what he started, a point that Lewis goes on to reiterate several times.[29]

Notice also that the perfection Christ is determined to accomplish in our lives may cost us "inconceivable purification" after death. Lewis does not elaborate on this point here, but it is clear that he thinks there will be postmortem work to be done in order to complete the project of our perfection. A few paragraphs after the long passage above, he repeats the striking vision of what God plans to do in our lives, insisting that nothing ever recorded of the greatest saints in terms of holiness or heroism is beyond what he finally intends to do in all of us. "The job will not be completed in this life; but he means to get us as far as possible before death."[30]

Now then, let us summarize. We have seen that on Lewis's view, the human plight is that we are desperately in need of assistance to get us out of a hole we have gotten ourselves into by our sinful choice to live as if we belong to ourselves. We need radical repentance, to return to God from the ground up, but are incapable of doing this on our own. God has provided exactly what we need in Christ, the "perfect penitent" who offered to God on our behalf the apology we could not by surrendering his will completely to God, even to the point of death on the cross. Christ's atonement does not, however, exempt us from the necessity of perfect repentance and transformation, but rather empowers and enables it. Consequently, faith in Christ does not mean that his righteousness is imputed to us, but rather, that we open our lives to him to let him have his way with us and allow him to do in and through us what we cannot pull off in our own power. His aim for us is nothing less than complete perfection, so much so that when it is accomplished we will be "little Christs." Our free assent to his work of transforming us must be ongoing, and if we grant it, he will carry the job forward as much as possible in this life. However, the job will not be finished in this life, and will require postmortem purification.

It is now apparent, I take it, why purgatory is a straightforward implication of Lewis's account of salvation, and integral to it. It is perhaps not surprising that many readers of Lewis would overlook this, particularly those whose primary interest may lie in the apologetic arguments of the first two books of *Mere Christianity*, and less so in his soteriology in book four. However, there is a straight line of thought from the striking argument for the deity of Christ, to the immediately following account of the atonement, to the final book on the Trinity. The deity of Christ shows us that God contains more than one person, and this is the ground of the Christian conviction that God is love in his eternal nature. God did not need the world to love since there is eternal love among the persons of the Trinity.[31] The transformational view of salvation that Lewis elaborates in this context emphasizes that God invites, indeed, entices us to join the eternal dance of love and thereby find the happiness for which we were created. But love cannot be forced, and unwilling dance partners cannot truly enjoy the dance.

Let us turn now to see how Lewis himself drew the implication of purgatory, and to look in more detail at how he understood the doctrine.

FRAMING LEWIS'S VIEW: MORE IS LESS, NEWMAN IS MORE

A good way to begin here is by returning to *Letters to Malcolm*, which we looked at earlier to establish that Lewis in fact believed in purgatory. That volume also provides us with Lewis's most explicit account of his rationale for the doctrine and how he understands it. Given our discussion above, we should not be surprised at his explanation:

Our souls *demand* Purgatory, don't they? Would it not break the heart if God said to us, "It is true, my son, that your breath smells and your rags drip with mud and slime, but we are charitable here and no one will upbraid you with these things, nor draw away from you. Enter into joy"? Should we not reply, "With submission, sir, and if there is no objection, I'd *rather* be cleansed first." "It may hurt, you know"—"Even so, sir."[32]

What is immediately striking about this passage is that the demand for purgatory comes from the soul itself. Its own desire to be purified transforms purgatory into a petition rather than a penalty to be undergone, even if there is pain involved. And if pain is involved, Lewis is convinced it will be exactly what is needed to accomplish the cure. His favorite image for this comes from the dentist after he has pulled a tooth, and tells us to " 'Rinse your mouth out with this.' *This* will be Purgatory. The rinsing may take longer than I can now imagine. The taste of *this* may be more fiery and astringent than my present sensibility could endure."[33]

It is also worth pointing out here that Lewis goes on to observe that the doctrine of purgatory implies that departed souls remain in time in some sense. The notion that the experience of the blessed dead is strictly timeless, he feels, is inconsistent with the (presumably future) resurrection of the body. By contrast, however, he believes that God has no experience of time as we know it, and this leads him to the conclusion that we are eternal in the eyes of God, in our deepest reality. "When I say we are 'in time' I don't mean that we are, impossibly, outside the endless present in which He beholds us as He beholds all else. I mean, our creaturely limitation is that our fundamentally timeless reality can be experienced by us only in the mode of succession."[34] The notion that our perception of time is merely a matter of our "creaturely limitation" is puzzling, and we shall come back to this issue later. For now, let us return to explore in more detail the theological substance of his view of purgatory.

Lewis gives us a large window into his view when he registers his opinion that the Reformers had good grounds for doubting "the Romish doctrine concerning Purgatory" in the form that was prevalent at the time of the Reformation.[35] The main issue for Lewis was not the "commercial scandal" but the appalling "degradation" of the doctrine between Dante and the sixteenth century. To illustrate this degradation, he cites two English theologians, namely, John Fisher and Thomas More, both of whom depict purgatory essentially as a temporary hell. The original etymology of the word "purgatory" has been so completely obscured in these writers that it is no longer a place of purification, but rather of excruciating retributive punishment.[36]

While Lewis dispenses with More and Fisher in a single paragraph in *Letters to Malcolm*, he discusses the views of both writers at more length in his scholarly work *English Literature in the Sixteenth Century Excluding Drama*. The work of More that he discusses in this connection is his little volume *The Supplication of Souls*, which was written in response to a book entitled *A Supplication for the Beggars* by Simon Fish. The latter volume was a polemical attack on clerical corruption, particularly as displayed in the financial exploitation of the doctrine of purgatory. Fish claimed to write on behalf of the poor suffering beggars who allegedly were neglected because money that should have been spent to relieve them was being plundered by greedy clergymen wielding threats of purgatory and promises of deliverance from its pains. His book was addressed to King Henry VIII, who gladly received its message, including the recommendation that the King seize Church property amassed in such a corrupt fashion.[37]

More's book in reply is an eloquent defense of purgatory, written as if it comes from souls who are currently there, suffering its pains, and imploring those yet alive on earth to remember them with compassion. More aims to convince his readers that the souls in purgatory suffer more grievously than any beggars in this life, so any efforts or resources spent on their behalf is more than justified. Echoing the classic idea, going back at least to Augustine, that the pain of purgatory exceeds any pain of this life, the souls there insist that "never have you known pain comparable to ours, whose fire as far surpasses in heat all the fires that ever burned upon earth as the hottest of all those surpasses an imaginary fire painted on the wall."[38] Indeed, these poor souls as More depicts them feel deeply neglected and ignored by their friends and loved ones on earth, and plead with them to be more mindful of their suffering and to do all they can to help free them from purgatory as soon as possible.

Lewis found it particularly objectionable that the torments in More's purgatory are inflicted by devils. On this point, he found More's account even worse than Fisher's, where the torments are meted out by angels, which preserved at least some minimal connection between purgatory and heaven. To designate devils as the tormentors, however, severed any final link with heaven, and thereby made purgatory a "department of hell."[39] And indeed, More paints the handiwork of these demons in lurid colors that are memorably macabre. The miserable souls in purgatory poignantly complain that the demons show them numerous cruel sights to intensify their anguish. For instance, they show them the possessions they previously valued and then mock them for the love they once had for such things. Moreover, they show them scenes of their wives flirting with other men, and their children dancing and singing with no more concern or thought for their dead father than for an old pair of shoes.[40] The following passage, cited by Lewis, sums up the sinister craft of these devilish tormentors and the role they play in magnifying the unspeakable misery of purgatory.

> Our keepers are such as may God keep you from—cruel damned spirits, odious, envious, hateful, pitiless enemies and vicious tormenters. Their company is more horrible and agonizing to us than the pain itself and the intolerable torment they inflict on us, with which they never cease to continually lacerate us from top to toe.[41]

When we recall that the fire of purgatory was already described as more painful than any fire in this life, we can appreciate Lewis's observation above that the Reformers had good reason to inveigh against "the Romish doctrine concerning Purgatory."

Lewis made similar observations in his discussion of John Fisher, the bishop of Rochester, and a cardinal who, like More, was martyred by Henry VIII. He sees in

Fisher a good representative of what the Reformers like Tyndale were attacking, beginning with his doctrine of penance which requires sinners to make satisfaction as a sort of balancing of accounts. Coupled with this notion was Fisher's rather extreme version of asceticism that was suspicious of the body and of physical pleasures, even within the confines of marriage. Beyond all this, however, was an issue that was still more deeply troubling:

> Even more important, if we are to understand why the Reformers, whether rightly or wrongly, felt that they were escaping from a prison, is Fisher's conception of purgatory. A modern tends to see purgatory through the eyes of Dante: so seen, the doctrine is profoundly religious. That purification must, in its own nature, be painful, we hardly dare to dispute. But in Fisher that pain seems to have no intrinsic connection with the purification at all: it is a pain which, while it lasts, separates us from God.[42]

Here, in modern English, is the passage, along with its larger context, that Lewis cites from Fisher to show this:

> Since the sorrows of this world occupy the mind more vehemently than its pleasures, and the pleasures of this world (if they are great and excessive) do not allow the soul to remember itself, much less, then, shall the soul abiding in torments have any remembrance. The pains of purgatory being much greater than the pains of this world, who in that painful place can remember God as he ought to? Therefore, the prophet says, *quoniam non est in morte, qui memor sit tui*, no creature being in purgatory may have you in remembrance as he should.[43]

As Lewis remarks, Dante's purgative pains appear to have become merely retributive in Fisher. He goes on to cite a line from Tyndale's answer to More that represents the Reformer's perception of this conception of purgatory: "To punish a man that has forsaken sin of his own accord is not to purge him but to satisfy the lust of a tyrant."[44]

After summarily rejecting the views of More and Fisher in *Letters to Malcolm*, Lewis goes on to commend another writer he saw as recovering the correct account of purgatory. "The right view returns magnificently in Newman's *Dream*," he writes, going on to add that Newman portrays the saved soul as begging to be cleansed, since it "cannot bear for a moment longer 'With its darkness to affront that light.'" This last line, which Lewis borrowed from Milton, explicates what he takes to be the cardinal shift that Newman represents: "Religion has reclaimed Purgatory."[45]

Recall from the quote above that Lewis described Dante's view of purgatory as "profoundly religious," which is the view he suggests has been reclaimed by Newman. Indeed, the passage about Newman just cited is immediately followed by the one quoted at the beginning of this section, which describes purgatory as something that is *demanded* by truly religious souls, rather than something imposed on them against their wishes.

The full title of Newman's book that Lewis mentions in abbreviated fashion is *The Dream of Gerontius*, a longish poem (by normal standards, not in comparison to Dante's *Comedy*), which was first published in 1865 and quickly became a best seller. This poem recounts in dramatic fashion the death of an old man and the journey of his soul to the throne of God. The passage Lewis alludes to is near the end, at the climactic moment when the soul, hastened by the energy of love, flies toward the feet of Christ on the throne. Before the soul reaches the throne, however, the sanctity it encounters from a single glance of God scorches and shrivels it. At this point, the soul prays to be sent to purgatory as it cannot bear "With its darkness to affront that light." Here is the full stanza in which the religious soul "demands" purgatory:

> Take me away, and in the lowest deep
> There let me be,
> And there in hope the lone night-watches keep,
> Told out for me.
> There, motionless and happy in my pain,
> Lone, not forlorn,—
> There will I sing my sad perpetual strain,
> Until the morn.
> There will I sing, and soothe my stricken breast,
> Which ne'er can cease
> To throb, and pine, and languish, till possest
> Of its Sole Peace.
> There will I sing my absent Lord and Love:—
> Take me away,
> That sooner I may rise, and go above,
> And see Him in the truth of everlasting day.[46]

Because the soul longs to be able to "see Him in the truth of everlasting day," to be able to bask forever in God's presence in complete peace and joy, it gladly embraces the necessary purification as an act of devotion and love.[47] Like the souls in Dante who sing as they climb the mountain, thereby celebrating the pain that heals, Gerontius, too, delights in the purging that will hasten his full entry into the presence of his Lord.[48]

We now have a pretty clear picture not only of how Lewis conceived purgatory positively, but also the sort of views he roundly rejects. Let us turn now to look at another suggestive account of purgatory in the Lewis corpus, namely, that found in his theological fantasy *The Great Divorce*.

SHADES OF GREY TOWN: PURGATORY IN *THE GREAT DIVORCE*

Lewis takes pains in the preface of this little volume to specify that the divorce he wants to depict in his fantasy is the inevitable conflict and ultimate divide between heaven and hell. It is totally misguided to imagine, as Blake did, that the two could possibly be married. This pernicious error presents itself in the facile notion that reality does not require of us a radical either/or choice in which we must choose definitively between good and evil. Contrary to this error, Lewis wants to insist that we cannot hold onto evil of any kind, we cannot retain any part of hell, but must reject it decisively if we want to choose heaven. This is not to say that every one who chooses evil is lost, but it is the case that all who do choose it must be put back on the right road to be saved. "A sum can be put right: but only by going back till you find the error and working it afresh from that point, never by simply *going on*. Evil can be undone, but it cannot 'develop' into good. Time does not heal it."[49] Lewis's point here is obviously reminiscent of his claim we noted above that salvation requires a thoroughgoing repentance from the ground floor. Lewis's aim in *The Great Divorce* is to depict for us the nature of the choice we must all finally make in deciding between the radically opposed alternatives of heaven and hell.

The fascinating premise of this volume is that a group of shades from hell take a bus ride to the outskirts of heaven and are invited, indeed encouraged in every way, to stay. Common sense dictates that, of course, the shades would gladly and gratefully accept the invitation and leave the misery of hell behind forever. The surprise, even shock, of this remarkable fantasy is that the dictates of common sense are confounded over and over again as the shades refuse the opportunity to remain in heaven and opt instead to return to hell.

After observing several such scenes, Lewis, as the narrator of the fantasy, encounters George McDonald, the Scottish writer whose works influenced him so profoundly. Lewis raises the question of whether the ghosts really can stay in heaven, or whether it is all an elaborate hoax. Heaven, after all, is quite uncomfortable for the ghosts from hell, and seems quite unsuited for them, as symbolized memorably, among other ways, by the fact that the grass hurts their insubstantial feet. Indeed, Lewis's narrative puts on dramatic display for us the observation of Newman, quoted in the introduction, that "Heaven would be hell to an irreligious man." One of the bright spirits in heaven acknowledges this reality, even as he offers encouragement to stay in heaven and become acclimatized to it. "Will you come with me to the mountains?" he asks. "It will hurt at first, until your feet are hardened. Reality is harsh to the feet of shadows. But will you come?"[50] Like most of the ghosts in the story, he declines.

McDonald initially answers Lewis's question as to whether the ghosts can actually stay in heaven by referring to the relatively obscure notion of the *refrigerium*, the idea that the damned occasionally experience relief from hell and even have temporary holidays or excursions elsewhere, including to the outskirts of heaven. Lewis persists in asking whether any of them really can stay, and McDonald cites the emperor Trajan as an example of someone who did. This is most interesting, particularly in light of our discussion of the emperor in the last chapter in connection with the idea of postmortem conversion. At this point Lewis is perplexed, and asks, "Is judgment not final? Is there really a way out of Hell into Heaven?"[51]

Now before considering McDonald's fascinating reply to this crucial question, let us note that Lewis raised this question elsewhere, in his scholarly work *A Preface to Paradise Lost*. In his discussion of "Satan's Followers" in that book, he draws some "mundane" comparisons to those fiends who have recently fallen out of heaven into hell. They are like a man who has been a traitor to his country, or has betrayed his friend and knows he is now a pariah, or like a man who has irrevocably hurt a woman he loves by some intolerable action. "For human beings there is often an escape from this Hell, but there is never more than one—the way of humiliation, repentance, and (where possible) restitution. For Milton's devils this way is closed. The poet very wisely never really allows the question 'What if they *did* repent?' to become actual."[52] The reason that he does not raise this question is because the devils have made it clear that they have no interest in repenting, which implies something most interesting about hell, but very much at odds with popular conceptions of it. "The door out of Hell is firmly locked, by the devils themselves, on the inside; whether it is also locked on the outside need not, therefore, be considered."[53]

The question that Milton never allowed to become actual is not only raised but persistently pressed by Lewis, as we have already seen. Moreover, he appears to return a positive answer to the question (through McDonald's character), as the example of Trajan appears to suggest. However, the matter is more complicated, as shown in the reply McDonald gives to the question of whether there is actually a way out of hell into heaven:

> "It depends on the way ye're using the words. If they leave that grey town behind it will not have been Hell. To any that leaves it, it is Purgatory. And perhaps ye had better not call this country Heaven. *Not Deep Heaven*, ye understand." (Here he smiled at me.) "Ye can call it the Valley of the Shadow of Life."[54]

Strictly speaking then, it appears there is no way out of hell into heaven, though it is possible to leave the grey town, and for those who choose to do so, it is purgatory.

Still, Lewis is not satisfied with this answer and persists in asking whether there is a genuine choice to be made after death. "My Roman Catholic friends would be surprised, for to them, souls in Purgatory are already saved. And my Protestant friends would like it no better, for they'd say that the tree lies as it falls."[55] To this, McDonald replies that perhaps both are right. The problem, he goes on to explain, is that it is very difficult to understand the relationship between our choices and time so long as we remain in time and continue to choose our eternal destiny. The point of the trip to heaven, however, is not to solve such mysteries, but rather to come to understand the nature of the fundamental choice involved. That, McDonald says, can be observed in the various characters as they decide whether to stay in heaven or return to hell.

Now this brings us to a central issue for Lewis. Just what is the nature of the essential choice, either for heaven or for hell? Here is his description of the fundamental choice of those who return to hell. "There is always something they insist on keeping even at the price of misery. There is always something they prefer to joy—that is, to reality."[56] The equation of joy with reality is striking, and echoes an earlier line where McDonald rejects out of hand the popular notion that heaven is merely a state of mind. While hell may rightly be called a state of mind, this is decidedly not true of heaven. "Heaven is reality itself. All that is fully real is Heavenly."[57]

Now if the choice of hell consists in preferring something to joy, to reality, then it is easy enough to see that the choice of heaven is the choice of reality, which is equivalent to choosing joy. And it is similarly easy to see that purgatory is a matter of coming to terms with reality by those who are out of sorts with it. Heaven is joyful in its very essence, but is not experienced as such by those who are at odds with it. "Reality is harsh to the feet of shadows," to all those who choose the lie of living as if they belong only to themselves and thereby cut themselves off from true joy. But those who are willing to embrace reality and become acclimatized to it can soon rollick in the grass that previously caused them pain.

Purgatory, then, appears to be the way out of the grey town and into heaven. And this way is open to anyone who truly wants to leave the grey town. This point is emphasized a bit later, when Lewis asks McDonald about the poor souls who never get to the bus to take the ride to heaven. McDonald assures him that he need not fear for such souls, for anyone who really wants to go to heaven will have the opportunity to do so.

"There are only two kinds of people in the end: those who say to God, 'Thy will be done,' and those to whom God says, in the end, 'Thy will be done.' All that are in Hell, choose it. Without that self-choice there could be no Hell. No soul that seriously and constantly desires joy will ever miss it. Those who seek find. To those who knock it is opened."[58]

It is clear, moreover, that in Lewis's vision, God's open door policy is fully sincere, and that God does everything he can, short of overriding freedom, to move his sinful creatures to knock at the door and enter his joy. This point is emphasized by the very next character to enter the narrative, a creature with a "thin" voice, who is speaking very rapidly in a soliloquy of self-pity. Lewis goes on to describe her as a "garrulous old woman" who doesn't seem even remotely to be the sort of creature who should be in danger of damnation. To the contrary, it seems that all she needs is a little kindness and rest and she would be fine. McDonald replies that if that is indeed the case, she most certainly will be cured. The crucial question, however, is whether she is still a grumbler, or has degenerated into merely a grumble. "If there is a real woman—even the least trace of one—still there inside the grumbling, it can be brought to life again. If there's one wee spark under all those ashes, we'll blow it till the whole pile is red and clear."[59]

The clear implication is that if there is any hope of rehabilitating a sinner, God will do whatever he can to accomplish this. If there is any spark of humanity left, "any germ of a desire for God" still remaining, then there is hope that the creature can yet be saved.[60] However, it is also suggested that a person can so resist God and refuse the invitation to joy that he loses all personality and reduces himself to mere ashes, or remains. In that case, the grumble may remain, but will have lost all hope or desire of ever unlocking the doors of hell and knocking on the doors of heaven. In any event, it is unclear whether there is any spark left in this woman, and we are not told whether she was saved or not.[61]

There is, however, one unequivocal example of a ghost who chooses to leave the grey town behind and to enter "deep heaven." For such a person, again, the grey town is purgatory, so we can learn from his example something of how Lewis conceives of the choice to pass through it on the way to heaven. This character appears near the end of the book, and is most distinguished by the fact that he has a red lizard perched on his shoulder and chattering in his ear. The lizard, which represents lust, is the thing he prefers to joy, and holds onto, even at the price of misery. His conflict is most memorable as he is deeply torn between his desire to give up his lust and enter heaven, and his reluctance to do so, fearing he will lose his very self if he does. A flaming Angel offers to dispose of the lizard, but he resists when he learns that the Angel means to kill it. It would be fine to silence it, he proposes by way of compromise, but killing it is too drastic a measure. The Angel insists there is no other way, and presses him to allow him to kill it, for he cannot do so without the man's consent. Finally, after a prolonged struggle, he grants the Angel permission to do so. "Next moment the Ghost gave a scream of agony such as I never heard on Earth. The Burning One closed his crimson grip on the reptile: twisted it, while it bit and writhed, and then flung it, broken-backed, on the turf."[62]

What follows is most remarkable, as the lizard is transformed into a shiny stallion with rippled flesh and muscle. The man, likewise transformed, throws himself at the feet of the Burning One in gratitude before joyously mounting the horse and riding off into the mountains. The lesson drawn from this incident is that our sinful substitutes for reality are poor, pitiful imitations of what God wishes to grant us if we will submit to his will and allow him fully to remake us. But the choice to submit to this transformation requires the death of our sinful self, and it is vain to look for a spiritual anesthesia that will make this process entirely pain free.

MERE PURGATORY?

We are now in a position to sum up Lewis's account of purgatory and to offer an answer to the question we raised at the outset of this chapter, namely, whether his views hold promise for an ecumenical version of the doctrine.

Let us begin by situating Lewis's view with respect to the issue of which model of the doctrine he affirms. Recall from an earlier chapter that there are various models of purgatory along a spectrum that has pure satisfaction on one end, and pure sanctification on the other. We also sketched a rough (tentative) history of the doctrine in this regard, in which early official versions of the doctrine were a combination in various degrees of satisfaction/sanctification, followed later by a lengthy period after Dante in which satisfaction was the primary, if not the sole emphasis. By the twentieth century, the pendulum had swung back in the direction of models that stressed sanctification over satisfaction, so much so that in contemporary Roman Catholic theology, it is arguable that a sanctification model has become fully dominant.

Now, it is clear in the first place that Lewis's model of purgatory is a thoroughgoing sanctification model. While he stoutly repudiates "the Romish doctrine concerning Purgatory," as that doctrine had degenerated by the time of the Reformation, he avoids the overreaction of throwing out the baby of purification with the murky bathwater of satisfaction and retribution. Lewis recognizes that the doctrine not only makes pastoral and devotional sense in terms of praying for the dead, but even more, he saw it as the natural "demand" of the soul on the way to perfection, and this is his primary reason for affirming the doctrine. Complete purification and sanctification is not only necessary for a fully restored relationship with God in the very nature of things, it is also the heart's cry of the converted person on the road of radical repentance, who can never be satisfied with anything less than the perfect fellowship with God for which we were created. The fact that Lewis sees this as the essence of the true understanding of purgatory points up the ecumenical promise of his view, for not only is it the case that many Protestants who are sympathetic to the doctrine see it as the completion of the sanctification process, but the same is true in contemporary Roman Catholic thought.

Second, while it is clear that Lewis rejects retributive punishment in purgatory as a distortion of the true doctrine, he does not shrink from the notion that there are certain kinds of pain intrinsically connected with purification. Coming to terms with truth and reality is unpleasant if we are at odds with it, as he shows so vividly in various ways in *The Great Divorce*. It is, however, the only way out of our self-imposed misery, and if we are unwilling to take that way, we remain in a prison constructed and maintained by own free choices. Recall Lewis's observation that those who have made treacherous choices have only one way out of their hell, "the way of humiliation, repentance, and (where possible) restitution." This way is undeniably a painful one, so those in this predicament have the option of embracing the productive pain that leads to reconciliation and healing, or remaining in the fruitless pain generated by perpetual impenitence.[63]

Sometimes this pain may be nothing more than the embarrassment of honest self-awareness, which may involve more than a touch of humor. We can see this in Lewis's amusing suggestion that one level of purgatory may involve men and women learning how they need to respond to a crisis in the kitchen, as well as his remark from *Reflections on the Psalms*, that we may see our own faces and hear our own voices as they really are, particularly when they are annoying. Seeing the truth about ourselves and our flaws and foibles is seldom to be relished, but it is essential to show us how we need to change, as well as to motivate us to make the necessary adjustments that are required if we are to be purged of those flaws.

At any rate, Lewis's recognition of the intrinsic connections between pain and purification retains an essential component of the traditional conception of purgatory, while repudiating the notion that the pain is arbitrarily imposed or meted out as a matter of punitive retribution. This not only avoids what he and many other Protestants find objectionable about the doctrine as it had degenerated at the time of the Reformation, but also accords with the emphasis on sanctification in current Roman Catholic theology. Consider this description of "interior penance" from the *Catechism of the Catholic Church*:

> Interior repentance is a radical re-orientation of our whole life, a return, a conversion to God with all our heart, an end of sin, a turning away from evil, with repugnance toward the evil we have committed.... This conversion of heart is accompanied by a salutary pain and sadness which the Fathers called *animi cruciatus* (affliction of spirit) and *compunction cordis* (repentance of heart).[64]

The "salutary pain" that is inherent in radical repentance is essentially the same as the profitable pain of the soul that demands purgatory in Lewis's sense.

Third, Lewis's view of purgatory is premised on a very strong view of human freedom, and the necessity of our cooperation for God to accomplish his purpose of perfecting us and making us like Christ. It is clear in his account, moreover, that God truly loves all persons and does all he can, consistent with human freedom, to rehabilitate lost sinners. It is the persistent choice of evil, and the corresponding rejection of grace, that defines the choice to remain in hell rather than to enter heaven, if that requires passing through the pain of purgatory. Lewis's view that God gives sinners every chance to repent that might be taken seems to be very much in agreement with the modified view of purgatory we examined in the previous chapter. That is, his views seem to allow that there could be postmortem repentance, and that God would welcome the repentance of any who still have even a germ of a desire for him.[65] This modification of purgatory has appealed to a number of Protestant thinkers, as well as contemporary Roman Catholics.

Whether in this life or the next, Lewis holds that our ultimate choice of heaven or hell is disclosed in a series of choices that we make over time, a series of choices that are often halting, uncertain, and even inconsistent. While time alone can never turn evil into good, the choice to turn away from evil and return to God does require time. Here it must be noted that there is a tension in Lewis's thought between the essentially temporal nature of this process, and his claim, noted above, that our fundamental reality is "timeless" since we are eternal in God's eyes.[66] What he seems to mean by this is that God, in his timeless knowledge of all things, sees all our choices as eternally present, and thereby views us in our settled final destiny.

In *The Great Divorce*, Lewis expresses this thought by saying that in a sense the saved have always been in heaven, and the damned have always been in hell. When good is fully grown, he suggests, it will work backward and transform even agonies into glories, and likewise when evil reaches full flower, it will retrospectively contaminate and corrupt all past pleasures. "And that is why, at the end of things, when the sun rises here and the twilight turns to blackness down there, the Blessed will say 'We have never lived anywhere except in Heaven,' and the Lost, 'We were always in Hell.' "[67] Lewis comes back to this issue at the end of the book, and again cautions (through the character of McDonald) that "every attempt to see the shape of eternity except through the lens of Time destroys your knowledge of Freedom." The choices we make in time really are choices in which we could have done otherwise, and freedom is "the gift whereby ye most resemble your Maker and are yourselves parts of eternal reality."[68]

Again, Lewis makes clear that he thinks our free choices are undetermined, and that God does everything he can, consistent with our freedom, to elicit from us a positive response to his love and grace. Our choice is not final until we have either decisively rejected evil and allowed God fully to perfect us, or until we have completely rejected all his overtures and put to death every last germ of desire for him.

This account accords very much with the summary observation we noted in the previous chapter that "purgatory is hope." Even more, it resonates deeply with Dante's vision of the God who "doth will to suffer conquest, who by His own love conquered, comes conquering and unconquerable." And while it is morally serious in highlighting God's uncompromising demand for holiness and perfection, it is clear that the demand is motivated by his love and his desire for our true happiness and satisfaction, a demand that is answered by the soul's own yearning for purification. This is not purgatory as a frightful threat, but as a gracious promise. He who has started a good work in us can be counted on to finish it as well. This is not purgatory as a playground for devils imposing their perverse will on hapless victims, but purgatory as the passage way to prepare us for our place in the eternal dance of joy.

It is important to be clear on this point, not only to represent Lewis accurately, but even more for a fair appraisal of the doctrine of purgatory. Critics of the doctrine often have a tendency, sometimes inveterately so, to depict it as a matter of salvation by works and then to reject it highhandedly in the name of grace. However, to pit purgatory against grace is to fail completely to grasp that purgatory itself is very much a matter of grace. To draw this contrast is to ignore the fact that grace is much more than forgiveness, that it is also sanctification and transformation, and finally, glorification. We need more than forgiveness and justification to purge our sinful dispositions and make us fully ready for heaven. Purgatory is nothing more than the continuation of the sanctifying grace we need, for as long as necessary to complete the job, as Lewis put it.

In view of this picture, it should come as no surprise that in one of his last letters before his death, Lewis mentions purgatory with something like amused anticipation. In a letter to Sister Penelope, dated September 17, 1963, he wrote: "When you die, and if 'prison visiting' is allowed, come down and look me up in Purgatory. It *is* all rather fun—solemn fun—isn't it?"[69]

Fun, understandably, is no doubt one of the last words anyone would associate with purgatory as popularly understood, not to mention More and Fisher's account of the doctrine. Anyone who understands Lewis's theology, however, can hardly accuse him of trivializing the matter. His view of the doctrine, as I have shown, flows naturally out of his vision of those profoundly beautiful truths that many believers readily recognize as "mere Christianity." As such, his view of purgatory is one that Protestants, no less than Roman Catholics and Eastern Orthodox, may find not only appealing, but theologically compatible with their deepest convictions about the Trinitarian God of love revealed in Christ and his extravagant gift of salvation.

7

∽

Looking Forward by Looking Back

From those most holy waters, born anew
I came, like trees by change of calendars
Renewed with new-sprung foliage through and through,
Pure and prepared to leap up to the stars.
　　　　　　　　　　　—Dante

As with purgatory itself, a book on the subject should leave those who have made it through with some sense of where their journey has taken them. Dante comes to the end of purgatory, led by the lovely Matilda, "pure and prepared to leap up to the stars." It is too much to expect from the concluding chapter of a mere book that it should evoke an experience of Matilda, let alone the beckoning stars, but we can perhaps recapitulate our journey to see where we have arrived and how we got there.

We began with a story of a cowboy, on the verge of entering eternity, who expected to arrive in heaven with his desires for revenge, along with his gun, intact. But heaven, we noted, is essentially morally perfect, and precludes the desire for revenge, along with other sinful dispositions and desires, whatever the case may be with guns. So if our cowboy has any realistic hopes of entering heaven, his sinful desires and other imperfections must somehow be purged and his character must be reformed in such a way that he is truly good and holy through and through. I have been arguing that the doctrine of purgatory makes best sense of how our cowboy, and countless other Christians who die far short of perfection, as well as others who have not yet accepted Christ, can be appropriately transformed and fitted for heaven.

I offer my defense of purgatory not as a dogma, but as a theological proposal that resolves issues and questions that no developed system of theology can ignore. I offer it, moreover, as a Protestant with a distinctive concern to articulate the doctrine in an ecumenical fashion that may appeal to Christians on both sides of the

Reformation divide. The prospects for such an ecumenical version of the doctrine are raised not only by the fact that a number of Protestant spokesmen have shown a willingness to reconsider it lately, but also by the fact that contemporary Catholic accounts of purgatory are much more amenable to Protestant theology than previously.

Like any substantive theological proposal, this one involves judgments on a number of controversial issues, none of which admit to a knockdown argument or a decisive resolution. There are good reasons in each case for taking the position that is favorable to purgatory, and insofar as one agrees with these judgments, he will be inclined to accept the doctrine. So let us briefly recapitulate those issues.

In the first place, purgatory involves issues of biblical interpretation, and for many Protestants, this is where the conversation not only starts but also ends, for they hold that scripture does not clearly support the doctrine, or worse, that it rules it out. While I agree that scripture does not clearly support the doctrine by way of explicit affirmation, I believe that it does not rule it out either, and that texts cited to show this do not carry nearly as much weight as often claimed. More positively, I believe the doctrine is a reasonable inference from things that are clearly taught in scripture. If so, the debate will have to range much wider, and deeper, than over a few controversial texts, and must address whether the doctrine is compatible with, or perhaps even follows from, one's larger theological commitments, particularly those pertaining to the nature and conditions of salvation.

A second issue is whether the doctrine is compatible with Protestant theology, even on the assumption that it is not explicitly ruled out by scripture. In particular, is it compatible with the doctrine of justification by faith, or is it in tension with this doctrine or does it even undermine it? Notably, the doctrine as attacked by the Reformers, as well as contemporary Protestant critics, is prominently a satisfaction model of purgatory, according to which it is necessary for sinners to pay part of the price of punishment in order to satisfy the justice of God. While we have seen that this model of purgatory is not merely a Protestant caricature of the doctrine, but has in fact been dominant in large stretches of history in Roman theology, it is not the only way the doctrine has been understood. Indeed, it is arguable that satisfaction models represent a significant departure from the original spirit and substance of the doctrine. Regardless, there are other ways of construing purgatory, particularly in terms of sanctification, and these models appear to be perfectly compatible with the Protestant doctrine of justification by faith. If the doctrine is understood in these terms, it is quite beside the point to appeal to the blood of Christ or the fact that justified sinners are no longer under condemnation as grounds for rejecting it.

As we have seen, moreover, it is arguable that the contemporary Roman Catholic account of the doctrine is a sanctification model that is essentially the same as the view of purgatory affirmed by a number of recent Protestant theologians. The current pope, Benedict XVI, has attempted to articulate the heart of the doctrine in a way that will have ecumenical appeal, and that will be consistent with the fundamental theological conviction that salvation is by grace through faith. He repudiates the punitive notion of purgatory, while affirming that a process of trans-formation is essential for final salvation. "Simply to look at people with any degree of realism at all is to grasp the necessity of such a process. It does not replace grace by works, but allows the former to achieve its full victory precisely as grace. What actually saves is the full assent of faith."[1]

In this connection, it is very much to the point to note that there is a lively debate currently going on, particularly among Protestants, about the doctrine of justifica-tion by faith. In particular, the notion of "imputed righteousness" has come under considerable scrutiny by critics who contend that this doctrine is not in fact taught in scripture, despite its impressive pedigree in Protestant tradition. One of the most prominent of these critics, N. T. Wright, has argued that a truly biblical doctrine of justification is fully trinitarian, and must include emphasis on the work of the Holy Spirit in our lives after our initial justification, and as we look forward to our final justification on judgment day:

> Virtue is what happens—I know many in the Reformation tradition shudder at the thought of the very word "virtue," but there is no help for it if we are to be true to Scripture and to trinitarian theology—when the Spirit enables the Christian freely to choose, freely to develop, freely to be shaped by God, freely to *become* that which is pleasing to God.[2]

As I have already noted, Wright is no fan of purgatory.[3] Nevertheless, his emphasis on sanctification and its relation to our final justification raises issues that require further exploration. In particular, if sanctification is essential, and not merely an optional luxury item for those on the way of salvation, the doctrine of purgatory may be crucial for a coherent account of this claim.

This brings us to the third question, which is perhaps the most crucial matter on which the whole issue turns, namely, what role does our free response play in our salvation? With respect to purgatory, this question pertains particularly to our sanc-tification. Is it necessary for us truly and actually to become holy that we undergo a process of moral transformation in which we freely cooperate, or can this transfor-mation be effected by a unilateral, instantaneous act of God the moment we die? Our judgment on this question will go a long way in deciding whether we find more plausible the doctrine of purgatory, or the characteristic Protestant view that we are perfected in the moment of death.

Closely related to this question, in the fourth place, are a cluster of issues per-taining to personal identity. One such issue is cast in epistemic terms as the question of whether there would be sufficient continuity that we could recognize ourselves as the same person were we to undergo dramatic instantaneous moral transforma-tion. The question can also be cast in metaphysical terms, namely, whether genuine moral change is temporal in its very essence. Is it the case that finite agents require time to come to see truth for themselves as it is disclosed to them, and moreover, to own it and internalize it? Furthermore, is moral change and character development essentially a process that takes place in a progressive fashion as we move through various stages which build on each other? Can certain insights and qualities of character only be gained incrementally after other insights and character growth has been achieved? To whatever extent one is inclined to return a positive answer to these questions, he will find it implausible that God can perfect our character with a unilateral act the instant we die.

Fifth, and finally, is God willing to do everything he can, short of overriding our freedom, to elicit from each of us a positive response to his offer of salvation provided by the death and resurrection of Christ? This question is particularly pertinent to the modification of purgatory involving postmortem grace and probation. If one answers this question positively, she will find postmortem probation a reasonable inference, but if she answers negatively, she likely will not.

The doctrine of purgatory is an appealing one because it brings into sharp focus the radiant beauty of the goodness of God, and the hope that entails for us. It is not, however, a frivolous hope, nor one that comes without a certain cost. C. S. Lewis pointed out that in one sense we are in a "terrible fix" if there is a perfectly good being behind the moral law.

> If the universe is not governed by an absolute goodness, then all our efforts are in the long run hopeless. But if it is, then we are making ourselves enemies to that goodness every day, and are not in the least likely to do any better tomorrow, and so our case is hopeless again. We cannot do without it, and we cannot do with it. God is the only comfort, He is also the supreme terror: the thing we most need and the thing we most want to hide from.[4]

If there is a perfectly good God, there is reason to hope that our lives will not end in death or ultimate futility, but rather that our lives have ultimate meaning. There is reason, moreover, to hope that our moral efforts are not in vain, that good will triumph. And this is so not only on the cosmic scale, but in our own individual lives as well. If there is a perfectly good God, then he can change us and give us the moral and spiritual renewal we need, and make us truly good, something we have no hope of pulling off on our own.

And yet, this hope is also deeply unsettling according to Lewis, for in our fallen condition, we are badly at odds with perfect goodness. The cost of the hope is recognizing that the transformation we require is not likely to be pain free. The "cost" that I emphasize comes at the expense of our sinful nature, which resists the Holy Spirit, and the work of sanctification in our lives.[5] Such a "cost," of course, is a paradoxical one, since it is in reality a gain, and one of immeasurable value at that.

I would suggest that the doctrine of purgatory can be thought of as casting Lewis's insight about the goodness of God into an eschatological setting. His perfect goodness grounds hope, and makes possible things that are otherwise unthinkable. He is good in the moral sense that he hates our evil, and demands our purity, but he is also good in the sense that he loves us and desires our happiness and true flourishing, which can only be complete when we are perfected in holiness. This reminds us one more time that purgatory, properly understood, is not an alternative to grace, but is itself an expression of grace.

Of course, we need not wait until purgatory to experience the goodness of God in his gracious work of salvation. It is his will even now that we accept his gifts of justification and sanctification. The more optimistic we are about the possibilities of grace, the more we may hope that even in this life he will carry forward the project of purifying us and conforming us to his likeness. But whether now, or in the life to come, his perfect love and goodness grounds our hope that "the one who began a good work in you will bring it to completion."[6]

NOTES

INTRODUCTION
1. Thanks to Karen Haserot for a comment that inspired this line.
2. Revelation 21:27.
3. Here and in the rest of this paragraph, I follow Justin D. Bernard, "Purgatory and the Dilemma of Sanctification," *Faith and Philosophy* 24 (2007): 312–314.
4. This does not mean, of course, that God would like to sin, but cannot. The desire to sin is itself sinful. For more on God's necessary goodness, see David Baggett and Jerry L. Walls, *Good God: The Theistic Foundations of Morality* (New York: Oxford University Press, 2011). See especially chapter 3.
5. I Peter 1:14–16.
6. Hebrews 12:14.
7. As the *Westminster Confession* puts it regarding original sin: "This corruption of nature, during this life, doth remain in those that are regenerated" (VI.5). And later it says that when a sinner is converted by God, although he is enabled to do good, "yet so that, by reason of his remaining corruption, he doth not perfectly, nor only, will that which is good, but doth also will that which is evil" (IX.4).
8. John Henry Newman, *Parochial and Plain Sermons* (San Francisco: Ignatius Press, 1987), 6–7. The scripture passage Newman quotes is Psalm 16:11.
9. *Plain and Parochial Sermons*, 8–9.
10. *Plain and Parochial Sermons*, 9.
11. Gary A. Anderson, *Sin: A History* (New Haven: Yale University Press, 2009), 3.
12. For these three effects of sin, see Thomas Aquinas, *Summa Contra Gentiles*, trans. Charles J. O'Neil (Notre Dame: University of Notre Dame Press, 1975): 4, 72, 3.
13. *Plain and Parochial Sermons*, 12.
14. *Plain and Parochial Sermons*, 721.
15. As we shall see in chapter 2, this could be the moment before death, or the instant after death. In the former case, it could due to an act of faith.

CHAPTER 1
1. Jacques Le Goff, *The Birth of Purgatory*, trans. Arthur Goldhammer, (Chicago: The University of Chicago Press, 1984), 58.
2. See Steven Tsoukalas, *Bhagavad Gita: Exegetical and Comparative Commentary with Sanskrit Text, Translation, Interlinear Transliteration with Parsing, Mini Lexicon and Text Critical Notes* (Lewiston, New York: Edwin Mellen Press, 2007), 1:88.
3. *Phaedo* 113d–114b. See also *Republic* 10:614b–616b.
4. Malachi 3:2b–3.
5. 2 Maccabees 12:41–43.
6. Matthew 12:31–32.

7. Matthew 5:25–26.

8. 1 Corinthians 3:11–15.

9. See Isabel Moreira, *Heaven's Purge: Purgatory in Late Antiquity* (New York: Oxford University Press, 2010), 18. The story appears in Daniel 3.

10. Thomas More, *The Supplication of Souls* in *The Four Last Things, The Supplication of Souls, A Dialogue on Conscience*, rendered in modern English by Mary Gottschalk (New York: Scepter Publishers, 2002), 138–140. The Hezekiah story is in 2 Kings 20 and 2 Chronicles 32. More also cites I Samuel 2:6 and Zechariah 9:11 in support of purgatory (pp. 140–141) along with other more commonly used proof texts.

11. Luke 16:19–26.

12. Matthew 12:40; Act 2:31; Romans 10:6–7.

13. Cited by Le Goff, *The Birth of Purgatory*, 49–50.

14. Matthew 5:26.

15. Joseph Ratzinger, *Eschatology: Death and Eternal Life*, 2nd ed. (The Catholic University of America Press, 1988), 224. Ratzinger notes that, earlier, Tertullian had deployed the text from Matthew in a more "rigorist" fashion, to teach that the intermediate state was a time of necessary purification for everyone. Whereas Ratzinger gives significant credit to Cyprian's contribution to the development of the doctrine of purgatory, Le Goff is more dubious. See *The Birth of Purgatory*, 57–58.

16. See *City of God*, 21.13 and 21.16.

17. *Confessions*, 9.13:34–37.

18. *The City of God*, 21.24.

19. Cited by Le Goff in *The Birth of Purgatory*, 68.

20. Le Goff, *The Birth of Purgatory*, 69.

21. As we shall see in chapter 5, according to a famous legend Gregory prayed for the salvation of the deceased Roman Emperor Trajan, and Trajan was delivered from hell and saved.

22. For an example of such a story, see Le Goff, *The Birth of Purgatory*, 92.

23. Moreira, *Heaven's Purge*, 159.

24. Moreira, *Heaven's Purge*, 165; cf 154,

25. Moreira, *Heaven's Purge*, 189. It is worth noting that Bede's theology of purgatory was useful for the missionary work of the Church at this time. See *Heaven's Purge*, 177–192.

26. The recent work of Moreira, just noted, and other historians, must qualify this claim at least to some degree.

27. Le Goff, *The Birth of Purgatory*, 125.

28. LeGoff, *The Birth of Purgatory*, 157. Moreira questions the claim that the word "purgatory" was first used as a noun at this time, suggesting that it was perhaps used as a noun in the passage from Bede cited in note 23.

29. Again, this claim may require qualification in light of Moreira's claim about the role of Bede in the history of the doctrine.

30. Le Goff, *The Birth of Purgatory*, 181. For an insightful analysis of the importance of this text for establishing purgatory in the popular imagination, see Stephen Greenblatt, *Hamlet in Purgatory* (Princeton: Princeton University Press, 2001), 73–101.

31. Le Goff, *The Birth of Purgatory*, 132.

32. Le Goff, *The Birth of Purgatory*, 225.

33. Indulgences are defined as follows: "'An indulgence is a remission before God of the temporal punishment due to sins whose guilt has already been forgiven, which the faithful Christian who is duly disposed gains under certain prescribed conditions through the action of the Church which, as the minister of redemption, dispenses and applies with authority the treasury of the satisfactions of Christ and the saints.' 'An indulgence is partial or plenary according as it removes either part or all of the temporary punishment due to

sin.' The faithful can gain indulgences for themselves or apply them to the dead." *The Catechism of the Catholic Church*, par. 1471.

34. Cited by LeGoff, *The Birth of Purgatory*, 214.

35. Le Goff traces this distinction to a gloss of one of Abelard's disciples as follows: "Sin, it must be said at the outset, has two aspects: that which involves guilt [*culpa*], which is the consent [*consensus*] or contempt of God [*contemptus Dei*], as when one says that a small child is without sin, and that which involves punishment, as when we say we have sinned in Adam that is, that we have incurred a punishment." *The Birth of Purgatory*, 214.

36. Le Goff, *The Birth of Purgatory*, 133; 230–234. See also Manuele Gragnolati, *Experiencing the Afterlife: Soul and Body in Dante and Medieval Culture* (Notre Dame: University of Notre Dame Press, 2005), xi–xii; 5.

37. Gragnolati, *Experiencing the Afterlife*, 92.

38. Le Goff, *The Birth of Purgatory*, 240.

39. Le Goff, *The Birth of Purgatory*, 259.

40. Cited by Le Goff, *The Birth of Purgatory*, 249.

41. Le Goff, *The Birth of Purgatory*, 284.

42. Cited by Le Goff, *The Birth of Purgatory*, 283–284.

43. Cited by Le Goff, *The Birth of Purgatory*, 285.

44. Greenblatt, *Hamlet in Purgatory*, 53–54. Greenblatt's volume includes several of these images.

45. See Le Goff, *The Birth of Purgatory*, 252, 259, 273 for his comments on Bonaventure, Albert, and Aquinas, respectively.

46. See Dorothy Sayers's comments on the looming influence of Boniface on *The Divine Comedy* in her Introduction to her translation of the *The Divine Comedy I: Hell* (London: Penguin, 1949), 34–36.

47. Dorothy Sayers takes exception to this common opinion and calls it a "libel" that Dante "was a peevish political exile who indulged his petty spites and prejudices by putting his enemies in Hell and his friends in Paradise." See her Introduction, 10, 14–15.

48. Introduction, 50. See also her Introduction to her translation of *The Divine Comedy II: Purgatory* (London: Penguin, 1955), 17ff.

49. Le Goff, *The Birth of Purgatory*, 346.

50. Le Goff, *The Birth of Purgatory*, 342. The term "ante-Purgatory" is Le Goff's.

51. For details, see J. Gill, "Florence, Council of" in *New Catholic Encyclopedia*, 2nd ed. (Detroit: Thompson Gale, 2003), 5:770–772.

52. Roland H. Bainton, *Here I Stand: A Life of Martin Luther* (New York: Abingdon-Cokesbury Press, 1950), 72.

53. Cited by Bainton, *Here I Stand*, 78.

54. *Martin Luther: Selections from His Writings*, ed. with an Introduction by John Dillenberger (New York: Anchor Books, 1961), 493. For a fascinating account of the role of purgatory in the English Reformation, particularly as it involved financial abuses, see Greenblatt, *Hamlet in Purgatory*, 10–32.

55. For Luther's final views on the doctrine of Purgatory, see "Widerruf vom Fegefeuer" [Rejection of Purgatory], in *Martin Luthers Werke*, (Weimar: Bohlaus, 1909), 30/2:360–390. For Calvin's view of Purgatory, see *Institutes of the Christian Religion*, trans. Ford Lewis Battles. (Philadelphia:Westminster, 1960), 3.5.1–10. It is noteworthy that some of Luther's fellow Reformers, such as Wycliffe and Latimer, were sympathetic to a modest account of purgatory, though equally critical of the Roman version of the doctrine and the associated abuses. See Greenblatt, *Hamlet in Purgatory*, 26, 33–34.

56. Carlos Eire, *A Very Brief History of Eternity* (Princeton: Princeton University Press, 2010), 119.

57. Richard K. Fenn, *The Persistence of Purgatory* (Cambridge: Cambridge University Press, 1995), 104. For his detailed discussion of Baxter and Locke, see pp. 73–110. Fenn's larger thesis includes the claim that "the modern self emerges directly from what I have been calling the secularization of purgatory" (p. 98). Fenn sees the secularization of purgatory in several facets of modern life, perhaps especially in the way modern life is dominated by the tyranny of time, and the fear of never having enough of it.

58. For more on the relationship between the denial of purgatory and the rise of secularism, see Eire, *A Very Brief History of Eternity*, 138–156.

59. "The Council of Trent: The Twenty-Fifth Session," http://history.hanover.edu/texts/trent/ct25.html

60. Eire, *A Very Brief History of Eternity*, 134.

61. Le Goff, *The Birth of Purgatory*, 356.

62. Charles Hodge, *Systematic Theology* (New York: Scribner, 1909), 3:751.

63. Karl Rahner, *Theological Investigations* (New York: Crossway Publishing, 1983), 19:181.

64. Rahner, *Theological Investigations*, 19:187.

65. *Documents of Vatican II*, ed. Austin P. Flannery (Grand Rapids: Eerdmans, 1975), 6.1.3. (p. 64).

CHAPTER 2

1. Martin Luther, Works, 32:96–97. Many Roman Catholics would likely have agreed with Luther's basic point about the lucrative benefits of purgatory. Writing in defense of purgatory in the 1560s, Cardinal William Allen contends that "this doctrine (as the whole world knoweth) founded all Bishoprics, builded all Churches, raised all Oratories, instituted all Colleges, endowed all Schools, maintained all hospitals, set forth all works of charity and religion, of what sort soever they be." Cited by Stephen Greenblatt, *Hamlet in Purgatory* (Princeton: Princeton University Press, 2001), 13.

2. Cited by Greenblatt, *Hamlet in Purgatory*, 45. For further discussion of the Protestant attack on purgatory as a piece of creative poetry, see Greenblatt, 3, 35–37, 161.

3. John Calvin, *Institutes of the Christian Religion*, ed. John T. McNeill, trans. Ford Lewis Battles (Philadelphia: Westminster, 1960), 3.5.6. See note 13 for the reference to Melanchthon.

4. John Fletcher, *Checks to Antinomianism* (New York: Hunt & Eaton), 2:488.

5. Martin Luther, *Martin Luther: Selections from His Writings*, ed. with an Introduction by John Dillenberger (New York: Anchor Books, 1961), 491.

6. See Thesis Twenty-six. *Martin Luther*, 492.

7. *Martin Luther*, 491.

8. I John 4:18.

9. Roland H. Bainton, *Here I Stand* (Nashville: Abingdon-Cokesbury Press, 1950), 28.

10. Formula of Concord, Part 2, Article 3, 32. This document is in *The Book of Concord*, trans. and ed. Theodore G. Tappert (Philadelphia: Fortress Press, 1959), 545.

11. See Formula of Concord, Part 2, Article 3, 26–27, 36, 41; Article 4. (*The Book of Concord*, 543; 545–546; 551–558.)

12. Apology of the Augsburg Confession, Article 12, 46. (*The Book of Concord*, 188).

13. Apology of the Augsburg Confession, Article 12, 148. (*The Book of Concord*, 205).

14. Apology of the Augsburg Confession, Article 12, 149. (*The Book of Concord*, 206) The Church of St. James in Spain was a favorite place of pilgrimage in the Middle Ages.

15. Apology of the Augsburg Confession, Article 12, 156. (*The Book of Concord*, 207).

16. Apology of the Augsburg Confession, Article 12, 167. (*The Book of Concord*, 209).

17. Large Catechism, Second Part, The Third Article, 57–58. (*The Book of Concord*, 418).

18. All quotes from this paragraph are from *Institutes*, 3.5.6.

19. See *Institutes*, 3.5.7–9.
20. The one notable exception is The Second Helvetic Confession, which rejects Purgatory in chapter 26.
21. All quotes in this paragraph are from *Westminster Confession*, 13.
22. *Westminster Confession*, 3.1.
23. *Westminster Confession*, 32.1.
24. Luther himself tended to believe in "soul sleep" and to hold that resurrection is of the whole person, not just the body. See Paul Althaus, *The Theology of Martin Luther*, trans. Robert C. Schultz (Philadelphia: Fortress Press, 1966), 410–417.
25. Charles Hodge, *Systematic Theology* (Grand Rapids: Eerdmans, 1968), 3:725.
26. Isaiah 35:8.
27. Jonathan Edwards, *The Works of Jonathan Edwards* (New Haven: Yale University Press, 1992), 10:471.
28. Edwards, *Works*, 10:472.
29. Edwards, *Works*, 10:478.
30. Edwards, *Works*, 10:476. Edwards goes on a bit later to exhort his readers to holiness, commenting with ironic philosophical understatement: "This is motive enough without any other; for what can be a greater motive than necessity?" See *Works*, 10:478.
31. Edwards, *Works*, 10:586.
32. The first quote in this sentence is from Edwards, *Works*, 10:584, and the second is from 10:586.
33. For an excellent exposition of Wesley's view of sanctification that takes care to show its subtleties and nuances, see Kenneth J. Collins, *The Theology of John Wesley: Holy Love and the Shape of Grace* (Nashville: Abingdon, 2007), 279–312. My account of Wesley draws heavily from Collins.
34. John Wesley, *The Works of John Wesley*, ed. Albert C. Outler (Nashville: Abingdon, 1985), 2:163.
35. Wesley, *Works* (1985), 2:167. Emphasis in original.
36. See his "A Letter to a Roman Catholic" in John Wesley, *The Works of John Wesley*, ed. Thomas Jackson (Grand Rapids: Baker Book House, 1979; reprint of the 1872 edition), 10:80–86.
37. Article 22, "Of Purgatory."
38. Cf. Wesley, *Works* (1872), 10:342–343.
39. In particular, Wesley cites Romans 8:1, 30, 33, 34.
40. Wesley, *Works* (1872), 10:98. cf. 144.
41. John Telford, ed. *The Letters of John Wesley, A.M.*, 8 vols. (London: Epworth Press, 1931), 4:10.
42. Telford, *Letters*, 4:13.
43. Wesley, *Works* (1872), 8:285.
44. Telford, *Letters*, 5:39.
45. For interesting reflections on this issue, see Collins, *The Theology of John Wesley*, 306–307.
46. Wesley, *Works* (1872), 11:394.
47. Fletcher, *Checks*, 2:489.
48. Fletcher, *Checks*, 2:516. The passage cited is from part 3 of the homily.
49. Fletcher, *Checks*, 2:570.
50. Fletcher, *Checks*, 2:571.
51. Fletcher, *Checks*, 2:566.
52. Millard J. Erickson, *Christian Theology* (Grand Rapids: Baker Book House, 1985), 3:1181.

53. Donald G. Bloesch, *The Last Things: Resurrection, Judgment, Glory* (Downers Grove: Intervarsity Press, 2004), 151–152.

54. Bloesch, *The Last Things,* 152.

55. Bloesch, *The Last Things,* 152. For more on his notion of hades as an intermediate state, see pp. 143–148.

56. N. T. Wright, *Surprised by Hope: Rethinking Heaven, the Resurrection and the Mission of the Church* (San Francisco: HarperOne, 2008), 170.

57. P. T. Forsyth, *This Life and the Next* (Boston: The Pilgrim Press, 1948), 37.

58. Jurgen Moltmann, "Is There Life after Death?" in *The End of the World and the Ends of God,* eds. John Polkinghorne and Michael Welker (Harrisburg, PA: Trinity Press International, 2000), 247.

59. Moltmann, "Is There Life after Death?" 252.

60. John Polkinghorne, "Eschatology: Some Questions and Some Insights from Science," in *The End of the World and the Ends of God,* 39–40.

61. Polkinghorne, "Eschatology," 41.

62. Clark H. Pinnock, "Response to Zachary J. Hayes," in *Four Views on Hell,* ed. William V. Crockett (Grand Rapids: Zondervan, 1992), 130.

63. Pinnock, "Response," 130. For an earlier example of a theologian in the Wesleyan tradition who was sympathetic to the doctrine of purgatory, while recognizing that Wesley and Fletcher were not, see W. E. Sangster, *The Path to Perfection* (New York: Abingdon, 1943), 65–70.

64. Hayes, "The Purgatorial View," 107–108. The nature of justification is very much at issue in contemporary Protestant and evangelical theology. See N. T. Wright, *Justification* (Downers Grove, IL: IVP Academic, 2009).

65. J. F. X. Cevetello, "Purgatory: In the Bible," in *New Catholic Encyclopedia,* 2nd ed. (Detroit: Thompson Gale, 2003), 11:825.

66. Zachary Hayes, "The Purgatorial View," in *Four Views of Hell,* 107.

67. We will look briefly at a few such texts in chapter 5.

68. For instance, Isaiah 14 and Ezekiel 28 have been read as teaching the fall of Satan, but contemporary interpreters read these texts as referring to human figures rather than to Satan.

CHAPTER 3

1. Clark H. Pinnock, "Response to Zachary J. Hayes," in *Four Views of Hell,* ed. William Crockett (Grand Rapids: Zondervan, 1992), 130.

2. Donald G. Bloesch, *The Last Things: Resurrection, Judgment, Glory* (Downers Grove: Intervarsity Press, 2004), 152–153. The quoted phrases in this passage are from Roman Catholic theologians Karl Rahner and Ludwig Ott, respectively.

3. Justin D. Bernard, "Purgatory and the Dilemma of Sanctification," *Faith and Philosophy* 24 (2007): 311–327.

4. Neal Judisch, "Sanctification, Satisfaction, and The Purpose of Purgatory," *Faith and Philosophy* 26 (2009): 169.

5. "Sanctification, Satisfaction, and the Purpose of Purgatory," 170.

6. M. F. Egan, "The Two Theories of Purgatory," *The Irish Theological Quarterly* 17 (1922): 24–34.

7. "Sanctification, Satisfaction, and The Purpose of Purgatory," 168.

8. "Sanctification, Satisfaction, and The Purpose of Purgatory," 169.

9. Cited by Le Goff, *The Birth of Purgatory,* 285. Bernard cites a similar passage from the Council of Florence in 1439 in support of his claim that Roman Catholic theology endorses a satisfaction model of purgatory. See "Purgatory and the Dilemma of Sanctification," 325.

10. Thomas Aquinas, *Summa Contra Gentiles* (hereafter SCG), trans. Charles J. O'Neil (Notre Dame: University of Notre Dame Press, 1975): 4, 91, 6.
11. Thomas Aquinas, *Summa Theologica*, (hereafter ST) Supplement, qu 2. art 1.
12. SCG, 4, 72, 6.
13. SCG, 4, 72, 8.
14. Matthew 16:19
15. SCG, 4, 72, 14.
16. It is worth noting, as paradoxical as it may seem, that in Catholic thought, the temporal punishment may be understood as a gift left to sinners. It is not an absolute good, but a relative one in the sense that it is an opportunity to battle, to participate meaningfully in the work of Christ, and express love to God. Thanks to Bryan R. Cross for this point.
17. This is related, of course, to how he understands satisfaction in the atonement of Christ. On this matter see Eleanore Stump, "Atonement According to Aquinas," in *Philosophy and the Christian Faith*, ed. Thomas V. Morris (Notre Dame: University of Notre Dame Press, 1988), 61–91; and Philip L. Quinn, "Aquinas on Atonement," in *Trinity, Incarnation and Atonement: Philosophical and Theological Essays*, eds. Ronald J. Feenstra and Cornelius Plantinga, Jr. (Notre Dame: University of Notre Dame Press, 1989), 153–177. As Stump interprets Aquinas, satisfaction is not about satisfying God's wrath or paying a debt of punishment to balance the divine books. She writes: "For Aquinas, then, the *aim* of any satisfaction (including vicarious satisfaction) is not to cancel a debt incurred by sin but to restore a sinner to harmony with God" (p. 69). Quinn's interpretation of Aquinas holds that the core of satisfaction is to pay the debt of punishment. He writes: "Hence a debt of satisfactory punishment may remain and be discharged even after the stain of sin has been removed (I-II 87, 6). Satisfaction in the strict sense, then, pertains to the voluntary payment of the debt of punishment (*Trinity, Incarnation and Atonement*, p. 158). The citation in the quote by Quinn is from *Summa theologiae*.
18. Cited by M. F. Egan, in "The Two Theories of Purgatory," 24.
19. See R. J. Bastian, "Purgatory," in *New Catholic Encyclopedia*, 2nd ed. (Detroit: Thomson Gale, 2003), 11: 827. See particularly on this page his account of this under his section on the "Purpose of the Suffering."
20. "The Two Theories of Purgatory," 26–27. Egan mentions Scotus as another first-rank theologian who may have held this view.
21. "The Two Theories of Purgatory," 27.
22. "The Two Theories of Purgatory," 30. Egan says this view is also shared by Bellarmine.
23. "Purgatory," in *New Catholic Encyclopedia*, 11: 827.
24. Martin Jugie, *Purgatory and the Means to Avoid It*, trans. from the 7th French edition by Malachy Gerard Carroll (Cork: The Mercier Press, 1949).
25. Jugie, *Purgatory and the Means to Avoid it*, 4.
26. Jugie, *Purgatory and the Means to Avoid it*, 5.
27. Jugie, *Purgatory and the Means to Avoid it*, 8.
28. Jugie, *Purgatory and the Means to Avoid it*, 45. cf. pp. 16, 21.
29. Jugie, *Purgatory and the Means to Avoid it*, 52
30. Jugie, *Purgatory and the Means to Avoid it*, 6.
31. Jugie, *Purgatory and the Means to Avoid it*, 9.
32. Jugie, *Purgatory and the Means to Avoid it*, 47. See also 73–78.
33. Charles Hodge, *Systematic Theology* (Grand Rapids: Eerdmans, 1968), 3: 726.
34. Jugie, *Purgatory and the Means to Avoid it*, 20.
35. Jugie, *Purgatory and the Means to Avoid it*, 24; cf 51.
36. Egan, "The Two Theories of Purgatory," 24.
37. SCG, 4, 72, 14.

38. SCG, 4, 72, 1.

39. SCG, 3, 158, 1.

40. SCG, 3, 151, 3.

41. Luke 22:42.

42. SCG, 3, 158, 6. Notice how his account of perfect repentance in this passage is nearly identical to what he says in 4, 72, 8.

43. ST, Ia IIae, 87, 6.

44. 4 Sentences d. 21, q. 1. a. 3. This passage is cited by Egan in support of the view that Aquinas held the view that purgatory involves a gradual purging of sins. "Two Theories of Purgatory," 27. Thanks to Fred Freddoso for translation of this line. Egan notes on the following page that those who hold that Aquinas supported the view that sin is immediately cleansed by an act of love upon entering purgatory cite De Malo, q. 7, art. 11.

45. Dorothy L. Sayers, "Introduction" to Dante, The Divine Comedy II: Purgatory, trans. Dorothy L. Sayers (London: Penguin, 1955), 59.

46. Sayers, "Introduction," 55, n3.

47. Sayers, "Introduction," 15.

48. Manuele Gragnolati, Experiencing the Afterlife: Soul and Body in Dante and Medieval Culture (Notre Dame: University of Notre Dame Press, 2005), 113.

49. Purgatory, 11, 67–72.

50. Purgatory 4, 130–135. For the passage on the excommunicates, see 3, 136–141.

51. Sayers, "Introduction," 64.

52. Sayers, "Introduction," 58.

53. Paul L. Griffiths, "Purgatory," in The Oxford Handbook of Eschatology, ed. Jerry L. Walls (New York: Oxford University Press, 2008), 432.

54. Gragnolati, Experiencing the Afterlife, 127.

55. Purgatory, 23, 61–75.

56. For description of the tree and water, see Purgatory, 22, 130–141; 23, 34–36.

57. Experiencing the Afterlife, 133.

58. Purgatory, 12, 109–117. The Latin phrase means, "Blessed are the poor in spirit," the first of the beatitudes. Matthew 5:3.

59. Matthew 27:46.

60. Gragnolati, Experiencing the Afterlife, 132.

61. Purgatory, 22, 7–9.

62. Purgatory, 24, 151–154. See also 22, 1–6.

63. Dante Alighieri, The Divine Comedy, trans. Allen Mandelbaum (New York: Alfred A. Knopf, 1995).

64. "Purgatory" in New Catholic Encyclopedia, 828. For another contemporary account of purgatory in this vein, see John Saward, Sweet and Blessed Country (Oxford: Oxford University Press, 2005), 108–124.

65. Documents of Vatican II, ed. Austin P. Flannery (Grand Rapids: Eerdmans, 1975), 6.1.3. (p. 64).

66. Thanks to Alan Rhoda for raising this point in conversation.

67. John Henry Newman, Parochial and Plain Sermons (San Francisco: Ignatius Press, 1987), 720.

68. Newman, Parochial and Plain Sermons, 721.

69. Bernard, "Purgatory and the Dilemma of Sanctification," 312.

70. Bernard, "Purgatory and the Dilemma of Sanctification," 316. For an interesting paper that raises similar issues, particularly what the authors call the "problem of heaven," see Yujin Nagasawa, Graham Oppy, and Nick Trakakis, "Salvation in Heaven," Philosophical Papers 33 (2004): 97–119. The authors never consider the possibility of purgatory as a way to form the sort of character that would freely choose only the good in heaven.

71. Bernard, "Purgatory and the Dilemma of Sanctification," 315.
72. Bernard, "Purgatory and the Dilemma of Sanctification," 326.
73. Richard L. Purtill, *Thinking about Religion: A Philosophical Introduction to Religion* (Englewood Cliffs, NJ: Prentice Hall, 1978), 148.
74. Charles Dickens, *A Christmas Carol and Other Christmas Books,* ed. Robert Douglas-Fairhurst (Oxford: Oxford University Press, 2006), 10.
75. Dickens, *A Christmas Carol and Other Christmas Books,* 14.
76. Dickens, *A Christmas Carol and Other Christmas Books,* 83.
77. Dickens, *A Christmas Carol and Other Christmas Books,* 52.
78. John 17:17.
79. In diagnosing the roots of sin, Paul writes, "for though they knew God, they did not honor him as God or give thanks to him, but they became futile in their thinking, and their senseless minds were darkened" Romans 1:21.
80. David Vander Laan, "The Sanctification Argument for Purgatory," *Faith and Philosophy* 24 (2007): 333.
81. Vander Laan, "The Sanctification Argument for Purgatory," 334.
82. Vander Laan, "The Sanctification Argument for Purgatory," 334.
83. Revelation 22:2.
84. Revelation 7:17; cf 21:4.
85. Vander Laan, "The Sanctification Argument for Purgatory," 335.
86. Dickens, *A Christmas Carol and Other Christmas Books,* 39.
87. Dickens, *A Christmas Carol and Other Christmas Books,* 39.
88. Dickens, *A Christmas Carol and Other Christmas Books,* 44.
89. For a defense of the claim that purgatorial cleansing involves pain, see David Brown, "No Heaven Without Purgatory," *Religious Studies* 21 (1985): 454–456.
90. "Sanctification, Satisfaction, and the Purpose of Purgatory," 184.
91. See, however, Gary A. Anderson, *Sin: A History* (New Haven: Yale University Press, 2009). Anderson explores the biblical background for the notion of a "treasury of merit" and of the notion of giving alms as a way of redeeming one's sins. He argues that this is not a matter of salvation by works, and in this context also defends the notion of indulgences. See pp. 135–188. On indulgences, see especially pp. 162–163.
92. "The Sanctification Argument for Purgatory," 336–337.
93. Refer, of course, to the chapter "Rebellion" in Dostoevsky's novel *The Brothers Karamazov.*
94. For a more detailed discussion of this point, see Jerry L. Walls, *Heaven: The Logic of Eternal Joy* (New York: Oxford University Press, 2002), 113–132.

CHAPTER 4
1. Dante Alighieri, *The Divine Comedy II: Purgatory,* trans. Dorothy L. Sayers (London: Penguin, 1955), 2: 76–90.
2. *Purgatory,* 2: 106–114.
3. Alasdair MacIntyre, *Three Rival Versions of Moral Inquiry* (Notre Dame: University of Notre Dame Press, 1990), 199; Charles Taylor, *Sources of the Self: The Making of the Modern Identity* (Cambridge: Harvard University Press, 1989), 48–50.
4. See Jerry L. Walls, *Heaven: The Logic of Eternal Joy* (New York: Oxford University Press, 2002), 92–112.
5. Thomists often reject the label of dualism, and see their view as alternative to that position, as we shall see. I classify it as a version of dualism, broadly speaking, since it holds that the separated soul persists in conscious form between death and resurrection.
6. A materialist who held a "gappy" view of personal identity could maintain that persons are resurrected and undergo purgatory before the final judgment. So, strictly speaking, the

gappy view is not inconsistent with purgatory. This suggestion is quite a departure from the traditional view of the doctrine, and I will not engage it further.

7. Paul Griffiths suggests the possibility of such a body in "Purgatory," in *The Oxford Handbook of Eschatology*, ed. Jerry L. Walls (New York: Oxford University Press, 2008), 436.

8. Kevin Corcoran, "Physical Persons and Postmortem Survival without Temporal Gaps," in *Soul, Body, and Survival: Essays on the Metaphysics of Human Persons*, ed. Kevin Corcoran (Ithaca: Cornell University Press, 2001), 209. Corcoran's principle is a restatement of a principle by Peter van Inwagen.

9. Corcoran, "Physical Persons and Postmortem Survival without Temporal Gaps," 210.

10. Corcoran, "Physical Persons and Postmortem Survival without Temporal Gaps," 210.

11. Corcoran, "Physical Persons and Postmortem Survival without Temporal Gaps," 214.

12. Joseph Ratzinger, *Eschatology: Death and Eternal Life*, 2nd ed., trans. Michael Waldstein (Washington, DC: Catholic University of America Press, 1988), 252.

13. Ratzinger, *Eschatology*, 108.

14. Ratzinger, *Eschatology*, 111. See pp. 109–111 for the discussion of the earlier points in this paragraph.

15. Ratzinger, *Eschatology*, 112.

16. Ratzinger, *Eschatology*, 267.

17. Ratzinger, *Eschatology*, 262, 269.

18. N. T. Wright, *Surprised by Hope: Rethinking Heaven, the Resurrection, and the Mission of the Church* (New York: HarperOne, 2008), 151.

19. Wright, *Surprised by Hope*, 171. See also 152, 162, 172. For St. Paul's reference to death as sleep, see I Corinthians 15:51.

20. Ratzinger, *Eschatology*, 261.

21. Ratzinger, *Eschatology*, 250. He goes on a few pages later to remark on "the fear engendered by the idea of the soul and the connected anxiety lest one receive a verdict of 'Guilty of dualism!'," p. 255.

22. See Philippians 1:21–23.

23. Ratzinger, *Eschatology*, 147.

24. Ratzinger, *Eschatology*, 258.

25. See J. P. Moreland and Scott Rae, *Body and Soul: Human Nature and the Crisis in Ethics* (Downers Grove: Intervarsity Press, 2000).

26. Christina Van Dyke, "Not Properly a Person: The Rational Soul and 'Thomistic Substance Dualism,'" *Faith and Philosophy* 26 (2009): 187.

27. Van Dyke, "Not Properly a Person," 189, 194.

28. Van Dyke, "Not Properly a Person," 190–91.

29. See Van Dyke, "Not Properly a Person," 201–203 for the details.

30. Van Dyke, "Not Properly a Person," 199.

31. Van Dyke, "Not Properly a Person," 194–195.

32. Dante, *Purgatory*, 25: 79–84. Lachesis is the fate who spins the thread of life.

33. Dante, *Purgatory*, 25: 100–108.

34. For more on Dante's view, and how it compares with that of Aquinas, see Manuele Gragnolati, *Experiencing the Afterlife: Body and Soul in Dante and Medieval Culture* (Notre Dame: University of Notre Dame Press, 2005), 67–87. It is worth noting that Aquinas held that separated souls can suffer from fire, though the suffering is not physical in nature. See Thomas Aquinas, *Summa Contra Gentiles*, trans. Charles J. O'Neil (Notre Dame: University of Notre Dame Press, 1975), 4: 90.

35. Cf, Dante, *Purgatory*, 3: 31–33.

36. John Polkinghorne, *The God of Hope and the End of the World* (New Haven: Yale University Press, 2002), 105.

37. Polkinghorne, *The God of Hope and the End of the World*, 106.
38. Polkinghorne, *The God of Hope and the End of the World*, 111.
39. Polkinghorne, *The God of Hope and the End of the World*, 108.
40. For a critique of compound dualism, and a defense of "pure dualism," the first interpretation of substance dualism we distinguished, see Eric T. Olson, "A Compound of Two Substances," in *Soul, Body and Survival*, ed. Kevin Corcoran, 73–88.
41. Richard Swinburne, *The Evolution of the Soul*, revised ed. (Oxford: Clarendon Press, 1986), 145–160.
42. Swinburne, *The Evolution of the Soul*, 262.
43. See his essay "Biblical Anthropology and the Body-Soul Problem" in *Soul, Body and Survival*, ed. Kevin Corcoran, 218–228. Cooper surveys the biblical data from both the Old and New Testaments in his essay.
44. Aquinas, SCG, 4, 91, 10.
45. Aquinas, SCG, 4, 91, 2.
46. Aquinas, SCG, 4, 91, 4, See also paragraph 5.
47. Aquinas, SCG, 4, 79, 11–12; 4, 85, 4.
48. Aquinas, SCG, 4, 95, 6.
49. Of course, not all Thomists agree that, for Aquinas, the person does not survive between death and resurrection. Eleanore Stump argues that, for Aquinas, the human person substantially exists, although deficiently, between death and resurrection. For assessment of her view, including relevant texts from Aquinas that support her interpretation, see Jason T. Eberl, "Do Human Persons Persist between Death and Resurrection?" in *Metaphysics and God*, ed. Kevin Tempe (New York: Routledge, 2009), 188–205.
50. Swinburne, *The Evolution of the Soul*, 267.
51. Swinburne, *The Evolution of the Soul*, 284.
52. Charles Dickens, *A Christmas Carol and Other Christmas Books*, ed. Robert Douglas-Fairhurst (Oxford: Oxford University Press, 2006), 52.
53. David Brown, "No Heaven Without Purgatory," *Religious Studies* 21 (1985), 451.
54. Brown, "No Heaven Without Purgatory," 452.
55. Taylor, *Sources of the Self*, 28.
56. Taylor, *Sources of the Self*, 48.
57. Taylor, *Sources of the Self*, 50.
58. Ratzinger, *Eschatology*, 182.
59. Ratzinger, *Eschatology*, 183–184.
60. Ratzinger, *Eschatology*, 189.
61. Ratzinger, *Eschatololgy*, 229.
62. Wright, *Surprised by Hope*, 167. The noted Lutheran theologian Wolfhart Pannenberg is sympathetic to Ratzinger's view that Christ himself is the eschatological fire, and suggests that when purgatory is understood in this fashion it should not be an issue for protestants. "The doctrine of purgatory is brought back into the Christian expectation of final judgment by the returning Christ. There is thus no more reason for the Reformation opposition." Wolfhart Pannenberg, *Systematic Theology* (Grand Rapids: Eerdmans, 1998). Vol. 3, p. 619.
63. Ratzinger, *Eschatology*, 230.
64. Ratzinger, *Eschatology*, 230.
65. Ratzinger, *Eschatology*, 232.
66. R. J. Bastian, "Purgatory," *New Catholic Encyclopedia* (Detroit: Thompson Gale, 2003), 11:828.
67. Dickens, *A Christmas Carol and Other Christmas Books*, 24.
68. Recall these lines from the previous chapter: And lighter-footed than I'd felt before At any pass, following with ease complete Those two swift spirits, on and up I bore. (Purgatory, 22:7–9.; see also 4:88–96; 12:115–126)

69. Justin D. Bernard, "Purgatory and the Dilemma of Sanctification," *Faith and Philosophy* 24 (2007). Bernard discusses this argument on pp. 318–325.
70. Ratzinger, *Eschatology*, 259.

CHAPTER 5

1. Jacques Le Goff, *The Birth of Purgatory*, trans. Arthur Goldhammer (Chicago: The University of Chicago Press, 1984), 306.
2. Le Goff, *The Birth of Purgatory*, 304.
3. Isabel Moreira, *Heaven's Purge: Purgatory in Late Antiquity* (New York: Oxford University Press, 2010), 165.
4. For a modern statement of this point, see Martin Jugie, *Purgatory and the Means to Avoid It,* trans. Malachy Gerard Carroll (Cork: The Mercier Press, 1949), 25–26.
5. Brian Hall has pressed me on the compatibility of purgatory with the parousia, at which time we are promised that "when he is revealed, we will be like him, for we will see him as he is" (1 John 3:2). How purgatory fits with the timeline of the parousia, the final judgment, and so on is not always clear and admittedly requires some degree of speculation. The assumption that this text is incompatible with purgatory assumes, however, that there is a singular moment of Christ's fully appearing to all believers, and that all will clearly and fully see him at this moment, and instantly become fully like him. However, the exact chronology, duration of time, and individual appropriation of this transformation is not explicitly clarified by this text. Rather, John writes economically, and his words leave these details uncertain. Thanks to Joe Dongell for insight (in conversation) on this text.
6. Le Goff, *The Birth of Purgatory*, 5.
7. Dorothy L. Sayers, "Introduction" to Dante, *The Divine Comedy II: Purgatory*, trans. Dorothy L. Sayers (Penguin: London, 1955), 60; 59.
8. Sayers, "Introduction," 59.
9. Sayers, "Introduction," 60. It is worth pointing out that Sayers conceives of the orthodox Catholic view of purgatory as including elements of both "satisfaction and purification."
10. Cf. Le Goff, *The Birth of Purgatory*, 134.
11. As Thomas Flint remarks: "Obviously, the safest thing to do here is to think of the circumstances as including all of the prior causal activity of all agents along with the simultaneous causal activity by all agents other than the agent the counterfactual is about." Thomas P. Flint, *Divine Providence: The Molinist Account* (Ithaca: Cornell University Press, 1998), 47.
12. For a more detailed account of this concept, see Jerry L. Walls, *Hell: The Logic of Damnation* (Notre Dame: University of Notre Dame Press, 1992), 88–94.
13. Cf the view of Terrance L. Tiessen, who holds that God extends to everyone at some point sufficient grace to enable them to believe. However, this grace does not suffice to save unless the person also receives efficacious grace, which is given only to the elect. What makes this grace sufficient for those who are not elect? "Its sufficiency lies particularly in its being enough to justify God's condemnation." *Who Can Be Saved?* (Downers Grove, IL: Intervarsity Press, 2004), 242. It is not clear how such grace is even sufficient to justify condemnation since apparently no one responds favorably to it without the additional efficacious grace.
14. It is worth noting that the concept of optimal grace disposes of the "vagueness" objection to hell, which contends that the boundary between those who are consigned to hell, and those who are saved, is vague and lacks any sort of clear distinction. On this objection, the individuals of our world are on a continuum with respect to their moral and spiritual choices, with no significant gaps along the way. See Theodore Sider, "Hell and Vagueness," *Faith and Philosophy* 19 (2002): 58–68. On my view, there is nothing vague about who

ends up in hell, and there is a yawning gap between any such persons and those on the other side of the divide. Those in hell separate and distinguish themselves by definitively and decisively rejecting the love of God and his offer of salvation.

15. Sayers, "Introduction," 17. See also Dante, *The Divine Comedy 1: Hell*, trans. Dorothy L. Sayers (Penguin: London, 1949), 95–96.

16. *Purgatory*, 77.

17. *Purgatory*, 3:37–45.

18. *Purgatory*, 3: 118–123.

19. *Purgatory*, 3: 133–135.

20. *Purgatory*, 7: 7–8. cf. *Hell*, 4: 25–42.

21. *Purgatory*, 7: 25–7; 30; 34–36.

22. *Purgatory*, 238.

23. *Purgatory*, 22: 67–69.

24. *Purgatory*, 10: 73–75.

25. Dante, *The Divine Comedy 3: Paradise*, trans. Dorothy L. Sayers and Barbara Reynolds (Penguin: London, 1962), 238.

26. *Paradise*, 20:106–117. The Trajan legend took different forms and was interpreted in significantly different ways in the Middle Ages. It was also a matter of debate among scholastic theologians, some of whom held only that Trajan's pains in hell were diminished, but that he was not saved. For details see Gordon Whatley, "The Uses of Hagiography: The Legend of Pope Gregory and the Emperor Trajan in the Middle Ages," *Viator* 15 (1984): 25–63. See especially pp. 43–50 for an account of Dante's interpretation of the story in comparison with others.

27. *Paradise*, 20:46–48.

28. *Paradise*, 19:70–78.

29. *Paradise*, 20:94–99. The Latin phrase in line 94 means "suffereth violence."

30. *Paradise*, 20:130–135. See also 19:79–99; 21: 91–99.

31. Whatley interprets Dante to be holding out hope for Virgil and others. See "The Uses of Hagiography," 47–49.

32. *Hell*, 20: 118–120.

33. Olin Alfred Curtis, *The Christian Faith: A System of Doctrine* (Grand Rapids: Kregal Publications, 1905), 400.

34. Curtis, *The Christian Faith*, 401.

35. Curtis, *The Christian Faith*, 401.

36. Curtis, *The Christian Faith*, 402.

37. Curtis, *The Christian Faith*, 403.

38. Curtis, *The Christian Faith*, 404.

39. Curtis, *The Christian Faith*, 404.

40. P. T. Forsyth, *This Life and the Next* (Boston: The Pilgrim Press, 1948), 36–37.

41. Forsyth, *This Life and the Next*, 37–42. See especially p. 40. The biblical texts Forsyth cites, but without giving the references, in support of the claim that we should pray for all nontrivial matters are apparently Philippians 4:6 and 1 Peter 5:7.

42. William H. Willimon, *Who Will Be Saved?* (Nashville: Abingdon, 2008), 36.

43. Willimon, *Who Will Be Saved?*, 84.

44. Willimon, *Who Will Be Saved?*, 84.

45. Karl Rahner, "Purgatory," in *Theological Investigations* (New York: Crossroad Publishing, 1983), vol. 19, p 191.

46. For details and critical analysis of Rahner's views, see Morwenna Ludlow, *Universal Salvation: Eschatology in the Thought of Gregory of Nyssa and Karl Rahner* (Oxford: Oxford University Press, 2000).

47. Joseph Ratzinger, *Eschatology: Death and Eternal Life*, 2nd ed., trans. Michael Waldstein (Washington, DC: The Catholic University of America Press, 1988), 188.

48. See Ratzinger, *Eschatology*, 185–190, for the larger context of this point. It is worth noting that Hans Urs Von Balthasar cited both Ratzinger and Rahner, along with other noted Roman Catholic theologians who agreed with him in hoping for universal salvation. See his *Dare We Hope "That All Men Be Saved"?*, trans. David Kipp (San Francisco: Ignatius, 1988), 168–169.

49. Another significant figure from an earlier era who suggested the possibility of postmortem probation to make up for the inequities of this life is Joseph Butler. Although he did not propose a doctrine of purgatory in this connection, the materials for such a proposal are arguably there. See his *Analogy of Religion, Natural and Revealed, to the Constitution and Course of Nature* (New York: Harper & Brothers, 1889), Pt. 1, ch. 3, pp. 119, 131; Pt. 2, ch. 6, p. 259.

50. For the details of Aquinas's argument, as well as criticism of it, see Charles Seymour, *A Theodicy of Hell* (Dordrecht: Kluwer Academic Press, 2000), 167–170. Seymour contends that Aquinas's argument in the end depends on a controversial ethical judgment, namely, that the damned deserve their fate so they will not be given bodies that allow them to repent.

51. Tiessen, *Who Can Be Saved?*, 219. His italics.

52. Tom Flint has suggested to me, in conversation, that it may be possible that persons could experience, subjectively, years of opportunities to repent and accept the gospel in the space of a mere moment of "objective" time in our world, right before they die. This would allow a full opportunity for all to repent before death. I am dubious of this, but if it is possible, it would allow for optimal grace for all persons in this life.

53. Tiessen, *Who Can Be Saved?*, 216.

54. Tiessen, *Who Can Be Saved?*, 215. See also 222.

55. Tiessen, *Who Can Be Saved?*, 218.

56. Tiessen, *Who Can Be Saved?*, 221.

57. Cf John Sanders, *No Other Name* (Grand Rapids: Eerdmans, 1992), 190–191.

58. Donald Bloesch, *The Last Things* (Downers Grove: Intervarsity Press, 2004), 227. Bloesch cites a number of other texts that he thinks support the idea of postmortem conversion including: Psalm 49:15, Isaiah 26:19, Matthew 12:31–32, 27:51–54, John 5:29, I Corinthians 15:29, I Peter 3:19–20, 4:6. See *The Last Things*, 144–145.

59. Ludlow, *Universal Salvation*, 205.

60. I am assuming, of course, that a hope has a certain propositional content, and may therefore be incoherent.

61. For instance, see Jeremy Taylor, *The Rules and Exercises of Holy Dying* (Whitefish, MT: Kessinger Publishing, 2007; reprint of 1710 ed.), 145, 152, 277. Taylor insisted that true repentance took time and could only be completed on one's deathbed, not begun there.

62. Thomas Aquinas, *Summa Contra Gentiles*, trans. Charles J. O'Neil (Notre Dame: University of Notre Dame Press, 1975), 4, 94, 1.

63. SCG, 4, 92, 8. See all of chapter 92 for more details of this argument. See also 3, 62–63. Recall from above his metaphysical argument that a separated soul cannot change its fundamental dispositions. The argument here is psychological rather than metaphysical.

64. Aquinas explains that the change of will can only take place by the grace of God but that "the damned are entirely excluded from grace. Therefore they will not be able to change their will for the better." SCG, 4, 93, 4.

65. Thomas Talbott, "Freedom, Damnation, and the Power to Sin with Impunity," *Religious Studies* 37 (2001): 420.

66. This of course blurs the lines between hell and purgatory. For another revisionist view of hell that argues that grace is extended to the damned in such a way that they could repent,

and also holds out the hope for universal salvation, see C. P. Ragland, "Love and Damnation," in Kevin Timpe, ed., *Metaphysics and God* (New York: Routledge, 2009), 206–224. Ragland comments that his view of hell "requires us to give up the traditional idea that there is no escape from hell, and thereby blurs some of the traditional distinctions between hell and purgatory" (p. 222).

67. For a critique of this line of argument, see Claire Brown and Jerry L. Walls, "Annihilationism: A Philosophical Dead End?" in Joel Buenting, ed., *The Problem of Hell* (Burlington, VT: Ashgate, 2010), 47–53.

68. For more on this, see Bloesch, *The Last Things*, 216–232.

69. I offer the tentative suggestion that purgatory might provide a possible rapprochement between those who hold to the perseverance of the saints, and those who do not. Perhaps those who reject this doctrine are correct in believing that the truly converted can turn away from God and die outside of a saving relationship with him, such that if there were no repentance after death, they would be lost. However, perhaps those who hold to perseverance are correct because in fact there is repentance after death, and any truly converted persons who fell away will eventually repent and turn back to God and be saved. For this to be known, it would have to be revealed by God, and for God to know it, he would have to have some way of knowing that all such truly converted persons would eventually repent. Molinism, of course, would readily explain how God could know this, and arrange things so that things would turn out this way. Molinism may not be the only way to account for this, but I will not argue that case now.

70. Tiessen points out that evangelicals who want to insist that explicit faith in Christ in this life is necessary for salvation have balked at the implication that all infants who die would be lost. So the issue of postmortem salvation for infants opens the question of postmortem salvation for adults who have never heard the gospel. See Tiessen, *Who Can Be Saved?*, 13–14.

71. The recent furor surrounding the book by Pastor Rob Bell was due to his defense of postmortem conversion, and the charge that this leads to universalism. However, Bell made clear that his view does not necessarily lead to universalism even if grace extends into the next life. See *Love Wins: A Book About Heaven, Hell and the Fate of Every Person who Ever Lived* (New York: Harper Collins, 2011), 64, 72, 79, 103-106, 113-114, 117, 173, 175, 177.

72. See Jerry L. Walls, *Hell: The Logic of Damnation* (Notre Dame: University of Notre Dame Press, 1992), 113–138; "A Hell of a Choice: Reply to Talbott," *Religious Studies* 40 (2004): 203–216; "A Hell of a Dilemma: Rejoinder to Talbott," *Religious Studies* 40 (2004): 225–257.

73. Whether it could be known that anyone had made such a choice depends, among other things, on one's view of God's knowledge of the future, particularly future free choices. One who holds that God knows future free choices with infallible certainty can readily claim that it is possible God may know that some persons who have chosen evil will never repent, so their choice is decisive. Those who deny such an understanding of foreknowledge will have to explain such a decisive choice of evil, and how God could know it, differently. See *Hell: The Logic of Damnation*, 49–55, 74–80, 93.

CHAPTER 6

1. C. S. Lewis, *Mere Christianity* (HarperSanFrancisco, 2001), ix.

2. For evidence of Lewis's awkward fit in many evangelical circles, consider this comment from popular pastor and writer John Piper in an article on what he has learned from Lewis. He acknowledges a certain irony in finding Lewis so significant "even though he is not Reformed in his doctrine, and could barely be called an *evangelical* by typical American

uses of that word." John Piper, "Lessons from an Inconsolable Soul: Learning from the Mind and Heart of C. S. Lewis," http://www.desiringgod.org/resource-library/resources/lessons-from-an-inconsolable-soul

3. Roger Olson, "Protestant Purgatory?" http://www.rogereolson.com/2010/09/07/protestant-purgatory/

4. C. S. Lewis, *Letters to Malcolm: Chiefly on Prayer* (London: Geoffrey Bles, 1964), 138.

5. Lewis, *Letters to Malcolm*, 139.

6. C. S. Lewis, *A Grief Observed* (HarperSanFrancisco, 2001), 42.

7. Lewis, *A Grief Observed*, 50. See also p. 27.

8. C. S. Lewis, *Reflections on the Psalms* (Glasgow: Fontana Books, 1961), 14.

9. C. S. Lewis, *Letters To An American Lady*, ed. Clyde S. Kilby (Grand Rapids: Eerdmans, 1967), 103. The letter is dated 31/7/62.

10. Wayne Martindale, *Beyond the Shadowlands: C. S. Lewis on Heaven & Hell* (Wheaton, IL: Crossway Books, 2005), 199. He cites Janine Goffer's *C. S. Lewis Index*, which has only eleven references to purgatory compared to seven pages of entries for heaven and two and a half for hell. Cf also Martindale's comment on his own relative indifference to the matter: "Purgatory I have put last because it is least important and can wait or be dispensed with as interest dictates" (p. 17).

11. Martindale, *Beyond the Shadowlands*, 204.

12. This, of course, is the argument that Christ must be either a liar, a lunatic, or the Lord of the universe, given the claims he made for himself. For a contemporary assessment of the argument, see David A. Horner, "Aut Deus Aut Malus Homo: A Defense of C. S. Lewis's 'Shocking Alternative'" in *C. S. Lewis as Philosopher*, eds. David Baggett, Gary R. Habermas and Jerry L. Walls (Downers Grove, IL: Intervarsity Press, 2008), 68–84.

13. Lewis, *Mere Christianity*, 56.

14. Lewis, *Mere Christianity*, 58.

15. Lewis, *Mere Christianity*, 58.

16. A likely historical influence for Lewis's view of the atonement is the nineteenth-century Scottish theologian McLeod Campbell. For an exposition and critical analysis of this view, see Oliver Crisp, "Non Penal Substitution," *International Journal of Systematic Theology* 9 (2007), 415–33. Crisp points out that a passage from Jonathan Edwards was the original inspiration for Campbell's work. It is also worth remarking that, while Lewis's view of the atonement lends itself readily to his transformational soteriology, his soteriology does not require his theory of atonement. I have argued elsewhere that there are several theories of atonement in contemporary philosophical theology that are amenable to a transformational view of salvation. See Jerry L. Walls, *Heaven: The Logic of Eternal Joy* (New York: Oxford University Press, 2002), 41–48.

17. Lewis, *Mere Christianity*, 57.

18. The doctrine of "imputed righteousness" is very much a matter of controversy among Protestant, particularly evangelical, theologians and biblical scholars. For an important critique, see N. T. Wright, *Justification* (Downers Grove, IL: IVP Academic, 2009).

19. For more on these points, see Scott R. Burson and Jerry L. Walls, *C. S. Lewis and Francis Schaeffer* (Downers Grove, IL: Intervarsity Press, 1998), 51–63.

20. Lewis, *Mere Christianity*, 208–209.

21. Lewis, *Mere Christianity*, 92. cf. 81, 118–120, 147–148, 176, 192.

22. Lewis, *Mere Christianity*, 141.

23. Lewis, *Mere Christianity*, 147.

24. Lewis, *Mere Christianity*, 175.

25. Lewis, *Mere Christianity*, 177. cf. 147, 195, 199.

26. Lewis, *Mere Christianity*, 191–2.

27. Lewis, *Mere Christianity*, 198.

28. Lewis, *Mere Christianity*, 202.

29. Lewis, *Mere Christianity*, 203, 205, 212, 221.

30. Lewis, *Mere Christianity*, 204.

31. Lewis, *Mere Christianity*, 174.

32. Lewis, *Letters to Malcolm*, 140.

33. Lewis, *Letters to Malcolm*, 141. Lewis also employs this image in *Letters to An American Lady*, 81. The letter is dated July 7, 1959.

34. Lewis, *Letters to Malcolm*, 142.

35. The phrase "The Romish doctrine concerning Purgatory" that Lewis quotes is from Article 22 of the Anglican Articles of Religion.

36. Lewis, *Letters to Malcolm,* 139–40.

37. For an account of Fish's book and its influence, see Stephen Greenblatt, *Hamlet in Purgatory* (Princeton: Princeton University Press, 2001), 10–14, 28–33, 133–150.

38. Thomas More, *The Supplication of Souls* (along with *The Four Last Things* and *A Dialogue on Conscience*, rendered in modern English by Mary Gottschalk (New York: Scepter Publishers, 2002), 190.

39. C. S. Lewis, *English Literature in the Sixteenth Century Excluding Drama* (Oxford: Clarendon Press, 1954), 173.

40. More, *The Supplication of Souls*, 186–187.

41. More, *Supplication of Souls*, 190. Lewis cites this passage in More's early modern English in *English Literature in the Sixteenth Century*, 172.

42. Lewis, *English Literature in the Sixteenth Century*, 163.

43. Saint John Fisher, *Exposition of the Seven Penitential Psalms*, in modern English with an introduction by Anne Barbeau Gardiner (San Francisco: Ignatius, 1998), 16. Lewis cites the passage in early modern English in *English Literature in the Sixteenth Century*, 163–164. Lewis cites part of this passage in *Letters to Malcolm* in support of his claim that Fisher's view is even more of a degradation of the doctrine than More's. See pp. 139–140.

44. Lewis, *English Literature in the Sixteenth Century*, 164.

45. Lewis, *Letters to Malcolm*, 140. The quote from Milton is *Paradise Lost*, I, 391. Another classic account of purgatory that conveys the same spirit is that of Catherine of Genoa. See her *Purgation and Purgatory, The Spiritual Dialogue*, trans. Serge Hughes (Mahwah, NJ: Paulist Press, 1979).

46. John Henry Newman, *The Dream of Gerontius* (Staten Island, NY: ST PAULS/Alba House, 2001), 68.

47. There are, however, passages in Newman's poem that suggest the pain of purgatory also involves paying off a moral debt. See pp. 59, 69, 71.

48. For another expression of the idea that the pain of purgatory is gladly embraced, see C. S. Lewis, *The Screwtape Letters* (HarperSanFrancisco, 2001), 174–175.

49. C. S. Lewis, *The Great Divorce* (HarperSanFrancisco, 2001), viii.

50. Lewis, *The Great Divorce*, 39. See also 20–21, 29.

51. Lewis, *The Great Divorce*, 68.

52. C. S. Lewis, *A Preface to Paradise Lost* (Oxford: Oxford University Press, 1942), 104–105.

53. Lewis, *A Preface to Paradise Lost*, 105. Lewis also expressed the view a few years before that the doors of hell are locked on the inside, so the damned are self-enslaved and lack any real will to repent. See *The Problem of Pain* (HarperSanFrancisco, 2001), 130. This book was first published in 1940.

54. Lewis, *The Great Divorce*, 68.

55. Lewis, *The Great Divorce*, 71.

56. Lewis, *The Great Divorce*, 71.
57. Lewis, *The Great Divorce*, 70. For further analysis of these themes, see Jerry L. Walls, "The Great Divorce," in *Cambridge Companion to C. S. Lewis*, eds. Robert MacSwain and Michael Ward (Cambridge: Cambridge University Press, 2010), 251–264.
58. Lewis, *The Great Divorce*, 75.
59. Lewis, *The Great Divorce*, 77.
60. Lewis, *The Great Divorce*, 98. cf. 104.
61. As this passage suggests, at times Lewis seems to say those who reject heaven will eventually be annihilated. See my essay "The Great Divorce," 259.
62. Lewis, *The Great Divorce*, 111.
63. Readers of *The Chronicles of Narnia* may be reminded here of Eustace, whose nasty behavior had turned him into a dragon. His painful cure involved Aslan tearing off his dragon skin layer by layer and then throwing him in the water. See C. S. Lewis, *The Voyage of the Dawn Treader* in *The Chronicles of Narnia* (HarperCollins: New York, 2001), 470–476.
64. *Catechism of the Catholic Church*, par. 1431.
65. Cf. Lewis, *The Great Divorce*, 139–40.
66. The problem particularly arises because he seems to hold both that God is timeless, and that he interacts with us in a dynamic way in the process or perfecting and sanctifying us. The nature of time, and of God's relationship to time, are of course extremely difficult issues which we cannot pursue here. I will simply register my opinion that it is doubtful that Lewis's views on these matters are coherent. For discussion of the difficulties faced by the notion that God is timeless, and also actively engaged with his creation, see William Lane Craig, "Divine Eternity," in *The Oxford Handbook of Philosophical Theology*, eds. Thomas P. Flint and Michael C. Rea (Oxford: Oxford University Press, 2009), 145–66. See especially pp. 155–163.
67. Lewis, *The Great Divorce*, 69.
68. Lewis, *The Great Divorce*, 141.
69. C. S. Lewis, *Letters of C. S. Lewis*, ed. W. H. Lewis (New York: Harcourt, Brace and World, 1966), 307.

CHAPTER 7

1. Joseph Ratzinger, *Eschatology: Death and Eternal Life* (Washington, D.C.: The Catholic University of America Press, 1988), 230–231.
2. N. T. Wright, *Justification* (Downers Grove: IVP Academic, 2009), 189. See also pp. 117, 144–147, 152, 156–157, 184, 187–189, 192–193, 224–225, 234–235, 237–239, 251.
3. It is perhaps no accident that Wright uses the phrase "treasury of merit" in reference to the doctrine of imputed righteousness. See pp. 135, 228, 231. The phrase "treasury of merit," of course, is used in Roman theology to refer to the merits achieved by Christ and the saints, which underwrite indulgences that may be applied to sinners to free them from temporal punishment in purgatory.
4. C. S. Lewis, *Mere Christianity* (HarperSanFrancisco, 2001), 31.
5. See Galatians 5:17.
6. Philippians 1:6.

INDEX

Abelard, Peter, 185n35
Abraham, 13, 18
abuses, financial, 185n54
Adam, 48, 185n35
afterlife
 geography of, 16–17, 18
 prison as, 12
Albert of Brandenburg, 27–28
Albert of Lauingen, 22, 25
Alexander of Hales, 22–23
Alighieri, Dante. See Dante
Allen, William (cardinal), 186n1
All Souls Day, 18
alms, as redeemer of sins, 191n91
Anderson, Gary A., 5, 191n91
angels, 24, 56, 165, 171
anger, Christ on dealing with conflict
 and, 12
Anglican Articles of Religion, 199n35
Anglican Church, 49–50
Anselm of Canterbury, 20–21
ante-purgatory, 75
Apocryphal Second Book of
 Maccabees, 11–12
apostles, 12–13, 69. See also specific apostles
Aquinas, Thomas, 25, 62, 68, 143, 189n17,
 196n50
 on change of will, 196n64
 on grace, 148
 on human persons survival in death and
 resurrection, 193n49
 penance doctrine of, 63–64, 71–74
 on sins purging gradually in
 purgatory, 190n44
 on souls suffering from fire, 192n34
 variations on Thomist view of
 survival, 105–7
 view of soul, 103

Aristotle, 131
Arras heretics, 26
Articles of Religion, 47
Aslan (fictional character), 200n63
assessments
 satisfaction model of purgatory, 68–71
 satisfaction/sanctification model of
 purgatory, 80–82
atonement
 Aquinas on satisfaction and, 189n17
 theories of, 198n16
Augsburg Confession, 36, 39, 41
Augustine, 14, 32, 81, 165
 on four classes of persons, 16, 18
 on salvation, 15–16, 17
auricular confession, 18–19, 21

babies. See infants
Babylon, 10
Bainton, Roland, 27, 38
Balthasar, Hans Urs Von, 123, 196n48
baptism, 18
Barth, Karl, 140
Baxter, Richard, 29
beatific vision, 68
Bede (saint), 17, 32, 124, 184n25, 184n28,
 184n29
Bell, Rob, 197n71
Benedict XVI (pope), 14–15, 32, 141, 178,
 200n3
 identity and views of, 99–100
 on purgatory, 117–18
 on soul, 102–3
benefits, purgatory's financial, 186n1
Bernard, Justin D., 60, 82–83, 86, 87, 121,
 183n3, 188n9
the Bible
 Colossians 2:11–12, 39

the Bible (*continued*)
I Corinthians, 196n58
Ezekiel 28, 188n68
forgiveness in, 12
Hebrews, 4, 145
hints of purgatory in, 11–13
Isaiah, 43–44, 188n68, 196n58
John 5:29, 196n58
I John, 19, 38
Leviticus, 25
Luke, 145, 146
Maccabees, 11–12
2 Maccabees, 35
Malachi, 11
Matthew, 184n15, 196n58
New Revised Standard Version, 19
Peter, 195n41
I Peter, 196n58
Philippians, 195n41
Psalms, 196n58
refining fire in, 11
Revelation, 3, 146
Romans, 185n55, 187n39, 191n79
sin in, 5
birth, of purgatory, 17–20, 21–22
The Birth of Purgatory (Le Goff), 184n15,
184n30
Blake, William, 167
blanket prayers, 120
Bloesch, Donald, 51–52, 80, 151
on postmortem conversion, 146,
196n58
purgatory rejected by, 59–60
Bodhisattva, 141
bodies. *See* human bodies
Bonaventure (saint), 25
Boniface VIII (pope), 25, 185n46
Brown, David, 114–16, 119
Buddhists, 141
Bunyan, John, 29
Butler, Joseph, 196n49

Calvin, John, 28–29, 39, 45, 154, 185n55
on purgatory's validity, 36, 41–42
Campbell, McLeod, 198n16
canon law, 18
Catechism of the Catholic Church, 87, 173
Cathari, 26
Catherine of Genoa, 199n45
character, time, identity, and, 114–19

Checks to Antinomianism (Fletcher), 49
choices, God's future free, 197n73
Christ. *See* Jesus Christ
Christianity, doctrines central to, 9
Christian perfection, 48
A Christmas Carol (Dickens), 84–85, 87,
112–13, 120–21
The Chronicles of Narnia (Lewis), 200n63
The City of God (Augustine), 15
Clement of Alexandria, 15, 16, 32
Cluny, France, 18
Cologne heretics, 26
Colossians 2:11–12, 39
Comestor, Peter, 18
Commentary on Psalm 37 (Augustine), 16
compound dualism, 107, 193n40
condemnation, 194n13
confession
auricular, 18–19, 21
as penance, 64
Confessions (Augustine), 15
conflict, Christ on dealing with anger
and, 12
consent, of God, 185n35
contempt, of God, 185n35
contrition
faith with, 39, 40, 64
as penance, 63
with penitence and faith, 39
conversion, postmortem, 52–53, 146,
196n58, 197n71
Cooper, John, 110
Corcoran, Kevin, 97–98, 100
I Corinthians, 15:29, 196n58
Council of Florence, 27, 188n9
Council of Trent, 29
Counter-Reformation, 29–30
Cross, Bryan R., 189n16
Curtis, Olin Alfred, 137–38
Cyprian of Carthage, 14, 32, 184n15

damnation, second-chance theories
with, 129–37
the damned
in hell, 199n53
universal salvation and souls of, 196n66
Dante, 3, 29, 96, 177, 185n46, 185n47,
195n26. *See also The Divine Comedy*
with hope for Virgil, 195n31
productive pain and, 76–77

on purgatory, 25–26, 74–78
second-chance theories with damnation,
 divine love and, 129–37
David (king), 40
Day of the Dead, 18
dead
 newly, 11
 suffrages for, 18, 22–23
death
 moment before or instant after,
  183n15
 prayers for, 155
 purgatory and repentance after, 197n69
 repentance in moment of, 126, 147,
  196n61
 sanctification process after, 6, 48
 sins forgiven after, 12
 as sleep, 192n19
 Thomists' views on human person's
  survival in resurrection and, 193n49
death purgatory, 49–51
debts, moral, 199n47
Decretum (Gratian), 18
demons, 24, 50, 165
Dialogues (Plato), 11
Dickens, Charles, 84–85, 87, 112–13,
 120–21
Dinocratus, 14
divine love, 129–37
The Divine Comedy (Dante), 25–26, 74–78,
 96, 185n46
 damnation and divine love in, 129–37
 embodied person in purgatory and,
  93–95
doctrines
 central Christian, 9
 penance, 63–64, 71–74
 Protestantism with imputed
  righteousness, 198n18
 purgatory, 4–33
Dongell, Joe, 194n5
Donne, John, 36
The Dream of Gerontius (Newman), 167
dualism, 192n21
 compound, 107, 193n40
 identity and survival with
  substance, 107–9
 pure, 193n40
 substance, 104, 112, 193n40
 Thomists and rejection of, 191n5

ecumenical councils, 9
Eden, garden of, 75
Edwards, Jonathan, 187n30, 187n32,
 198n16
 on holiness, 43–45
efficacious grace, 194n13
Egan, M. F., 60, 65, 66, 71, 81, 190n44
Egypt, 10
Eire, Carlos, 29, 30
*English Literature in the Sixteenth Century
 Excluding Drama* (Lewis), 164
entire sanctification, 46–49, 51
Erickson, Millard, 51
eschatological fire, 13, 193n62
Eschatology: Death and Eternal Life
 (Ratzinger), 184n15
Eudes of Chateauroux (cardinal), 23
Eustace (fictional character), 200n63
evangelicalism, justification in Protestantism
 theology, 188n64
Eve, 48
evil, 56, 121–22
evildoers, 146
expiation, 67
Ezekiel 28, human figures in, 188n68

faith
 contrition with, 39, 40, 64
 justification received by, 38–39, 45, 46,
  51, 54–55, 80, 82, 159, 178–79
 with penitence, 39
 sanctification received by, 46, 48–51
 saving, 135, 142–43, 150
 two levels of, 160
fathers, purgatory's mothers and, 14–17
fear, 192n21
Fenn, Richard K., 29, 186n57
final judgment, purgatory compatible
 with, 194n5
financial abuses, Reformation and role of
 purgatory, 185n54
financial benefits, purgatory's, 186n1
fire
 eschatological, 13, 193n62
 Malachi and imagery of refining, 11
 purgatorial, 13, 16
 souls suffering in, 192n34
 as transformative power of God, 118
Fish, Simon, 164–65
Fisher, John (saint), 164, 165, 199n43

fission, 100–101
Fletcher, John, 188n63
  on death purgatory, 49–51
  on purgatory, 36–37
Flint, Thomas, 194n11, 196n52
forgiveness, 12
Formula of Concord, 39
Forsyth, P. T., 52–53, 139–40, 195n41
France, 18
Freddoso, Fred, 190n44
Frederick II (emperor), 131
free choice, 197n73
free will, 56–57
future, purgatory in, 30–32
future free choices, God's knowledge
  of, 197n73

gappy view, 97–98, 109
  of personal identity, 191n6
gastronomic indulgence, 76, 83–84
geography
  of afterlife, 16–17, 18
  purgatory rooted in, 23–24, 75
glorification, 41
Gnilka, J., 118
God
  consent and contempt of, 185n35
  with fire of refinement and
    purification, 11
  with fire of transformative powers, 118
  future free choices known by, 197n73
  molinism with, 197n69
  sinning and necessary goodness
    of, 183n4
  timeless knowledge of, 173–74
  time's relationship to, 200n66
godless, 16
Goffer, Janine, 198n10
goodness, 56, 183n4
grace, 197n71
  Aquinas on, 148
  Catholic view of, 131
  efficacious, 194n13
  optimal, 129, 151, 194n14, 196n52
  salvation by, 51
  universal salvation, damned souls
    and, 196n66
gradual sanctification, 46
Gragnolati, Manuele, 21, 74–75, 78
Gratian, 18

The Great Divorce (Lewis)
  God's timeless knowledge in, 173–74
  purgatory in, 167–71
Greece, 10
Greek Church, 23, 27
Greenblatt, Stephen, 24–25
Gregory (pope), 16–17, 32, 184n21
Gregory the Great. *See* Gregory (pope)
Gresham, Joy, 156
Griffiths, Paul, 42, 76, 83–84
guilt (*culpa*), 21, 141
  sin as cause of, 5, 185n35
  unresolved, 117

hades, 52, 146
halfway sanctification, 46
Hall, Brian, 194n5
Handy, Jack, 3
Hayes, Zachary, 54, 55
heaven
  Newman on, 4–5
  problem of, 190n70
  sin absent in, 4
  visions of, 3–5
Hebrews, 4
  9:27–28, 145
hell
  Lewis on, 199n53
  Limbo as most pleasant part of,
    131, 135
  reasons for being in, 194n14
Henry VIII (king), 165
heretics, 26
Hezekiah, 13
Hinduism, 11
Hodge, Charles, 31, 43, 69
holiness, 4
  Edwards on, 43–45
  sinful natures transformed into, 6
Holy Spirit, 51, 52. *See also* God; Jesus
  Christ
  forgiveness for speaking against, 12
  trinity and, 9, 22
Homilies (Bede), 17
hope, 123, 196n60
Hugh of Saint-Cher, 23
human bodies, 65. *See also* resurrection
  in Dante's purgatory, 93–95
  physicalist views of survival and,
    100–102

post mortem physical identity and,
  97–98
as rotten, filthy and loathsome, 45
sin tied to, 44–45, 52
as temporal, 116–17
as vehicle for repenting, 196n50
human nature, 95–97
Hume, David, 95

identity
  Benedict XVI's view on, 99–100
  character, time and, 114–19
  physicalist view of survival with,
    100–102
  postmortem physical, 97–98
  purgatory and issues with, 95–97
  Thomist view of, 102–5
  substance dualism's survival and, 107–9
  survival options in purgatory with,
    109–14
  time, purgatory and personal, 93–122
  variations on Thomism with, 105–7
identity argument, 115
ignorance, sin due to, 21
imputed righteousness doctrine, in
    Protestantism, 198n18
Incarnation, as central Christian
    doctrine, 9
India, 10
indulgences, 191n91
  definition, 184n33
  to pardon sins, 22–23
infants, 18, 138
  postmortem salvation for, 144–45, 151,
    197n70
initial sanctification, 45
Innocent IV (pope), 23, 24, 33
intensity, purgatory's pain and, 69–70,
    76–77, 81
intentionality, sin and, 21
intermediate state, 184n15
Isaiah, 43–44
  26:19, 196n58
  human figures in, 188n68
Ivan Karamazov (fictional character),
    89–90

James (saint), 40
Jesus Christ, 19. *See also* God
  on forgiveness, anger and conflict, 12

as liar or lunatic, 198n12
perfection and, 162
purgatorial fire of, 13
purgatory at odds with sacrifice
    of, 41–42
repentance and, 137–38
Jews, 11–12
John, 196n58
John (saint), 50
I John, 19, 38
John Paul II (pope), 88
joy, reality with, 170
judgment, final, 194n5
Judisch, Neal, 60, 61, 87
Jugie, Martin, 66, 67–68
  on pain and intensity of purgatory,
    69–70, 76
jurisdiction, of priests over purgatory,
    22–23
justification
  by faith, 38–39, 45, 46, 51, 54–55, 80,
    82, 159, 178–79
  Protestant and evangelical theology with
    nature of, 188n64
  sanctification compared to, 39

Klosterman, Chuck, 35

Latimer, Hugh, 185n55
law, canon, 18
Laws of Manu, 11
Lazarus, 13
Le Goff, Jacques, 9, 15, 16, 21, 32, 74,
    184n15, 184n30
  on doctrine of purgatory, 17, 23
  on dual birth certificates of purgatory, 33
  on glory days of purgatory, 30
  on guilt and punishment as aspects of
    sin, 185n35
  on hope and purgatory, 123
  purgatory as second chance,
    125–26
  on purgatory in literature, 19–20
  on "purgatory" used as noun, 18
Leo X (pope), 27–28
Letters to An American Lady (Lewis), 166,
    199n33
Letters to Malcolm: Chiefly on Prayer
    (Lewis), 155, 163
Leviticus, 25

Lewis, C. S., 7, 199n33, 199n35, 200n63
   on atonement, 198n16
   evangelical circles and awkward fit
      of, 197n2
   on hell, 199n53
   mere purgatory and, 171–75
   more as less, Newman as more, and view
      of, 163–67
   with prospect of mere purgatory,
      153–75
   purgatory affirmed by, 154–57
   purgatory in *The Great Divorce*, 167–71
   on salvation, 158–63
liar, Christ as lunatic or, 198n12
Limbo, 131, 135
literature, purgatory in, 19–20, 25–26
Locke, John, 29
Lombard, Peter, 18
Lord. *See* God
Louismet, Dom S., 65
love, 141
   second-chance theories with Dante,
      damnation and divine, 129–37
Ludlow, Morwenna, 146
Luke
   13:23–30, 145
   16:26, 146
lunatic, Christ as liar or, 198n12
Luther, Martin, 28–29, 45, 154, 185n55.
     See also Protestantism
   perspectives on purgatory, 37–41
   on purgatory's biblical validity, 35–36
   on purgatory's lucrative benefits, 186n1
   on resurrection and soul sleep, 187n24
Lutherans. *See also* Luther, Martin
   penitence and, 39–40

Maccabees, Apocryphal Second Book
     of, 11–12
2 Maccabees, 35
Maccabeus, Judas, 11–12
magic, 53
Magnus, Albertus, 22, 25. *See also* Albert of
     Lauingen
Malachi, fire as refining in, 11
Mandelbaum, Allen, 78
Manfred, 131–32
Martindale, Wayne, 157
martyrs, 14, 16. *See also specific martyrs*
Mary. *See* Virgin Mary

matter, 53
Matthew
   12:31–32 and 27:51–54, 196n58
   purification and intermediate state
      with, 184n15
McDonald, George, 168–69
Melanchthon, 36, 39–40, 41, 64
Mere Christianity (Lewis), 153, 156, 158
Milton, John, 166, 169, 199n45
minds, distortion of reality and, 5
misery, sin as cause of, 46
missionaries, 184n25
models of purgatory. *See* purgatory models
molinism, 197n69
Moltmann, Jurgen, 53
moral debts, 199n47
moral space, orientation in, 116
More, Thomas (saint), 13, 164–65,
     165–66, 199n43
Moreira, Isabel, 17, 32, 124, 184n26,
     184n29
   on purgatory, 184n28
Moreland, J. P., 104
mortal sins, 19, 63, 65
mothers, purgatory's fathers and, 14–17

Nagasawa, Yujin, 190n70
New Catholic Encyclopedia, 55, 66, 79, 120
newly dead, 11
Newman, John Henry (cardinal), 82,
     199n47
   on heaven, 4–5
   Lewis's view of more as less and more
     as, 163–67
   on purgatory, 4
   on sinful natures transformed into
     holiness, 6
   on taste and perception, 5
New Revised Standard Version Bible, 19
New Testament. *See also* the Bible
   forgiveness of sins in, 12
Ninety-five Theses, 37. *See also* Luther,
     Martin; Lutherans
Notre Dame school, 18, 32
noun, purgatory as, 18, 24, 184n28
numbers, 20

objective time, 196n52
Old Testament. *See also* the Bible
   Malachi, 11

purgatory in, 13
  sin in, 5
Olson, Roger, 154, 157
Oppy, Graham, 190n70
optimal grace, 129, 151, 194n14, 196n52
orientation, in moral space, 116
Origen, 15, 16, 17, 32
original sin, in *Westminster
    Confession*, 183n7
Ott, Ludwig, 188n2

pain
  productive, 76–77
  purgatory's intensity and, 69–70,
    76–77, 81
Pannenberg, Wolfhart, 193n62
Paradise Lost (Milton), 199n45
parousia, purgatory compatible
    with, 194n5
partial sanctification, 46
The Passion of Perpetua and Felicitas, 14
Patrick (saint), 19
Paul (saint), 12–13, 28, 40, 52, 69
  on roots of sin, 191n79
penance, 71–74
  confession as, 64
  contrition as, 63
  rationale for purgatory with, 61–64
  satisfaction as, 64
Penelope (nun), 174
penitence, 16
  contrition and faith with, 39
  Lutherans and, 39–40
  punishment as necessary for, 40
perception, 5
perfection, 43, 69, 162
  blanket prayer for, 120
  Christian, 48
Perpetua, 14
Persia, 10
The Persistence of Purgatory (Fenn), 186n57
personal identity, gappy view of, 191n6
persons, Augustine's four classes of, 16, 18
Peter, 195n41
Peter (saint), 28, 40
I Peter, 196n58
Peter the Chanter, 19
Phaedo (Plato), 11
Philip II (king), 30
Philip III (king), 30

Philip IV (king), 30
Philippians, 195n41
physical identity, postmortem, 97–98
Pinnock, Clark, 54, 56, 59
Piper, John, 197n2
Plato, 11, 39, 131
Polkinghorne, John, 53, 106–7
postmortem conversion, 146
  purgatory as place of, 52–53
  texts citing, 196n58
  universalism influenced by, 197n71
postmortem physical identity, 97–98
postmortem probation, 7
  critical analysis of purgatory as, 142–47
  purgatory as, 137–42, 196n49
postmortem repentance, 7
postmortem salvation, for infants, 144–45,
    151, 197n70
power
  God with fires of transformative, 118
  to pardon sins, 22–23
prayers
  appeal to, 88
  blanket, 120
  for dead, 155
predestinarian views, 42
A Preface to Paradise Lost (Lewis), 169
priests, with jurisdiction over
    purgatory, 22–23
prison, as afterlife, 12
probation, purgatory as postmortem, 7,
    137–47, 196n49
productive pain, 76–77
Protestantism
  biblical readings of Roman Catholicism
    differing from, 11–13
  on Catholic view of purgatory, 61–62
  imputed righteousness doctrine
    in, 198n18
  justification in evangelical theology
    and, 188n64
  Lutheran perspectives on purgatory,
    37–41
  objections and alternatives to purgatory
    in, 35–57
  purgatory and contemporary
    perspectives on, 51–54
  purgatory doctrine rejected by, 26–28
  reformed perspectives on purgatory
    in, 41–45

Protestantism (*continued*)
  Wesley, John, and perspectives on
    purgatory in, 45–51
Psalms, 196n58
punishment (*poena*), 21
  as aspect of sin, 185n35
  as necessary for penitence, 40
  suffering to pay debt of, 75
  temporal, 189n16, 200n3
pure dualism, 193n40
purgatorial fire, 13, 18
  Augustine on, 16
purgatory, 184n30, 185n55, 193n68
  ancient intimations and non-Christian
    views of, 10–11
  Bede's theology of, 184n25
  biblical hints of, 11–13
  birth of, 17–20
  doctrine, 4–33
  as eschatological fire, 13, 193n62
  fathers and mothers of, 14–17
  financial abuses in English Reformation
    and role of, 185n54
  five factors conducive to birth of, 20–22
  in *The Great Divorce*, 167–71
  history of, 9–33
  identity issues with, 95–97
  identity with survival options in, 109–14
  Lewis and mere, 171–75
  Lewis and prospect of mere, 153–75
  Lewis's affirmation of, 154–57
  Luther on lucrative benefits of, 186n1
  models of, 59–91
  Newman on, 4
  as noun, 18, 24, 184n28
  penance and rationale for, 61–64
  personal identity, time and, 93–122
  as postmortem probation, 137–42,
    196n49
  as postmortem probation with critical
    analysis, 142–47
  Protestants objections and alternatives
    to, 35–57
  rejected and reaffirmed, 26–30
  repentance after death and, 197n69
  Roman Catholics and satisfaction model
    of, 188n9
  second-chance theories with, 123–52
  secularization of, 186n57
  into twenty-first century, 30–32

Wesley, John, and perspectives on,
    45–51
purgatory models, 59–60, 91
  penance and rationale for purgatory
    with, 61–64
  sanctification, 82–87
  sanctification assessment, 87–90
  satisfaction, 64–68
  satisfaction assessment, 68–71
  satisfaction/sanctification, 71–79
  satisfaction/sanctification
    assessment, 80–82
purification, 67, 184n15
purity, of souls, 45
Purtill, Richard, 84

questions, second-chance theories and
    unavoidable, 147–50

Rae, Scott, 104
Ragland, C. P., 196n66
Rahner, Karl, 31, 140, 188n2, 196n48
rationale, for purgatory with penance,
    61–64
Ratzinger, Joseph, 14–15, 93, 184n15,
    193n62, 196n48. *See also* Benedict
    XVI (pope)
  on purgatory, 32
reaffirmation, of purgatory after
    rejection, 26–30
reality
  joy with, 170
  sin and distortion of minds and, 5
refining fire, 11
reflection, 112
Reflections on the Psalms (Lewis), 156
the Reformation, 27
  purgatory's role in financial abuses
    of, 185n54
Reformed
  perspectives on purgatory, 41–45
  sanctification views of, 42–45
refrigerium interim (interim
    refreshment), 13–14, 18
rejection, of purgatory before
    reaffirmation, 26–30
relativity theory, 53
repentance, 147
  to be completed on deathbed, not
    begun, 196n61

after death, 197n69
human bodies as vehicle for, 196n50
Jesus Christ and, 137–38
in moment of death, 126
Wesley, John, on, 46
resurrection, 95–97, 100
bodies, 101
Luther on soul sleep and, 187n24
Thomists' views on human person's
survival in death and, 193n49
Wright on, 101–2
Revelation, 3
1:18, 146
revisionists, 196n66
righteous persons, 16
Roman Catholic Church
grace viewed by, 131
on Protestant view of purgatory, 61–62
purgatory doctrine's history with, 9–10
purgatory viewed by, 140–41
Roman Catholics
biblical readings of Protestants differing
from, 11–13
gift of temporal punishment to, 189n16
purgatory's lucrative benefits and, 186n1
satisfaction model of purgatory
with, 188n9
Romans, 185n55, 187n39, 191n79
Rome, 10

Saint Patrick's Purgatory, 19, 33
saints, 16. *See also specific saints*
salvation, 42
Augustine on, 15–16, 17
by grace, 51
infants and postmortem, 144–45, 151,
197n70
Lewis on, 158–63
universal, 15, 16, 17, 196n48, 196n66
sanctification, 187n33
assessment with purgatory models, 87–90
entire, 46–49, 51
by faith, 46, 48–51
gradual, 46
as incomplete in life, 41
initial, 45
justification compared to, 39
partial or halfway, 46
process after death, 6, 48
Reformed views of, 43–45

sanctification model, 60. *See also*
satisfaction/sanctification model
assessment, 87–90
of purgatory, 82–87
Satan, fall of, 56, 188n68
satisfaction
Aquinas on atonement and, 189n17
as penance, 64
satisfaction model, 60
assessment, 68–71
of purgatory, 64–68
satisfaction/sanctification model
assessment, 80–82
of purgatory, 71–79
Sayers, Dorothy, 59, 136–37, 142, 147, 156,
185n46
on Catholic view of purgatory, 125–26
on Dante, 26, 75–76, 185n47
freedom of will, 129–30
Scholasticism, 19
second-chance theories
critical analysis of purgatory as
postmortem probation and, 142–47
Dante, damnation, divine love and,
129–37
purgatory and, 123–52
purgatory as postmortem probation
and, 137–42
unavoidable questions with, 147–50
when seconds matter and, 127–29
Second Council of Lyons, 9, 24, 27. *See also*
Roman Catholic Church
secularization, of purgatory, 186n57
self-acceptance argument, 114–15
Sentences (Lombard), 18
separated souls, 110
Seymour, Charles, 196n50
sins
alms as redeemer of, 191n91
death and forgiveness of, 12
due to ignorance, 21
God's necessary goodness and, 183n4
gradual purging of, 190n44
guilt as aspect of, 5, 185n35
heaven and absence of, 4
holiness transformed from, 6
human body tied to, 44–45, 52
misery caused by, 46
mortal or venial, 19, 63, 65
original, 183n7

sins (*continued*)
  Paul on roots of, 191n79
  power to pardon, 22–23
  punishment as aspect of, 185n35
  three destructive effects of, 5
  willful, 21
sleep, death as, 192n19
soteriology, 45, 198n16
souls, 65
  Aquinas' view of, 103
  Benedict XVI on, 102–3
  filth of human bodies and pure, 45
  fire with suffering, 192n34
  grace and universal salvation for
    damned, 196n66
  reasons for being in purgatory, 66–67
  separated, 110
soul sleep, Luther on resurrection
    and, 187n24
space, 20, 53
  moral, 116
Statius, 133–34
Stump, Eleanore, 189n17, 193n49
Suarez, Francisco, 65–66, 70, 81
substance dualism, 104, 112, 193n40
  identity and survival with, 107–9
suffering
  to pay debt of punishment, 75
  souls in fire, 192n34
suffrages, 18, 22–23
A Supplication for the Beggars (Fish), 164
The Supplication of Souls (Lewis), 164
survival
  identity and physicalist view of,
    100–102
  identity and purgatory with options
    for, 109–14
  of substance dualism, 107–9
survivors, identity and self-identified
    Thomist, 102–5
Swinburne, Richard, 107–8, 112

Talbott, Thomas, 149
Tartarus, 11
taste, 5
Taylor, Charles, 116
Taylor, Jeremy, 196n61
temporal argument, 114–15
temporal punishment, 200n3
  Roman Catholics and gift of, 189n16

Tertullian, 13, 184n15
Tetzel, 27–28, 29
texts
  postmortem conversion cited in,
    196n58
  purgatory supported in biblical, 11–13
Theodoric (king), 17
Therese of Lisieux, 141
Thomas (saint), 66
Thomistic Substance Dualism, 104
Thomists, 191n5
  on human person's survival in death and
    resurrection, 193n49
  identity and variations on, 105–7
  survivors and identity, 102–5
Tiessen, Terrance L., 151, 194n13
  on postmortem salvation for
    infants, 197n70
  on saved infants, 144–45
time, 20, 53
  dispensing with, 119–22
  God's relationship to, 200n66
  identity, character, and, 114–19
  objective, 196n52
  personal identity, purgatory and, 93–122
  when seconds matter and, 127–29
timelessness, God and, 200n66
Tolkien, J. R. R., 156
Trajan (emperor), 134–36, 143, 168,
    184n21, 195n26
Trakakis, Nick, 190n70
treasury of merit, 191n91, 200n3
Trinity, 9, 122
Tyndale, William, 166

universalism, postmortem conversion
    leading to, 197n71
universal salvation, 196n48
  Origen on, 15, 16, 17
  revisionists on grace, damned souls
    and, 196n66
usurers, 123–24

Vander Laan, David, 86–87, 89
Van Dyke, Christina, 104, 105, 111
Vatican II, 31, 79
Venerable Bede. *See* Bede (saint)
venial sins, 19, 63, 65
Virgil, 195n31
Virgin Mary, 23

visions
   beatific, 68
   of heaven, 3–5

Waldensians, 26
weaknesses, sin as fortifying, 5
Wesley, Charles, 48
Wesley, John, 187n33, 187n39, 188n63
   on entire sanctification, 46–49, 51
   on gradual sanctification, 46
   perspectives on purgatory, 45–51
   on repentance, 46
Wesleyans. *See* Wesley, John
Westminster Confession, 42
   on original sin, 183n7

on perfection, 43
Whatley, Gordon, 195n31
will
   Aquinas on change of, 196n64
   free, 56–57, 129–30
   sin with intentionality and, 21
Williams, Charles, 156
Willimon, William H., 140
Wright, N. T., 52, 53, 109, 179
   on Benedict XVI's views of
      purgatory, 118, 200n3
   on resurrection, 101–2
Wycliffe, John, 185n55

Zwingli, Ulrich, 154